James P. Lusardi

THE ORIGINS OF
SHAKESPEARE

THE ORIGINS OF SHAKESPEARE

EMRYS JONES

OXFORD

At the Clarendon Press

1977

Oxford University Press, Walton Street, Oxford OX2 6DP

OXFORD LONDON GLASGOW NEW YORK
TORONTO MELBOURNE WELLINGTON CAPE TOWN
IBADAN NAIROBI DAR ES SALAAM LUSAKA ADDIS ABABA
KUALA LUMPUR SINGAPORE JAKARTA HONG KONG TOKYO
DELHI BOMBAY CALCUTTA MADRAS KARACHI

ISBN 0 19 812080 X

Printed in Great Britain
at the University Press, Oxford
by Vivian Ridler
Printer to the University

Preface

THE mid-Tudor period was one of exceptionally rapid social change. England was well into the process of becoming Protestant, but remained Catholic in its deepest memories and traditions. Humanism with its stress on colloquial latinity was fermenting an already vigorous vernacular culture. Out of this period of national upheaval, though after an interval of Elizabethan peace, came the great writers, including Shakespeare. His emergence from that mid-Tudor world is the subject of this book.

The opening chapter states the theme by describing the highly literate culture created by the humanists, and suggests a few of the ways in which Shakespeare both drew upon and contributed to it. But if the sixteenth century was the first to feel the impact of humanism, it was also the last to give allegiance to medieval ideals. Accordingly the second chapter adjusts the balance by examining a neglected factor in Shakespeare's immediate background: the still surviving mystery play tradition and its bearing on the writing of the tragedies. The third and fourth chapters go together as parts of a single argument: they propose a connection with a remoter past, making a case for Shakespeare's knowledge, so often denied, of Greek tragedy. Indeed a concern throughout the book has been to bring out the wide range of intellectual materials and opportunities open to him from the beginning of his career. The remaining chapters are on a distinct group of plays, the early histories, which were probably all written within two or three years of each other. I have approached each of them very differently in response to their own diversity, since they are much more various in substance and in form than is often supposed; at the same time I have tried to bring them into sharper focus by relating them in some very specific ways to the life of the age. My intention throughout has been to explore some neglected areas so as to give a sense of the extraordinary fusion of original force and acquired learning in Shakespeare's genius.

I am much indebted to the advisers and staff of the Oxford University Press for their careful work on this book. A section of Chapter 10, in a slightly different form, has previously appeared in *Essays in Criticism*.

My greatest debt throughout has been to my wife Barbara Everett, and to her the book is dedicated.

Magdalen College
Oxford

Contents

1. A Tudor Genius

I

THE life of Shakespeare presents a challenge to the biographer which shows no sign of losing its power. A biography appears every few years. The best of them serve a real purpose: they are informative; they do what can be done to make the thin documentary materials take on life. But they all suffer from one serious defect. The man we encounter in their pages can hardly ever be imagined as actually writing the plays which for us mean 'Shakespeare'. They are lives of Shakespeare which leave 'Shakespeare' out. What is always missing is what most matters, his mind— the mind that created such things as the Falstaff plays, *Hamlet*, *Lear*, and *Macbeth*, and such fantastically brilliant oddities as *Cymbeline*. These lives have a void at the centre which leaves the reader finally more perplexed than enlightened. If anything they increase the sense of unfathomable mystery surrounding Shakespeare. They leave us once again romantically marvelling at the genius, but not much wiser as to how the miracle happened.[1]

One is tempted to say that such biographies are over-imaginative. But the truth is different. They are not imaginative enough. They have failed to break through the tough fabric of the Shakespeare myth. To some extent, perhaps, no one is altogether free of it. Four centuries after his birth, Shakespeare has become more than an author: he is an institution, a part of the national mythology. He attracts to himself a mass of prejudice and emotion, so that anyone's conscious idea of him is likely to involve unconscious assumptions about a great many other things besides. Forces with their origins far back in English history have helped to fashion the myth, disposing us to think of him as fundamentally anomalous and inexplicable. The Shakespeare myth should be dissipated in favour of history. What we need is a more historically adequate idea not only of the man himself but of the age which produced him.

[1] See S. Schoenbaum, *Shakespeare's Lives*, Oxford, 1970, for an excellent survey of Shakespearian biography.

In most accounts of Elizabethan England Shakespeare looms out with an extraordinary abruptness, a suddenness that puts an end to thought rather than inviting attempts to understand. There is of course always a sense in which genius is beyond explanation. Genius *is* characterized by an abruptness in the way it arrives. We are suddenly in the presence of a mind of incomparably greater powers than anything that had gone immediately before, and a feeling of shock, of being taken by surprise, is not out of place but the only right response. Even so, with due allowance for the suddenness of genius, it remains true that the wrong sort of mystery has attached itself to Shakespeare. It amounts to mystification, an unnecessary vagueness as to how the man Shakespeare achieved what he did, how he became equipped to write his works. Many scholars have in fact addressed themselves to answering these very questions, but for various reasons their findings have not on the whole been absorbed by a more general public. Shakespeare is still under-intellectualized, his mental powers still underestimated.

There are many reasons for this state of affairs. We inherit Romantic assumptions about the autonomy of genius, its capacity to create its works out of itself; and from this point of view Shakespeare is our supreme specimen of self-determining genius, magnificently inexplicable. But Romantic critical theories can hardly be the whole explanation, since this way of thinking about Shakespeare is much older than Romanticism. It begins in the seventeenth century and goes back to Ben Jonson's verse tribute to Shakespeare in the First Folio of 1623. Jonson's too-memorable phrase 'though thou hadst small *Latine*, and lesse *Greeke*' inaugurates a whole tradition of assumptions about Shakespeare. By 1668 Dryden was saying that he 'needed not the spectacles of books to read Nature; he looked inwards, and found her there'. Shakespeare was being fixed in his place as our great natural genius, the English Homer, an untaught 'wit' who created his own laws. Ever since that time he has been regarded as the great exception to all the rules. It may be that in being so regarded he was meeting some profound English need, an instinct that—especially after the Cromwellian Interregnum—disapproved of intellect and was suspicious of too much learning. There was certainly no doubt as to which of the two— Shakespeare and Jonson—the public preferred, and from the

Restoration onwards the over-simple labels have stuck and the rift between what they stood for widened: Shakespeare for unlearned Nature, Jonson for learned Art. The one needed no books at all; the other was—to his cost—all books and nothing else. The evidence embedded in Shakespeare's plays could not be ignored for long. In the eighteenth century the investigation began in earnest into the question of Shakespeare's learning. It reached a climax some two hundred years later with T. W. Baldwin's 1,500-page work *Shakspere's Small Latine & Lesse Greeke* (1944). Baldwin closely examined the curricula of Tudor grammar-schools, and came to the conclusion that Shakespeare, though indeed not learned by the standards of such scholar-poets as Jonson, Milton, and Dryden, was none the less a 'learned grammarian'—a favourable specimen of the kind turned out by the grammar-schools. By twentieth-century standards he had absorbed a considerable amount of Latin, and possibly even a little Greek. After Baldwin, no one should have been able to quote Jonson's phrase without knowing that it might not mean what it apparently says. Baldwin's work was in every sense monumental, and any student of Shakespeare must pay tribute to it. At the same time it is much to be regretted that economy was not one of Baldwin's virtues. His several formidably thick volumes have as deterrent a look as the novels of Samuel Richardson. One suspects, as a result, that his important findings have failed to reach many readers.

Despite Baldwin's work and the work of many others, before him and after,[1] the myth of Shakespeare as a comparatively book-less natural genius has persisted, and it has had secret oblique effects of a somewhat pernicious kind. It was assumed that, if he was unlearned, he was also perhaps not remarkable for intelligence. The assumption, unconsciously arrived at, still has power, so that when, in an essay on Shakespeare's learning, Professor Frank Kermode says of him that 'he was a person of enormously superior intelligence', one does not feel him to be saying

---

[1] Among Baldwin's predecessors two may be singled out: J. S. Smart, *Shakespeare: Truth and Tradition*, 1928, and E. I. Fripp, *Shakespeare Man and Artist*, Oxford, 1938. Later contributors include J. A. K. Thomson, *Shakespeare and the Classics*, 1952; V. K. Whitaker, *Shakespeare's Use of Learning*, 1953; and Reuben A. Brower, *Hero and Saint: Shakespeare and the Graeco-Roman Heroic Tradition*, Oxford, 1971.

something utterly commonplace.[1] The remark ought to be trite, but is not. Shakespeare's intelligence and knowledge are both commonly underestimated, and the fact that they are has far-reaching results. It sets up presuppositions which affect us even before we have started reading a play or walked into a theatre. It often appears in a tendency to find his effects accidental rather than designed or to whittle down what would appear to be implausibly large artistic ambitions. The unwillingness on the part of scholars to believe that he could as a young man plan and execute a complete trilogy is a case in point. It was in keeping with this failure to notice the quality of mind they were dealing with that so many scholars, until recently, thought Shakespeare a 'late developer', his early plays of only slight interest and in any case often no more than adapted from the work of other men. Shakespeare's extreme quickness of mind is one of the few things we know about him as a man—not only Jonson but Heminge and Condell mention it—yet it could be assumed that until his late twenties he was the tardy disciple of such clear intellectual inferiors as Greene and Peele. (Something of this misunderstanding of his intellectual calibre runs through those many volumes of the New Cambridge Shakespeare edited by Quiller-Couch and Dover Wilson.)

The belief that Shakespeare needed the tuition of the University Wits went with an ignorance of the contents of his grammar-school education. It was assumed that a Cambridge graduate such as Greene must have known more about the art of writing than one who had not been to a university. The true state of affairs is nowadays better understood. Now that we know more of what a grammar school might have taught him, it has become possible to move Shakespeare away from the shadow of the Wits and to recognize that he was already well equipped to embark upon his career before any of them had written a single play. The only one of the Wits with anything substantial to teach him was Marlowe (and Marlowe later returned the compliment by modelling *Edward II* on *2 Henry VI*). Indeed by the time he arrived in London, Shakespeare must already have absorbed the bulk of his intellectual and literary materials. He was now almost ready to write the plays discussed

---

[1] Frank Kermode, 'Shakespeare's Learning', in *Shakespeare, Spenser, Donne*, 1971, p. 183.

later in this book; what he needed was the stimulus of the London theatre itself, and particularly the experience of acting, the example of Marlowe, and perhaps the further prompting of a few literary works which were printed or reprinted just before he began to write.

Our thinking about Shakespeare at this hypothetical moment at the outset of his career must be closely related to what we think of his cultural hinterland, that mental world which was his natural inheritance. If we underestimate that inheritance we shall make his appearance as puzzlingly—and implausibly—abrupt as accounts in the past so often did. If we give it due weight, however, we shall be closer to understanding how the 'miracle' happened. That in another way it remains a miracle is not in question.

II

Too often we have confined Shakespeare to a narrow setting in the belief that his intellectual milieu was in fact narrow. It has taken a long time to rid ourselves of inherited conceptions of the Tudor age which made it seem smaller than it was, saw it indeed as impoverished and provincial when it was, far more than England became later, still part of Western Christendom and wide open to continental influences. Although the only literary work by a Tudor Englishman to win European fame was More's Latin *Utopia*, the great intellectual effort of the century in England was to put Englishmen in touch with all that was good in classical and modern continental writing. Much of the best recent scholarly work on Elizabethan literature has been given to tracing connections formerly unsuspected, or if considered at all rejected as unlikely on the usual grounds that Elizabethan writers were provincial and inward-looking, not much exposed to foreign developments. But what these rediscovered connections suggest is that, intellectually, the Tudor sky was higher, the horizons more distant, than had often been thought. We need to expand our sense of the size of the Tudor intellectual world.

One way of doing this is to ponder the staggering advances in education made in England from about ten or twenty years before Shakespeare was born until about twenty years after his death. The point can be made by contrasting two views of the

Tudor age, the first written in the eighteenth century and blinkered by the unavoidable historical ignorance of its period, the
second by an authoritative historian of our own time. The first
is Dr. Johnson's in his *Preface to Shakespeare* (1765). Johnson is
trying to persuade his readers to 'make some allowance' for
Shakespeare's 'ignorance': 'Every man's performances, to be
rightly estimated, must be compared with the state of the age in
which he lived, and with his own particular opportunities . . .':

The English nation, in the time of *Shakespeare*, was yet struggling to
emerge from barbarity. The philology of *Italy* had been transplanted
hither in the reign of *Henry* the Eighth; and the learned languages
had been successfully cultivated by *Lilly*, *Linacer*, and *More*; by *Pole*,
Cheke, and *Gardiner*; and afterwards by *Smith*, *Clerk*, *Haddon*, and
Ascham . . . But literature was yet confined to professed scholars, or
to men and women of high rank. The publick was gross and dark;
and to be able to read and write, was an accomplishment still valued
for its rarity.[1]

According to Johnson, the common people had a childish and
uncritical appetite for fabulous entertainments; as he winds up
the survey, a note of Augustan contempt enters his voice: '*The
Death of Arthur* was the favourite volume.' In a recent study,
'The Educational Revolution in England, 1560–1640', Professor
Lawrence Stone comes to rather different conclusions about the
literacy and the general intellectual attainments of the Elizabethan populace. He is admittedly more interested in the seventeenth-century end of his eighty-year period, but his findings
certainly cover the whole of Shakespeare's life-time. There was,
he says, 'an astonishing expansion of education between 1560
and 1640':

If it is accepted that over half the male population of London was
literate, that a high proportion of the one third of adult males who
could sign their names in the home counties could read, and that $2\frac{1}{2}\%$
of the annual male seventeen-year-old age-group was going on to
higher education, then the English in 1640 were infinitely better
educated than they had been before. It was a quantitative change of
such magnitude that it can only be described as a revolution. How the
new pattern compared with that of other European countries we
simply do not know, for the social history of education has hardly

---

[1] *Johnson on Shakespeare*, ed. W. Raleigh, Oxford, 1949 rep., pp. 30–1.

begun. But it may well be that early seventeenth-century England was at all levels the most literate society the world had ever known.[1]

As a dramatist, Shakespeare was dependent on there being a large audience in existence that would support his plays in the theatre. Professor Stone may be quoted in this connection too:

> It was precisely between 1590 and 1690 that England boiled and bubbled with new ideas as no other country in Europe. What is so striking about this period is not the appearance of individual men of genius, who may bloom in the most unpromising soil, but rather the widespread public participation in significant intellectual debate on every front. It is no accident that the monarchs, Elizabeth, James I, Charles I and even Charles II, were more interested in things of the mind than any before or since; that James was even flattered to be called 'King of the Academicians'.[2]

One may add in qualification that a popular dramatist cannot 'bloom in the most unpromising soil': unless he finds prompt and widespread sympathy from other people, his plays will languish unperformed, more probably remain unwritten.

If Professor Stone's conclusions are even only approximately right, it is clear that Johnson, and those many others who have thought as he did, misunderstood the intellectual temper of Shakespeare's time. It should indeed be obvious that the plays of Shakespeare and Jonson are the most intellectually demanding entertainments ever put before a large audience in the history of England. But this period of 'unprecedented intellectual vitality' (as Professor Stone calls it) did not happen suddenly: the foundations for it had been laid much earlier in the sixteenth century. When we turn from social to literary history, however, we find that the conventions usually adopted by literary historians have not much helped to clarify the historical processes involved, for the desire to impose manageable period-divisions has put more stress on superficial discontinuity than continuity at a deeper level. And so the 'Elizabethan' period—the last twenty years of Elizabeth's reign—is usually treated in isolation from the earlier part of the century. The attention of literary historians tends in any case to be focused on to the more 'imaginative' poetical kinds; writing of a more utilitarian order often gets little notice. (C. S. Lewis's brilliant Oxford volume is outstandingly

---

[1] *Past and Present*, vol. 28, 1964, p. 68.   [2] Ibid., p. 80.

— More's polemics, etc.

good here in casting its net much wider than is usual.) According to the common scheme, the century begins promisingly under Henry VIII; it then collapses into sectarian strife and the poetically dull middle decades under Edward, Mary, and the young Elizabeth; and at last comes to fruition in the 80s and 90s, the years of 'Golden' literary and dramatic achievement. But such schematic contrasts disguise the fact that, in education, continuity was the rule, and that despite the immense upheaval of the Reformation the new impulses associated with humanism gathered headway. If anything, of course, the Reformation in England assisted the spread of the critical spirit of humanism. Instead of regarding the late Elizabethan flowering as a more or less separate movement, we should see it as in many ways the fulfilment of what had been prepared earlier—not only in the Henrician period by the early humanists, but also in the Edwardian years when so much else was initiated in the field of education. Indeed the reign of Edward, which the historian of poetry is likely to consider a low point (unless he admits The Book of Common Prayer), is from the educational point of view a richly potential moment of direct relevance to the late Elizabethan achievement.

Christian humanism is the primary cultural fact of the sixteenth century in England. Those literary historians who, like C. S. Lewis, disparage humanism on the grounds that it fostered a sterile pedantry, or was anti-intellectual, or even that it 'created a new literary quality—vulgarity', are thinking more of continental variants than of the kind that was dominant in England. Lewis indeed explicitly portrays humanists as destructive or inhibitive influences who would have put a stop to genuinely imaginative writing if they had been able: 'all the facts seem consistent with the view that the great literature of the fifteen-eighties and nineties was something which humanism, with its unities and *Gorboducs* and English hexameters, would have prevented if it could, but failed to prevent because the high tide of native talent was then too strong for it. Later, when we were weaker, it had its way and our pseudo-classical period set in.'[1] But this 'view', far from clarifying what happened in the sixteenth century, in fact obscures it, for it distracts attention from

---

[1] *English Literature in the Sixteenth Century Excluding Drama*, Oxford, 1954, pp. 19–20.

what humanists in England actually did—and it makes things worse by chopping the century into 'Late Medieval', 'Drab', and 'Golden', a scheme which, no doubt deliberately, proclaims Lewis's scepticism about attempts to 'explain' literary phenomena. 'I do not claim to know', he says, 'why there were many men of genius at that time.'

If one regards Lewis as mistaken on this issue, it is because he focuses on the less important doctrines of some humanists, and neglects those which were, or could be, really beneficial and of a nature to foster good writing. And he directs his attack against certain humanists, mostly Italian, but gives no special attention to the one humanist who was superlatively important for Tudor civilization: Erasmus. No one would gather from his massive book the commanding position Erasmus held in the world of northern humanism: France, Germany, the Low Countries, and England (and though not 'northern', Spain may be added to the list). Indeed northern—or Erasmian—humanism receives no recognition at all. Yet the history of sixteenth-century England would have been profoundly different if Erasmus had never lived.[1] Colet founded St. Paul's School, but Erasmus was its presiding spirit. He wrote textbooks for it and helped with the standard Latin grammar, which eventually became standard for all England; and possibly the plan of studies in the school was of Erasmian inspiration. All this has been amply demonstrated by T. W. Baldwin. One of Baldwin's chapter-titles, 'Erasmus laid the Egg', suggests part of the book's argument. Erasmus's educational and literary theories were put into practice at St. Paul's, and St. Paul's soon became the prototype of many, perhaps most, Tudor grammar-schools. In this way Erasmian ideals, values, and practices quickly spread through the country to affect a large number of those who received a grammar-school education. Among these must be included Shakespeare at Stratford.

Erasmus and his followers are the inaugurators of the classical, or neo-classical, phase of our literature, which lasted for nearly three hundred years. In its full extent neo-classicism is a phenomenon of immense complexity and diversity. It gives rise to the

---

[1] See, e.g., M. M. Phillips, *Erasmus and the Northern Renaissance*, 1949. For a recent survey, with bibliography, see Margaret Aston, 'The Northern Renaissance', in *The Meaning of the Renaissance and Reformation*, ed. Richard L. De Molen, Boston, 1974, pp. 71–129. For Erasmianism in England, see J. K. McConica, *English Humanism and Reformation Politics*, Oxford, 1965.

Italian-influenced Milton as well as the French-influenced Pope.
It includes not only theoretical and doctrinaire writers but those
less given to enunciating programmes: not only Jonson but
Shakespeare. For Shakespeare too must be seen as a writer who
unavoidably breathed the neo-classical atmosphere, however
much one would want to qualify any attempt to brand him in
too downright a way as an imitator of the classics. But writing
comedies and tragedies in five acts in itself relates him to the
dramatists of Roman antiquity; and much more did besides.
Humanism, as it worked in practice in Tudor schools and
colleges, was not just a matter of the more extreme doctrines
mentioned by Lewis, like the three unities and English hexameters. It had much more to do with the cultivation of idiom,
a skill in varying phrases by saying the same thing in as many
different ways as possible, translating from Latin into English
and back again—and in the process discovering the finer potentialities of one's own vernacular, even at its best inspiring the
student to extend those potentialities. The sillier extremes of
stylistic purism, like the Ciceronianism of those Italian humanists
who confined themselves to words taken from Cicero, found no
exponent in Tudor England. Erasmus was in this sense an anti-
Ciceronian. He had written a famous dialogue holding the cult
up to ridicule. He was in any case by temperament untheoretical,
unmetaphysical, averse to doctrinaire pronouncements. The
movement of his mind was quick, direct, terse, light. Erasmus
was in short not in the least like the humanists who in Lewis's
handling emerge as such a reprehensible lot. And yet so much of
what is distinctive in Tudor literary culture can be traced back
to Erasmus. For it would be absurd to suggest that humanism in
England was a matter mainly of style and verbal expression,
important though they were. The entire temper of northern
humanism was one of sober practicality, usefulness, and service-
ableness; which explains why it achieved so much. The humanist
impulse quickly merged with religious, political, and educational
activity; it was never concerned to keep itself separate from everyday affairs. Its whole purpose was to improve the quality of lay
life; its workings therefore rapidly become invisible and hard to
trace. In more specifically literary terms, Erasmus's own writings
and his astringent critical spirit had a fertilizing influence which
has never been properly assessed. He was not only More's close

friend and stimulus in the brief period of his richest literary activity, the years of *Richard III* and *Utopia*, but he also inspired More's later antagonist, Tyndale, to his momentous New Testament translations. His *Praise of Folly* is an acknowledged seminal work for Western literature generally: Rabelais and Cervantes were deeply indebted to it. And among the Elizabethans Shakespeare responded more deeply than anyone to the Erasmian paradoxes of the wisdom of folly and the folly of wisdom.[1]

Erasmus's most widely influential work was done through editions, translations from Greek into Latin, and compilations. He was essentially a mediator of classical thought and experience. He performed his task with superb and astonishing efficiency. His huge collections of idioms, sayings, proverbs, and anecdotes which fill such volumes as his *Adagia* and *Apophthegmata* were the most effective kind of reference books, clearly arranged and well indexed. They transmitted from the classical to the modern world thousands of easily remembered, easily absorbed units of linguistically shaped experience. Many of these transplantations proved instantly fertile, for they were promptly translated, so enriching the English language and English life, adding flavour to the commonest of linguistic transactions. 'To call a spade a spade' from 'Ligonem ligonem vocat' ('to call a hoe a hoe') is often cited to illustrate this process; among others are 'to leave no stone unturned', 'his heart was in his boots', 'to be in the same boat', and 'to die laughing'.[2] But scores of other phrases included in the *Adagia*, while not enjoying quite the same popular success, were copied into notebooks by students, emerging later to add force and lustre to their style, as well as a quality less easily defined but suggesting a traditional human wisdom. One example may serve for many: 'sea of troubles' from Hamlet's 'take arms against a sea of troubles'. This was noted, along with many others, by J. Churton Collins as a phrase which seemed to him derived from a Greek source.[3] He quoted examples from Homer and

---

[1] Walter Kaiser, *Praisers of Folly*, 1964.

[2] M. M. Phillips, *The 'Adages' of Erasmus*, Cambridge, 1964, p. 7. Cf. F. P. Wilson: 'consider the number of translations from that great disseminator of proverbs Erasmus: the *Dicta Sapientum* of *c.* 1526, Taverner in 1539, Nicholas Udall in 1542, William Baldwin in 1547, Robert Burrant's *Precepts of Cato*, with the annotations of Erasmus, in 1545, and so on.' ('The Proverbial Wisdom of Shakespeare', reprinted in *Shakespearian and Other Studies*, ed. Helen Gardner, Oxford, 1969, p. 147.)

[3] 'Shakespeare as a Classical Scholar', in *Studies in Shakespeare*, 1904, p. 51.

Aeschylus, adding that it was used more than once in the Greek drama. The phrase occurs, however, in Erasmus's *Adagia*, and while it is extremely unlikely that Shakespeare had a first-hand knowledge of Homer or Aeschylus, he might well have consulted, at some stage of his life, either the *Adagia* themselves or one of the many selections from them. Under 'Mare malorum' Erasmus quotes the *Hippolytus* of Euripides: 'Tantum malorum pelagus aspicio miser'.[1] In this instance, as in others, Churton Collins was probably right to suggest a Greek source, but he omitted the Erasmian link. Many other details of Shakespeare's diction, which we assume to be original, could probably also be traced to this or a similar source. On another page of the *Adagia* one comes across the phrase 'Multae regum aures atque oculi' ('The ears and eyes of kings are many in number'), a political common-place; but Erasmus goes on to quote from the *Andromache* of Euripides the phrase 'vitae oculus', applied by Andromache to her son, and comments: 'what is unique in life gives delight. For nothing is dearer than eyesight' ('Nam oculo nihil carius').[2] The notion appears more than once in Shakespeare, as when Goneril protests her love for Lear: 'Dearer than eyesight . . .', or when Othello urges Desdemona to take care of her handker-chief: 'Make it a darling like your precious eye.' On yet another page one's eye is caught by the phrase 'Delphino lascivior' ('more lascivious than the dolphin').[3] One wonders whether Shakespeare recalled it when he made Cleopatra say of Antony 'His delights / Were dolphin-like' and whether for him it coloured the meaning of the simile.

Any single examples of this kind of influence look insignificant. Only when hundreds are taken into account can the magnitude of the humanist revolution be grasped. We need to envisage a society, numerically small by modern standards, but culturally homogeneous to a high degree. By modern standards, it was pedantically bookish. Those who had been through a grammar-school had been saturated in the literature of classical Rome. There was an immense amount of learning by rote. Boys who had spent the best part of six long days a week for perhaps as many as ten or eleven years reading, translating, analysing, and expli-cating Latin literature would have memorized hundreds, perhaps

[1] Erasmus, *Opera*, Leyden, 1703–6, ii. 123.
[2] Ibid., p. 69.   [3] Ibid., p. 12.

thousands, of lines or scraps of lines from the poets, as well as
having innumerable phrases, constructions, and rhythms from
the prose writers impressed on their minds. A classical colouring
would be cast over everything they read or wrote. During these
years the entire effort of schoolmasters was directed towards
awakening the linguistic awareness of their pupils and stretching
their linguistic capacities. And so for all its alarming narrowness,
its quite excessive orientation to the classical past, Tudor education proved itself wonderfully adapted to producing not merely
competent classical scholars but endlessly resourceful prac-
titioners in English.

The number of good writers to appear in the second half of
Elizabeth's reign is more than surprising: it astonishes. But if one
bears in mind the formidably well-organized campaign conducted
for so long by the educational reformers, astonishment is likely
to be tempered by a recognition that it all makes historical sense.
It remains true that literary talent, and especially poetic talent,
is always exceptional, an unexpected bonus, a gift. But the conditions in which it may flourish can perhaps be prepared, and in
this instance it seems that they were. Without the intensive new
study of language and literature which the grammar schools
provided, the major writers at the turn of the century would not
have been equipped to do their work. Without humanism,
in short, there could have been no Elizabethan literature: without
Erasmus, no Shakespeare.

III

Shakespeare's writings betray their humanistic cultural align-
ments in innumerable ways. A striking feature of a very early
play like *1 Henry VI* is the constant comparativeness of its
method: we are never allowed to become identified with the
point of view of any one of its characters. Although Talbot is
a famous soldier-hero, he is only one of several main figures.
The play's vision of reality is never less than complex: all viewpoints are partial. Hence the endless oscillation from one nation,
one group, one individual, to another. England and France are
at war; England is divided by faction; and within any group of
men—such is the lesson Shakespeare's dialogue method enforces
—a conversation must become a contest, an exchange of views,

a struggle for precedence. Hence too the play's rotatory scenic technique: each party has its turn, but only for a while. Of course the French are treated jingoistically: they are hardly given a fair chance of voicing their own viewpoint—although quite a lot comes through which is not particularly favourable to the English. We are presented with a number of conflicting voices, and although it is possible to pick out some unexceptionable sentiments (like Exeter's choric comments), few positions are not exposed to the questioning gaze of other positions nearby.

This dramatic method is clearly the product of academic rhetorical training in the writing of *controversiae*. In these exercises the pupil took up one side in a debate situation. He would try to win his audience's favour by using the most intellectually and emotionally suasive means. Or rather, he would be told to defend each position in turn, so acquiring in the process a versatile technique. Such a teaching method would militate against the dogmatic espousal of a single position. Shakespeare at any rate seems to have profited from this method more than any one else in his time. It was peculiarly congenial to his mind; no one else exploited relativistic (or as C. O. McDonald calls them, anti-logistic) modes as resourcefully as he.[1]

In such an educational context, *1 Henry VI* is almost a copy-book product of this rhetorical method of study. Such a training in the writing of *controversiae*, the devising of situations which could be broken down into a structure of division and opposition and then treated with the utmost emotional force of which the writer was capable, would undoubtedly make for the kind of drama we find in early Shakespeare. This is essentially a structure of interaction, more dualistic than monistic, antipathetic to the single unchallenged way of looking at things or to the single hero. Marlowe's *Tamburlaine*, by contrast, invites us—compels us—to contemplate its hero and accept him. There are one or two dissentient views, like those of Calyphas, Tamburlaine's degenerate son. But such opposing estimates of the central situation are peripheral: even in Part Two they hardly challenge the validity for himself of the hero's life-style. Tamburlaine is never demonstrably wrong in any of his actions; he is never

[1] C. O. McDonald, *The Rhetoric of Tragedy*, University of Massachusetts, 1966. See also David Riggs, *Shakespeare's Heroical Histories: Henry VI and its Literary Tradition*, Cambridge, Mass., 1971.

an oversimple view of *Tamb.*

measured against a standard outside himself and found wanting. In Shakespeare there is no such immunity from law; and in *1 Henry VI* it can be seen as following from the rhetorical method just described—its readiness to give a hearing to a wide range of positions—which results in a genuinely multi-voiced dramatic spectrum. Shakespeare's whole-hearted submission to this principle of rhetorical dialectic—his willingness to lend a voice of the utmost eloquence to every point of view—is his dramatic secret. It was this power that so awed Romantic critics of Shakespeare: his wide, almost universal, sympathies; his 'myriad-mindedness'; what Coleridge noted as 'the alienation, and, if I may hazard such an expression, the utter *aloofness* of the poet's own feelings, from those of which he is at once the painter and the analyst'.[1] What they did not notice was the encouragement his school training must have given to this almost divinely detached—and attached—dramatic posture. There was complete continuity between his rhetorical training and his dramatic practice.

Another way in which Shakespeare shows his humanistic affiliations is not so much through his treatment of subject as through his choice of subject, his initial decision as to where to locate his dramatic action. This side of an artist's work is usually taken for granted and seldom discussed; yet it is surely of fundamental importance. Much of Shakespeare's power comes from his skill in choosing subjects that arouse interest and attention—they did so at the time and have done so ever since.

Any good dramatist's choice of subject must have something deeply intuitive about it. He must somehow locate his action in a psychic region shared by himself and those contemporaries of his likely to become his audience. He has to know where the powerful centres of interest are, those magnetic areas which infallibly excite a strong human response. Shakespeare has an extraordinary knack of choosing subjects of this kind. And what is distinctive about them, or many of them, is a tendency to look back, as if appealing to his audience's memory of what they have already experienced. Some of his subjects seem to surface as if by a kind of inevitability from earlier in the century. In his early histories and tragedies, for instance, he had a strong predilection for what had often been treated before—not

---

[1] *Biographia Literaria*, ed. J. Shawcross, 1907, ii. 15–16.

— doctrine of imitation ?

necessarily on the stage, but at least in some literary form, whether in non-dramatic poetry, in history, or prose fiction, or as part of the study of rhetoric as it was taught in the schools. By the time he put them on the stage they had often acquired a kind of mythic aura, a penumbra, of familiar associations. Such subjects, however, were not merely familiar; they were also matter for debate—they provoked contrary interpretations and arguments. We can take an example from the educational use of rhetorical exercises. In his inaugural address at the opening of the new high school at Nuremberg in 1526, the great Lutheran educational reformer Melanchthon outlined the new teaching syllabus. For rhetorical practice the school would use, he said, Erasmus's *De Copia*, some Cicero, and Quintilian. He adds in a footnote: 'The master will, for example, take a question from history. Was Brutus right or wrong in murdering Caesar? or, was Manlius right or wrong in slaying his son for accepting the challenge of the Samnite chief?'[1] The reference to Brutus is interesting, since it suggests that the subject of Shakespeare's *Julius Caesar*—the rights and wrongs of the conspiracy and assassination—was used for rhetorical purposes at school. The boys would be trained to find arguments for and against Brutus' act: there was no question of coming down simple-mindedly on one side. We can pick up another clue to the Tudor antecedents of the early plays from a remark of Thomas Wilson's in *The Art of Rhetoric* (1560). Under the heading 'Description of Persons' he suggests drawing a comparison between Henry VI and Richard III.[2] The evidence is slight, but it suggests that such personages as these two kings were not necessarily thought of as confined to the pages of the chroniclers. Their characters might be impersonated and their conflicts acted out by schoolboys acquiring the arts of speech-making. So although it is not known for certain that there were any English plays before Shakespeare's on the reigns of Henry VI and Richard III, the idea of imitating their persons in rhetorical performances (or in civic ceremonies or pageants) was not at all new.

It is altogether in keeping with Shakespeare's conservative tendency that he should have chosen the reign of King John as the subject for a play. John figured prominently in anti-papal

---

[1] W. H. Woodward, *Studies in Education during the Age of the Renaissance 1400–1600*, Cambridge, 1924, p. 225. [2] *The Art of Rhetoric*, ed. G. H. Mair, 1909, p. 179.

More's mode in Hist. of R III — Mirror for Magistrates?

propaganda and so was a well-known symbolic type, even if
Bale's morality *Kynge Johan* had been forgotten by Shakespeare's
time. Similarly with *Romeo and Juliet*: there seems to have been
at least one English play on this subject before Shakespeare's;
the story was known in various non-dramatic forms, so that the
lovers had already acquired something of their legendary status
before Shakespeare wrote his play. This willingness to follow
rather than initiate helps to account for Shakespeare's deep
popularity. He is in an entirely good sense a derivative writer,
never affecting singularity but going after the classical view of
his subject, the inherited 'right' way of treating it. Hence his
invisibility; he is lost in his works.

A contrast can again be drawn with Marlowe, or with Marlowe's heir, Jonson. Both men, for all their great gifts, had the
ill luck or poor judgement to choose subjects which are often,
rightly or wrongly, found wanting in interest; or if interest is
aroused, as it is in their best plays, something is yet felt to be
lacking. *Tamburlaine*, especially if Part One is taken as a single
play, throws down a challenge to its audience. It makes a break
with the past. It astounds and disconcerts and altogether scorns
compromise:

> View but his picture in this tragic glass,
> And then applaud his fortune as you please.

Shakespeare never speaks in so inflexibly haughty a voice. When
Marlowe does tread in Shakespeare's footsteps, in *Edward II*,
it is revealing that he chooses a reign oddly lacking in significance
and which had not attracted much literary attention. Marlowe's
plays pay a price for their slightly eccentric originality: they
suffer from a certain emptiness, which is the effect of the over-
assertion of will. Shakespeare's fullness, on the other hand,
follows from his naturalness, with its constant invitation to the
audience to complete the dramatist's suggestions and to fill out
from its own experience the forms adumbrated by the action.
His plays seem 'full' to us because we help to fill them. If Marlowe's plays seem comparatively empty, it is because we are not
made to do enough work: we are, like any audience, ready to
co-operate, but are not sufficiently called upon to play our part.[1]

---

[1] For an acute comparison between Shakespeare and Marlowe, see the concluding
essay, 'Artist and Ethos', in Wilbur Sanders's *The Dramatist and the Received Idea*,

In all this Shakespeare recalls the earlier humanists, and Erasmus especially. Like Erasmus he is a transmitter—he lets others speak through him. He lacks egoism and self-assertiveness, and is all the more original for seeming not to seek after originality. If he was bent on 'making it new', he did it by making new what was already traditional or even archaic—hence the rootedness, what must have seemed the old-fashionedness, of many of his subjects. In *Richard III*, characteristically, he was dramatizing what was almost an old favourite, an episode which had been studied over and over again ever since that earliest of Tudor masterpieces More's *History of Richard III*. But the new play which Shakespeare made from such old materials was forward-looking. It remains the only play of these years (the four or five years centring on 1588) which has continuously held the stage down to our own times.

IV

'I believe that the conditions of the twenty years which precede a man's birth set the pattern of his early thinking, and leave a permanent mark upon him.'[1] So writes a modern historian, and with Shakespeare in mind. Professor Hurstfield is thinking of the mid-sixteenth century, with its assumptions of 'social instability, ideological conflict, a frequently re-enacted struggle for personal and political power'. But we may extend the bearing of his observation. For it is also true that the 1540s and 50s were years of radical change in another way. England, under Protestant Edward, saw the beginnings of that immense educational revolution which transformed the following hundred years.[2] And the informing principle of that fervent educational campaign was the doctrine of Imitation. Roger Ascham, himself a characteristic voice of these Edwardian years, declared in *The Schoolmaster*: 'This foresaid order and doctrine of *Imitation* would bring forth more learning, and breed up trewer judgement, than any other exercise that can be used . . .'[3] Of all principles it is the one

Cambridge, 1968. The book is itself in the nature of an extended comparison between the two.

[1] Joel Hurstfield, 'The Elizabethan People in the Age of Shakespeare', in *Shakespeare's World*, 1964, ed. James Sutherland and Joel Hurstfield, pp. 27–8.

[2] Joan Simon, *Education and Society in Tudor England*, Cambridge, 1966, pp. 268 ff.

[3] *Elizabethan Critical Essays*, ed. Gregory Smith, 1904, i. 10.

which most distinguishes Renaissance from modern classical teaching.

Imitation was something quite distinct from either reproduction or translation. It was a principle of real assimilation. The best writers of the past were studied by making the student produce not a copy of the original but a work both similar and different. The difference, the element of novelty and originality, was vital. A good early statement of this principle occurs as a set piece on Imitation in a letter from Petrarch to Boccaccio:

A proper imitator should take care that what he writes resembles the original without reproducing it. The resemblance should not be that of a portrait to the sitter—in that case the closer the likeness the better —but it should be the resemblance of a son to his father. Therein is often a great divergence in particular features, but there is a certain suggestion, what our painters call an 'air', most noticeable in the face and eyes, which makes the resemblance. As soon as we see the son, he recalls the father to us, although if we should measure every feature we should find them all different. But there is a mysterious something which has this power.

Thus we writers must look to it that with a basis of similarity there should be many dissimilarities. And the similarity should be planted so deep that it can only be extracted by quiet meditation. The quality is to be felt rather than defined. Thus we may use another man's conceptions and the color of his style, but not his words. In the first case the resemblance is hidden deep; in the second it is glaring. The first procedure makes poets, the second makes apes.[1]

Or as Ascham put it: 'This *Imitatio* is *dissimilis materiei similis tractatio*; and, also, *similis materiei dissimilis tractatio*' ('similar treatment of dissimilar material, and dissimilar treatment of similar material').[2] The element of difference ensured that the imitation had at least a chance of independent life.

Like all his contemporaries, Shakespeare was nourished on this doctrine. As R. R. Bolgar puts it in his excellent chapter on Imitation, Shakespeare was 'a product of a world that had learnt through imitation. The fragments which others had excerpted from the classics had come to him along a thousand devious paths to form the essential fabric of his outlook.'[3] He was amazingly

---

[1] *Letters from Petrarch*, selected and translated by Morris Bishop, Bloomington, 1966, pp. 198–9. E. M. Gombrich quotes this same letter in 'The Style *all'antica*: Imitation and Assimilation', in *Norm and Form*, 1966, p. 122.

[2] Gregory Smith, op. cit., i. 8.

[3] *The Classical Heritage and Its Beneficiaries*, Cambridge, 1954, p. 329.

resourceful in finding ways of converting to wholly original ends what was so abundantly supplied by the printing presses of his time. Admittedly on only one or two early occasions does he model entire plays on earlier ones. *The Comedy of Errors* is plainly based on Plautus' *Menaechmi*, though with so many departures from and additions to it that the new play is in no sense a copy of the old but rather a larger, denser, and altogether more interesting transformation of it. I shall argue in a later chapter that *Titus Andronicus* is also modelled on a famous classical play. But usually the imitations are on a much smaller scale. It may be a matter of giving English form to Latin phrases or tacitly absorbing elements of situation or character so as to thicken the dramatic medium. Often it gives it a richly allusive feel, a suggestion of further possible significance, which adds its own degree of implication to the text's plain and obvious meaning. So, for example, in the Hostess's description of the death of Falstaff in *Henry V* we may be momentarily reminded of one of the most famous deaths in classical antiquity—the death of Socrates. In the words of the Hostess: 'So a' bade me lay more clothes on his feet; I put my hand into the bed and felt them, and they were as cold as any stone; then I felt to his knees, and so upward, and all was as cold as any stone.'[1] In the *Phaedo* Plato says that 'the man who gave him the poison now and then looked at his feet and legs; and after a while he pressed his foot hard, and asked him if he could feel; and he said, No; and then his legs, and so upwards and upwards, and showed us that he was cold and stiff.'[2] There seems a clear resemblance between the two accounts in this one circumstance: a bystander feels from the foot up the leg of a dying man. But it is not at all obvious what we are to make of it, though there are affinities of a general kind between Falstaff and Socrates, especially in the light in which Socrates was sometimes regarded in the sixteenth century. Erasmus called him a jester, saying that 'his eternal jesting gave him the air of a clown', and pointing out that he drank the hemlock 'with as cheerful a face as he wore when he was drinking wine, and

---

[1] Quotations from Shakespeare are from the single volume edition by Peter Alexander (1951). The resemblance between Falstaff and Socrates was noted by J. Dover Wilson, New Cambridge *Henry V*, 1947, p. 147. Cf. W. Kaiser, *Praisers of Folly*, p. 252.

[2] *Phaedo*, tr. B. Jowett, *The Four Socratic Dialogues of Plato*, Oxford, 1903, p. 273.

joking with his friend Phaedo even as he lay dying . . . So it was
not unjust that in a time when philosophers abounded, this
jester alone should have been declared by the oracle to be wise,
and to know more—he who said he knew nothing—than those
who prided themselves on knowing everything.'[1] On the other
hand, if Socrates could be called the supreme exponent of wisdom,
we could hardly extend that title to Falstaff. Shakespeare's glancing collocation of their final moments seems teasingly indeter-
minate, something less than a deliberately pointed allusion, but
more than a mere accident. Conceivably he used the detail of the
dying man's cold feet and legs simply as a memorable image,
as a way of defining the moment in which life surrenders, without
implying anything about the mingling of wisdom and folly in
Falstaff. What is Shakespearian about such a passage is the
freedom and casualness and audacity with which the classical
text is put to work in a new vernacular context and then used in
such a way as to stimulate the mind into entertaining a number of
different possibilities.

There is in Shakespeare—and this is typical of several of the
most remarkable literary minds of this intensely literary age—
an astonishing ease and rapidity of commerce between literature
and life, between literary texts and the life of spontaneous feeling.
It is often as if, at some deep level of his mind, Shakespeare
thought and felt in quotations. Sometimes (and if we knew
enough about his reading the occasions would doubtless multiply),
when he is writing with great power, his mind will revert,
unconsciously no doubt, to a whole complex of literary passages,
perhaps learned at school or entered into a notebook, according
to the method prescribed by schoolmasters and learned from the
earlier humanists. For like his contemporaries, Shakespeare
must have kept copious literary notebooks which, under classified
topics, would preserve an analytical summary of his reading.
If this does not square with our usual notions of Shakespeare
as a practising playwright, that is because reading habits have
changed so radically since the sixteenth century.[2]

[1] M. M. Phillips, The 'Adages' of Erasmus, pp. 270–1.
[2] For the notebook method see R. R. Bolgar, The Classical Heritage, pp. 265–75.
The De Copia of Erasmus was, as Dr. Bolgar stresses, a crucial text for sixteenth-
century education: 'The student is to take a note book divided into sections under
headings, which are then further varied by sub-headings and by stock themes
entered under the latter. Reading is then done with a view to extrapolating; and it is

A speech from *Hamlet* can be taken as illustrating this literariness of mind, with its adhesive mnemonic devices and its profusion of well-tried topics all available for instant use.[1] Hamlet's soliloquy 'O, what a rogue and peasant slave am I!' comes at the end of the very long scene with Polonius, Rosencrantz and Guildenstern, and the Players, and it makes an effect of impatiently restrained passion suddenly released. In performance it sounds like a spontaneous outpouring. It gives a convincing impression of a mind actually in motion, thinking and feeling from moment to moment. But for all its lifelike effect of making itself up as it goes along, it can be shown to have at least three major sources. At first Hamlet is still under the impact of the experience he has just undergone (the Player's recital of his speech and his collapse in tears); next, a sense of helpless indecision seizes him while he upbraids himself for his lethargy; and finally he hits upon a solution, the performance of the play before the King. For the dramatic occasion of the soliloquy, the emotion of the Player, Shakespeare drew upon a much-quoted passage from Quintilian: 'I have often seen actors, both in tragedy and comedy, leave the theatre still drowned in tears after concluding the performance of some moving role. But if the mere delivery of words written by another has the power to set our souls on fire with fictitious emotions, what will the orator do whose duty it is to picture to himself the facts and who has it in his power to feel the same emotion as his client whose interests are at stake?'[2] This passage, it seems, gave Shakespeare the idea both for the Players' episode in itself, in which the Player is moved to tears by his own speech, and for Hamlet's subsequent soliloquy which applies it to his own situation. In his opening lines Hamlet comments on the Player's emotion in a tone of incredulous amazement. For this passage Shakespeare took over something from the speech in his own *Richard III* (I. ii. 230 ff.) in which Richard scornfully comments on Lady Anne's weakness in submitting

suggested that every intending writer should go through the whole of classical literature in this way at least once in his life, presumably before he starts seriously to write.' (p. 274.)

[1] Cf. J. Walter Ong, S.J., 'Oral Residue in Tudor Prose Style', *P.M.L.A.*, vol. 80, 1965, pp. 145–54.

[2] Quintilian, *Institutio Oratoria*, VI. ii. 35, tr. H. E. Butler. This was pointed out by T. W. Baldwin, *Small Latine*, Vol. 2, pp. 204–5. Cf. C. O. McDonald, *The Rhetoric of Tragedy*, pp. 127–9.

to his wooing. Women and actors are alike in their emotional
susceptibility:

> What! I that kill'd her husband and her father,
> To take her in her heart's extremest hate,
> With curses in her mouth, tears in her eyes . . .
> And yet to win her, all the world to nothing!
> Ha!
>
> Is it not monstrous that this player here,
> But in a fiction, in a dream of passion,
> Could force his soul so to his own conceit
> That from her working all his visage wann'd;
> Tears in his eyes, distraction in's aspect . . .
> For Hecuba!

The shaping of both passages, the cumulated clauses and the
sudden abrupt halt, are very close. For the middle part of the
soliloquy, where Hamlet's frustration rises to a climax of self-
vilification, Shakespeare drew on the first monologue of the
revenger Atreus in Seneca's *Thyestes*. Again, what is recalled is
not so much the exact words as the shape and movement of the
passage:

> Ignave, iners, enervis et (quod maximum
> probrum tyranno rebus in summis reor)
> inulte, post tot scelera, post fratris dolos
> fasque omne ruptum questibus vanis agis
> iratus Atreus? (176–80)

> Am I a coward, sluggard, impotent,
> And—what I count the worst of weaknesses
> In a successful king—still unavenged?
> After so many crimes, so many sleights
> Committed on me by that miscreant brother
> In violation of all sacred law,
> Is there no more to do but make vain protests?
> Is this your anger, Atreus? . . .[1]

> Am I a coward?
> Who calls me villain, breaks my pate across,
> Plucks off my beard and blows it in my face . . .

---

[1] *Five Tragedies and 'Octavia'*, tr. E. P. Watling, Harmonsdworth, 1966, p. 53.
The translator's incorporation of a sentence from *Hamlet* ('Am I a coward?') seems
unintentional since *Hamlet* is not mentioned in the Appendix which discusses
Seneca and Elizabethan drama. See Appendix A below.

'Swounds, I should take it, for it cannot be
But I am pigeon-livered and lack gall
To make oppression bitter, or ere this
I should a' fatted all the region kites
With this slave's offal . . .

Like Hamlet, Atreus opens in a self-lacerating mood: he too has
been dilatory, or so he thinks, and he heaps up reproaches against
himself. But then Hamlet, disgusted by his own flow of historionic
words—one might say he is tearing a passion to tatters in the
manner of a Senecan revenger—pulls himself up short: 'About,
my brains.' But even in doing this, his phrase—seeming so
natural and unpremeditated—translates Atreus' 'age, anime'
('work, my mind'). For a few lines the movement of feeling has
been Senecan. Finally, for the conclusion of Hamlet's speech,
Shakespeare drops Seneca and makes use of a commonplace about
the moral ends to which the drama could be put: 'I have heard /
That guilty creatures sitting at a play . . .' If there was a precise
source for this, it is impossible to ascertain. Examined in this way,
Hamlet's soliloquy is seen to be a tissue of submerged and no
doubt unconscious literary memories and quotations. It would be
absurd to suppose that Shakespeare needed to consult Quintilian,
Seneca, and perhaps others; it seems altogether likelier that he
carried these scraps in his head, perhaps looking up a notebook,
but knowing what their gist and shape and tone were and in what
sort of context they could be put to work.

Grammar-school pupils were expected to show their skill
through innumerable like-yet-unlike imitations. Unavoidably the
more gifted products of such a high-pressured system became
accomplished parodists and *pasticheurs*. They had learned to imitate the styles of all the poets and prose writers they had studied.
One of the ways in which we can respond sensitively to such early
plays as the three Parts of *Henry VI* is to recognize the many
verbal styles deployed by Shakespeare in different scenes. In *2
Henry VI*, III. i. for example, when Margaret and her exiled lover
Suffolk take leave of each other, they do so in a style derived,
though with impressionistic freedom, from Qvid's *Heroides*. Later
in the same play (v. ii), when civil war in the full military sense at
last breaks out, the theme is announced in sombrely fuliginous
terms and with harshly abrasive epigrams—this time in the manner
of Lucan, the poet of civil war. But whether or not the styles used

are associated with a particular poet, a special style is in fact being chosen for each unit of the play. For each unit is a kind of set piece for which a certain recognizable style is appropriate. To the Shakespearian scholar today there is perhaps a temptation to be over-ingenious in tracing Shakespeare's memory of what he had once read or heard. Notoriously, of the tracing of Shakespeare's sources there is no end. Yet it must be insisted that the situation, by modern standards, was a remarkable one. The sheer extent of Shakespeare's verbal indebtednesses will appear incredible only so long as we forget that his culture was massively orientated towards acquiring certain kinds of linguistic and literary skills. Even now, after so much work has been done on his sources, one can safely say that many of them have still gone unnoticed. In many cases our ignorance is probably of no importance. But in others, knowing the source can increase understanding; it may give us a firmer grip on the *raison d'être* for some detail or other of the conception of a play. Two final examples may support this contention. Each of them shows Shakespeare transforming classical material in a completely personal way; and each of them also, as it happens, shows him at his greatest as a tragic writer.

On more than one occasion in *Othello* Desdemona swerves from telling the sober truth. Even at the moment of her death she tells a lie. The fact that she is—if we wish to use the harsh word— a liar is usually glossed over by critics of the play. But we have no excuse for avoiding it, since Othello insists on it in his bitter exchange with Emilia:

Othello. Why, how should she be murder'd?
Emilia. Alas, who knows?
Othello. You heard her say herself it was not I.
Emilia. She said so. I must needs report a truth.
Othello. She's like a liar gone to burning hell:
'Twas I that kill'd her.
Emilia. O, the more angel she,
And you the blacker devil.

A famous phrase comes to mind as possibly underlying this passage, indeed giving Shakespeare the idea for it: Horace's 'splendide mendax'. (The phrase was no doubt used in Shakespeare's day, as it still is, as a textbook example of oxymoron.) Desdemona is, as Othello says, a liar; she is also, as Emilia says, an angelic one. When we look up the source of the phrase, we find the context surprisingly relevant. The eleventh Ode of Horace's third Book is about the fifty daughters of Danaus. He commanded them to kill their husbands on their wedding night. All of them complied save one, who woke her husband in the night and urged him to flee:

> una de multis face nuptiali
> digna periurum fuit in parentem
> splendide mendax at in omne virgo
> nobilis aevum . . .

> One bride alone, among the many, honoured
> The torch of marriage, proved a shining liar
> To her oath-breaking father and for all time
> Stands as a paragon.[1]

In Horace the girl who is 'splendide mendax' is a heroically faithful wife, a 'virgo nobilis'—like Desdemona. Perhaps instinctively, Shakespeare refrains from including some such phrase as 'radiant liar' which would have directly rendered Horace's famous two words (one remembers what Petrarch said about avoiding word-for-word imitations). Instead Horace's sense is conveyed by the entire situation. But later in the scene Othello applies to himself a closely comparable oxymoron—'honourable murderer'—which further suggests that Shakespeare had Horace's phrase at the back of his mind. These oxymora are not trivial or insignificant: they are part of the entire conception and meaning of *Othello*. The play's world forces its lovers into self-contradiction, so that Othello is at best an 'honourable murderer', Desdemona at worst 'splendide mendax'.

The classical affiliations of *Macbeth* have often been noticed—especially with Seneca's tragedies. A convincing source for the banquet scene, however, has never been discovered. The scene comes as the climax to the third act, which is largely given to the disposal of Banquo. Macbeth urges Banquo to attend the 'solemn supper' he is giving that evening, but as soon as he has left arranges for him to be murdered. In his scene with his wife he shows a similar division of mind: he presses her to give special attention to Banquo that evening and yet warns her that a 'deed of dreadful note' is imminent. At the feast itself these apparent contradictions are clarified. Knowing that Banquo is dead, Macbeth

---

[1] *The Odes of Horace*, tr. James Michie, Harmondsworth, 1967, p. 177.

repeatedly expresses the wish that he were present—a wish ironically granted by the repeated appearance of Banquo's Ghost. The question arises where, if anywhere, Shakespeare could have found the idea for Macbeth's strange division of purpose: the desire, almost expectation, that a guest should attend his feast who had already been put to death. The idea for this came, I suggest, from Suetonius' Life of the Emperor Claudius—which Shakespeare may have consulted a few years before writing *Macbeth* for some traits of his own Claudius in *Hamlet*.[1] In the sixteenth century Suetonius, along with Tacitus and the tragedies of Seneca, was ransacked for material suitable for the portrayal of tyrants. Claudius was seen as belonging to the same gallery of monsters as Tiberius, Caligula, and Nero. Incidents from his life could therefore assume more generally representative or symbolic qualities: this is what tyrants are like. Suetonius has the following passage (the flippant sarcasm of tone is wholly characteristic):

> Claudius's scatter-brainedness and shortsightedness—or if you prefer the Greek terms, his *meteoria* and *ablepsia*—were truly remarkable. After executing Messalina, he went in to dinner, and presently asked: 'Why is her ladyship not here?' On several occasions he sent for men to give him advice or throw dice with him; and, when they did not appear, followed this up with a reproachful message calling them slugabeds— quite unaware that he had just sentenced them to death.[2]

In wondering why Banquo has failed to attend his feast, having just received an assurance of his death from his murderer, Macbeth is running true to type. He has become a tyrant in the classical mould. Of course Shakespeare deepens the psychological effect of the incident: the banquet scene is one of his most searching dramatic conceptions. He converts Claudius' 'scatterbrainedness' into a profound self-alienation: Macbeth's psyche is fragmented. But the idea of the tyrant's inhuman forgetfulness was yet another thrown up by his classical reading—or, to be more cautious, by his reading some book or other which derived this detail from Suetonius. The lives of the Roman emperors were constantly

---

[1] See William Montgomerie, 'More an Antique Roman than a Dane', *Hibbert Journal*, vol. 59, 1960, pp. 67–77. (I owe this reference to John W. Velz's valuable critical bibliography *Shakespeare and the Classical Tradition*, Minneapolis, 1968.) Suetonius was one of the classical authors edited by Erasmus.

[2] *The Twelve Caesars*, tr. Robert Graves, Harmondsworth, 1957, p. 204.

referred to by Tudor writers, Claudius' along with the rest. So, for example, in his *Governor*, Elyot says of Claudius that 'moved with wrath he caused divers to be slain, for whom after he demanded and would send for to supper'.[1] And in the 1587 edition of *The Mirror for Magistrates*, Claudius is given a monologue in which he says of himself (closely paraphrasing Suetonius):

> And so forgetful, such my negligence,
> I would eftsoones enquire for these full rife,
> As for *Messalina* of late my wanton wife:
> Eke for such others I enquirde agayne,
> As I before commaunded should be slayne.[2]

There is therefore a chance that at least a few members of Shakespeare's audience might have recognized the Claudian model for Macbeth's tyrannical behaviour.

V

These are some of the ways in which Shakespeare might be called a 'Tudor' genius. The habits he acquired as a 'grammarian' persisted throughout his work, early and late. The chapters that follow, however, are centred on a group of his earliest plays. With the exception of *Richard III*, these plays are rarely acted and perhaps little read; in comparison with those that came later they have not received much appreciative criticism. Such neglect is not altogether surprising, since they are among the least accessible of Shakespeare's works. The chief reason for this is simply that the whole of the later and greater Shakespeare comes between us and them. Shakespeare's development was so prodigiously rapid that his earlier work has always to some extent been eclipsed by it, and to many readers has even seemed not Shakespearian at all but the work of someone else. Most of the plays discussed in this book have at different times been rejected from the canon or admitted to it only on special terms. But this reluctance to acknowledge them is just another sign that the early Shakespeare is still for most people the unknown Shakespeare, certainly the least appreciated. It takes an effort to see them not as 'early works', or

---

[1] *The Book named The Governor*, ed. S. E. Lehmberg, 1962, Bk. 2, chap. 6, p. 113.
[2] *Parts Added to The Mirror for Magistrates*, ed. Lily B. Campbell, Cambridge, 1946, p. 317.

'apprentice pieces', or as 'forerunners' of later things, but as
plays which were once new, and which bear the full impress of
Shakespeare's mind as it was in his middle twenties.

It is of course quite proper for special purposes to approach
them for what they foreshadow of the later tragedies. To a
remarkable extent the later plays can be said to grow out of them.
They are a storehouse of dramatic forms, themes, motifs, which
far from forgetting Shakespeare continued to draw upon until late
in his career. We can see, at least in retrospect, that *King Lear*
builds on *Titus Andronicus* and *King John*, *Macbeth* on *Richard III*.
As late as *Antony and Cleopatra*, Shakespeare is adapting the
scenic forms of *1 Henry VI*. In these early plays he was staking
out the area within which he would continue to work in his
mature tragedies and at the same time doing some radical thinking
about the drama. But they are more than precursors and sources,
and it is not in that light that they will be considered here. They
form a distinct category in the Shakespearian canon and have their
own peculiar character. Yet we need to get a sense of their
variety as well as of what they have in common, and so the approaches adopted here vary both according to the play and according to the present state of criticism. A sympathetic reading should
find all these plays bigger and more original than they are usually
thought to be, wider in scope, more thoughtful, and more artistically resourceful. But it needs to be remembered that of all
Shakespeare's plays they are the closest to the mid-Tudor, pre-
'Golden' world of his childhood and his parents' youth. Inevitably
therefore they have kept something of the academic cast of mid-
Tudor literary culture. At first glance they may seem more book-
ishly artificial, less 'natural', than their more lyrical successors.
(*Richard III* and *Richard II* can hardly be more than two or three
years apart, yet they belong to different stylistic systems: by the
time of the later play Shakespeare has crossed a frontier and entered
his 'second period'.) The earlier plays, less sensuously ingratiat-
ing, may even strike a reader new to them as merely 'rhetorical'
compositions—not because the later plays do without rhetoric,
but because here the rhetoric is used with all its devices frankly
visible, whereas later, when fashion changed, Shakespeare learned
to conceal them. Even so, that early stylistic system is being used
by a poet who could not help extending its resources, discovering
new means of expression and exploring a far wider tonality than

he is usually credited with. These plays deserve to be read more sensitively.

I have chosen to stress the humanistic impetus of the culture which formed Shakespeare. Indeed its importance can hardly be overstated. But humanism came into contact with and modified an already rich native culture which, for convenience, we designate 'medieval'. Much is now known of course of the medieval heritage of the Elizabethans, and nothing I have said should be taken as attempting to minimize that heritage. The Elizabethan achievement was nothing if not the product of an astonishingly capacious synthesis. If, for example, the banquet scene of *Macbeth* owes something crucial to a historian of classical Rome, it is also, as I hope to show in the next chapter, quite as indebted to medieval Christian forms. And what is true of the banquet scene is true of Shakespeare more generally. The theme of the next chapter is in fact not humanistic at all but medieval. For the point to stress in conclusion is not simply that Shakespeare was a child of humanism, but that he was the heir to two distinct traditions at whose convergence he had the good fortune to be born and both of which he had the genius to fructify.

2. *Shakespeare and the Mystery Cycles*

I. *The Mysteries in Protestant England*

A MAJOR obstacle to a close historical understanding of Shakespearian drama, and particularly the histories and tragedies, has
been the failure to bring into relation with it the great body of
dramatic writing known as the mystery plays, the Corpus Christi
cycles written in the later fourteenth and the fifteenth centuries.
During the last twenty years or so the morality play tradition and
its effect on late sixteenth-century dramatists has been well studied.
We have become used to noticing morality elements put to fresh
use in Marlowe, Shakespeare, Jonson, and others. We have had
Iago's dramatic ancestry traced back through the Vice and Devil
derivatives of the earlier popular drama.[1] We know too (the
example has become trite) that Kent in the stocks in *Lear*, like the
authoritarian trio Overdo, Busy, and Waspe in *Bartholomew Fair*
who are also put in the stocks, are from this point of view simply
late eminent examples of a well tried morality play routine: in
such plays the virtuous often *were* put in the stocks.[2] The mystery
plays, however, although attracting increasingly sympathetic and
expert attention for themselves, continue for the most part to be
treated as if they were without much relevance to the Elizabethan
dramatic imagination. Or, more probably, the later mutations of
mystery play forms have been little studied because they have not
been recognized. The truth is that Shakespeare was the heir to
this late-medieval achievement and would have written differently
if he had not known of it. His mature tragedies would have been
to some extent impoverished if this tradition had not been open
to him. Without it, he might have been—I think he would have
been—less great than he is.

The existence of the mystery cycles has always been known to
Shakespearian scholars, but that large body of drama was until

---

[1] Bernard Spivack, *Shakespeare and the Allegory of Evil*, New York, 1958. See also
Leah Scragg, 'Iago—Vice or Devil?', *Shakespeare Survey*, 21, 1968, pp. 53–65.

[2] The example was not trite when T. W. Craik described the routine in *The Tudor
Interlude*, Leicester, 1958.

recently more known about than known with much first-hand intimacy. Few scholars had given it close study, so that the more general ignorance of it shown by the larger literate public was wholly understandable. Only during the last few years of the nineteenth century and later were the four great cycles adequately edited: the York Plays in 1885, the Chester Plays in 1892, the Townley Plays in 1897, and *Ludus Coventriae* not until 1922.[1] Even so they were still confined to a fairly narrow academic public. Three of the cycles were issued in the restricted Early English Text Society edition, while only in recent years, since 1950, have modernized, easily readable versions of York, Townley, and *Ludus Coventriae* appeared, so attracting for the first time the non-academic public.

The inaccessibility of the texts was one obstacle, but there was also the sheer difficulty of reaching a close familiarity with such extensive works. The immediate literary rewards are often not great. These plays were not meant for close reading, and until recently many of their dramaturgical conventions were not understood. Readers could get little help towards imagining a performance. In any case there was the dominant feeling that the plays which made up the great mystery cycles and the plays of Shakespeare and his contemporaries belonged to quite different dramatic species. They seemed incommensurate with each other, as if Elizabethan dramatists really had made a fresh start. On the other hand, it has always been known that Shakespeare was to some extent aware of the mysteries. Macbeth's Porter is in himself a pointed allusion to the Harrowing of Hell plays, while through such phrases as Hamlet's 'it out-Herods Herod' Shakespeare could remind his audience of a stock figure of the old cycles. But as far as the salient structural features of his histories and tragedies were concerned, it was felt to be unnecessary to search for origins in the native medieval drama.

Another reason why the contribution of the mysteries has been neglected is that the history of Tudor England has lent itself all too easily to simple schematization—to an unrealistically abrupt division between the Catholic, or largely Catholic, earlier half

---

[1] *York Plays*, ed. Lucy Toulmin Smith; *Chester Plays*, ed. H. Deimling and J. B. Matthews; *Townley Plays*, ed. G. W. England and A. W. Pollard; *Ludus Coventriae*, ed. K. S. Block. The provenance of the last is not agreed: Lincolnshire and Norfolk are possible.

more important perhaps, whose quality we cannot know, was destroyed by the authorities. It is this above all that makes it so hard to account, in historical terms, for Shakespeare's achievement. He seems to us to emerge suddenly out of the 'drab' middle decades of the century. But they were precisely the years which saw the worst of reformist zeal, the most uninhibited waves of iconoclastic destruction. As a result, the loss of so many unique texts of the Catholic drama has made it exceptionally difficult to trace continuity in the drama. We can only be negatively sure that if they had all survived, our picture of Elizabethan drama would be very different.

This difficulty determines the oblique and tentative nature of what follows. Although I shall be comparing some of Shakespeare's plays with some of the mysteries (those which happen to survive), the likelihood that Shakespeare knew these particular texts is highly questionable. But there is a strong generic likeness between all the texts we have; in their own ways the authors followed the same scriptural accounts, expounding the same doctrines. What I shall assume—what, I believe, the evidence obliges us to assume—is that Shakespeare knew something sufficiently like the four great cycles to justify our positing a deep indebtedness on his part.

II. *The Passion Sequence: the Fall of Duke Humphrey*

2 Henry VI is not only one of Shakespeare's earliest history plays: it also contains, in its first three acts, a very early example of Shakespeare's tragic writing: the fall and death of Duke Humphrey of Gloucester. This forms a tragic movement complete in itself, a tragedy in little, which, given its narrower dimensions in keeping with its place within the *Henry VI* trilogy, can be compared with the fully extended actions of such formal tragedies as *Titus Andronicus, Lear,* and *Coriolanus. Titus Andronicus* may have been written earlier than the *Henry VI* plays: if it was, Shakespeare wrote tragedy first in a classical style and then, in *2 Henry VI*, in a more native manner. This is the interest of the 'tragedy' of Duke Humphrey: it shows Shakespeare taking over late medieval tragic forms and giving them his own distinctive stamp. But what those forms were needs first to be established.

The action of Humphrey's tragedy is as follows. Henry VI has undertaken to marry Margaret of Anjou, on the prompting of Suffolk, and against the advice of Humphrey, who had already arranged a marriage for him. The arrival of the new Queen adds further virulence to the court factions, for she is herself power-seeking and Humphrey, as the King's Protector, stands in her way. The Queen and Suffolk her lover (as he soon proves himself to be) join forces with Humphrey's old enemy Cardinal Beaufort. Humphrey is first made to relinquish power—ostensibly to the King, but in reality to the Queen and her allies—and is then toppled to his fall. First Humphrey's ambitious wife Eleanor is discovered to be practising witchcraft: she is tried, found guilty, and banished. Then Humphrey himself is accused by his concerted enemies of various malpractices, is summoned to a Parliament at Bury St. Edmunds, and is there murdered.

Such a bald summary conveys very little; it says nothing at all about the way Shakespeare chose to dramatize this series of events. A glance at a few passages from Hall, the chief historical source, will bring us closer to the play as we have it. These are the key sentences (he is speaking of Margaret):

This woman perceivyng that her husbande did not frankely rule as he would, but did all thyng by thadvise and counsaill of Humfrey duke of Gloucester, and that he passed not muche on the aucthoritie and governaunce of the realme, determined with her self, to take upon her the rule and regiment, bothe of the kyng and his kyngdome, & to deprive & evict out of al rule and aucthoritie, thesaid duke, then called the lord protector of the realme . . . This . . . invencion . . . was furthered and set forward by suche, as of long tyme had borne malice to the duke. . . . Whiche venomous serpentes, and malicious Tygers, perswaded, incensed, and exhorted the quene, to loke well upon the expenses and revenues of the realme, and thereof to call an accompt: affirmyng plainly that she should evidently perceive, that the Duke of Gloucester, had not so muche advaunced & preferred the common wealth and publique utilitie, as his awne private thinges & peculier estate. . . . And although she joyned her husbande with hir in name, yet she did all, she saied all, and she bare the whole swynge . . . and first of all she excluded the duke of Gloucester, from all rule and governaunce, not prohibityng suche as she knewe to be his mortal enemies, to invent and imagyne, causes and griefes, against hym and his: so that by her permission, and favor, diverse noblemen conspired against hym, of the whiche . . . the Marques of Suffolke, and the duke of Buckyngham to be the chief, not unprocured by the Cardinall of

Winchester, and the Archebishop of Yorke. Diverse articles, bothe heynous and odious, were laied to his charge in open counsaill, and in especiall one, that he had caused men adjudged to dye, to be put to other execucion, then the law of the land had ordered or assigned. . . . But his capitall enemies and mortal foes, fearyng that some tumulte or commocion might arise, if a prince so well beloved of the people, should bee openly executed, and put to death, determined to trappe & undoo hym. . . . So for the furtheraunce of their purpose, a parliament was somoned to be kept at Bery, whether resorted all the peres of the realme, and emongst them, the duke of Gloucester, whiche on the seconde daie of the session, was by the lorde Beaumond, then high Constable of Englande, accompanied by the duke of Buckyngham, and other, arrested, apprehended, and put in warde, and all his servauntes sequestered from hym . . .. The duke the night after his emprisonment, was found dedde in bed. . . .[1]

Hall's account can be reduced to this : the Queen and the rest conspired against Humphrey with the object of removing him from the scene. Straightforward violence, however, was not open to them : they had to use legal means to get Humphrey isolated and away from his own people. Once this was done, his death was arranged and presented to the people 'as though he had died of a palsey or empostume : but all indifferent persons', continues Hall, 'well knewe, that he died of no natural death but of some violent force : some judged hym to be strangled . . . other write, that he was stiffeled or smoldered betwene two fetherbeddes.' Two features stand out : first, there was a conspiracy against Humphrey; second, the conspirators felt obliged to use legalistic means to do away with him. These features determined the way Shakespeare transformed the narrative into stage terms.

Duke Humphrey himself is conceived in such a way as to mark him as the protagonist of this three-act tragedy. In the chronicles we learn that Humphrey was himself capable of less than ideal conduct : he was, according to Hall at one point, 'either blynded with ambicion or dotyng for love'; and later, his first marriage was 'very wilfull, either blinded with dotage, or inflamed with covetousness of his wife's possessions'.[2] Such details are suppressed by Shakespeare, who in 2 Henry VI needs only a counsellor devoted to his country's good but shamefully made victim

[1] New Arden 2 Henry VI, ed. A. S. Cairncross, 1957, pp. 163-4.
[2] Hall, Chronicle, 1809 rep., pp. 116, 128.

of the malice and greed of others. But he endows the vague presence we faintly discern in the chronicles with a more positive form suiting his tragic purposes. The Humphrey we meet in these first three acts is a *passionate* man, one subject to strong, even violent, feeling. All the chief characters of this play express themselves passionately to some extent. The Henry VI plays are composed according to a system of highly conventional rhetoric which does not allow much subtlety of intonation (though there is more than appears at first); it seems to place a high value on sustained vehemence of denunciation—forcibleness is all. Yet even so, with due allowance for this general loudness of voice, Humphrey is set apart from the others by the clearly deliberate way he is marked, by Shakespeare, as a man of passion. There are several clear signs. Near the beginning of the play (I. i. 49) Humphrey, reading the 'articles of contracted peace' between England and France, is dramatically overcome by sudden feeling:

> *Lets the paper fall.*
> *King.* Uncle, how now!
> *Glouc.*   Pardon me, gracious lord;
>   Some sudden qualm hath struck me at the heart,
>   And dimm'd mine eyes, that I can read no further.

Shortly after, the King, Margaret, and Suffolk leave, and Gloucester initiates the main movement of the play with a long address to the nobles ('To you Duke Humphrey must unload his grief', 71 ff.), a speech whose full-bodied emotional burden is immediately pointed up by Beaufort's reply:

> Nephew, what means this passionate discourse,
> This peroration with such circumstance?

Gloucester's subsequent attack on Suffolk again receives comment in Beaufort's 'My lord of Gloucester, now ye grow too hot' (131); similarly, when Gloucester leaves the stage, Beaufort again calls attention to his passionate nature: 'So there goes our Protector in a rage' (142). The following scene is differently pitched: this is a private colloquy between Gloucester and his wife. But when he chides her for her ambitious 'dream', her reply has the effect, like Beaufort's malicious comments, of bringing out the same distinguishing mark in Humphrey's nature:

> What, what my lord! Are you so choleric
> With Eleanor for telling but her dream?   (i. ii. 51–2)

The next scene is set at court and shows the first stage of the conspiracy against Humphrey. His enemies make a concerted attack on him in a series of hard-hitting accusatory speeches (the speakers are Suffolk, Beaufort, Somerset, Buckingham, and finally the Queen). Humphrey makes no reply, but simply exits. A few lines later he returns saying:

> Now, lords, my choler being overblown
> With walking once about the quadrangle,
> I come to talk of commonwealth affairs.   (i. iii. 150–2)

Again, 'choler' recalls Eleanor's 'choleric' in the previous scene. In II. i, after Eleanor's arrest, he protests that 'sorrow and grief have vanquish'd all my powers' (178), and after her sentence of banishment, 'Mine eyes are full of tears, my heart of grief' (ii. iii. 17). In both these last scenes Humphrey mentions his heart: one instance has just been quoted, while to Beaufort he says, 'Ambitious churchman, leave to afflict my heart'. Throughout these three acts he seems in fact to be suffering from palpitations of painful grief. He is also conscious of his coming end, even though in a moment's overconfidence he shrugs aside Eleanor's warning. At his first exit in i. i, he sounds a clear premonitory note:

> Lordings, farewell; and say, when I am gone,
> I prophesied France will be lost ere long.   (140–1)

And this is *before* the conspiracy against him has been formed. The couplet is repeated, with variations, in ii. iii, when he gives up his staff of office to the King:

> Farewell, good King; when I am dead and gone,
> May honourable peace attend thy throne!   (37–8)

Humphrey's apparent foreknowledge and acquiescence—which are not incompatible with indignation and a will to resist—together with the confident purposefulness of his enemies give his fall a measure of inevitability; the outcome seems already determined.

It seems clear that Shakespeare deliberately presented Humphrey as a man of passion—'passion' in more than one sense of the

word. He both suffers, and is also given to spasms of violent
feeling. He is 'afflicted', 'vanquish'd' by 'sorrow and grief', his
eyes are 'full of tears'; he speaks 'a passionate discourse', and is
also—or is said to be—'too hot', 'in a rage', 'choleric'. He himself
states that he has left the company until his 'choler' was 'overblown', and here his abrupt exit and sudden re-entry are a way
of demonstrating in visible stage terms that he is carried away by
passion. There is, it seems, both an active and a passive side to
'passion': Humphrey is both an agent, who indulges feeling, as
well as one who suffers pain. It is these two aspects of passion
which suggest something mysterious about the process of his fall,
something which we do not find in the obvious narrative and
poetic sources and analogues which Shakespeare either did consult or could have consulted (the chronicles, *The Mirror for Magistrates*, etc.). It is in fact precisely this dimension of non-naturalistic
formality—a suggestion that the action is adhering to a predeter-
mined pattern—that makes his fall tragic in quality rather than
merely pathetic.

This dimension of 'formality' (however we describe it), which
runs through the entire action of Humphrey's fall, is crucial to our
sense of what as a dramatist Shakespeare was doing. At this point
I can return to the passage I quoted from Hall. I remarked that
Humphrey's enemies plotted against him in a conspiracy, and that
their way of ensnaring him was through legal processes. We can
now look more closely at Shakespeare's way of working up this
situation into dramatic form.

There are two scenes in particular (I. iii and III. i) which carry
the conspiratorial process to a high point of verbal violence and
which make a powerful dramatic effect. At the beginning of the
first of them (I. iii. 40 ff), in a private dialogue with Suffolk,
Margaret is near boiling-point: she is enraged that the King
should so neglect her, and also—but on this issue she sees a
possibility of action—that he should still be under the governance
of Duke Humphrey. To make matters worse, Eleanor behaves at
court like a queen and treats her, Margaret, as a poverty-stricken
immigrant. Suffolk soothes Margaret, assuring her that Eleanor is
already on the brink of ruin. Now the rest of the court enter,
already squabbling about whether Somerset or York should be
given the Regency of France. Gloucester unwisely snubs Margaret
and in so doing, precipitates a concerted attack on himself:

Glouc. Madam, the King is old enough himself
   To give his censure. These are no women's matters.
Queen. If he be old enough, what needs your Grace
   To be Protector of his Excellence?
Glouc. Madam, I am Protector of the realm;
   And at his pleasure will resign my place.
Suff. Resign it then, and leave thine insolence.

Suffolk's attack (6 lines) is backed up by Beaufort (2 lines), Somerset (2 lines), Buckingham (3 lines), and finally Margaret (3 lines). Her words are the most personally aggressive of all, since they for the first time show Humphrey's life to be in danger:

> Thy sale of offices and towns in France,
> If they were known, as the suspect is great,
> Would make thee quickly hop without thy head.

At this point Humphrey goes out without saying a word in reply and with a consequent effect of disconcerting abruptness. But the explosive violence latent in the stage situation is at once converted into physical terms: Margaret drops her fan:

> *Queen.* Give me my fan. What, minion, can ye not?
>   (*She gives the Duchess a box on the ear.*)
> I cry your mercy, madam; was it you?
> *Duch.* Was't I? Yea, I it was, proud Frenchwoman. . . .
> Could I come near your beauty with my nails,
> I could set my ten commandments in your face.

The two women, who occupy the highest positions in the country, almost come to blows in an undignified brawl.

The most interesting passage in the scene is the menacing group-attack on Humphrey which leads up to his exit. It is relatively brief (120–35), but it packs considerable force. Five speakers join in the attack, rapidly transferring the burden from one to the other. Humphrey is in effect baited, overcome by an unexpected wave of group-hatred. The promptness with which his enemies line up against him and the rapidity with which their accusations are run off are an important part of the effect. It is not necessary to postulate that the attack is prearranged in detail (in 'real life' such a concerted action would have had to be planned or even rehearsed beforehand): what seems clear is that while it lasts in performance we recognize it—through its repetitive rhythms—as a set-piece of some kind, a movement of heightened formality in which the speakers—Suffolk, Beaufort, Somerset, Buckingham, Margaret—surrender some of their personal individuality while they assume the more fixed lineaments of given roles. These are quite simply the roles of accusers, taunters, insulters. For Margaret, Suffolk, and the rest are engaged in more than a quarrel with Humphrey which happened to flare up as the result of his imprudent remark. They have become for a few moments participants in a ritual of spite and malice, a disturbingly formalized group-act of execration—with Humphrey as the foreordained victim. The violence of the act is precariously contained within the ritual's form. That the violence is there can be gauged first from the fact that Humphrey is for a short time physically removed from the stage and secondly from the physical blow which Margaret inflicts on Eleanor (who in this instance serves as surrogate for her husband).

The second of the two crucial scenes is III. i, another court scene, this time at Bury, where the Parliament has been called and where it is intended that Humphrey shall be impeached. This is another scene in which Humphrey is victimized by a group, and like the first it makes an effect of heightened formality. It is after all a Parliament scene, but the impression made is one of a trial in which the verdict has already been decided. Shakespeare varies the scenic structure: this time we are made to wait for Humphrey's appearance. Accordingly the scene opens with the King saying 'I muse my lord of Gloucester be not come'—the Court have already been waiting for him before the scene begins. This time most of the accusations are made in Humphrey's absence: Margaret leads off with a long elaborate diatribe, intended to win over the weakly compliant but still loyal King. Suffolk, Beaufort, York, and Buckingham back her up, as before, with an effect as of dogs spitefully yapping. The King tries to reply on Humphrey's behalf, but is promptly countered by a second attack from Margaret, which ends

> Take heed, my lord; the welfare of us all
> Hangs on the cutting short that fraudful man.

At this point, however, there is a short interruption to the Gloucester theme: it is not Humphrey but Somerset who now appears, to announce the complete loss of the French territories. It sounds at first like a rather maladroit insertion, designed solely to enable York to remind us in an aside of his latent claim to the throne:

> Cold news for me: for I had hope of France
> As firmly as I hope for fertile England.

But that *is* the point: at this critical moment in Henry's—and England's—destiny, when Henry's right-hand man, his chief counsellor and former Protector, is about to be cast away, we are alerted, with fine economy, to the coming Lancaster–York death struggle. Immediately after York's aside, Humphrey enters for the last time.

It is now line 91; by line 221 Humphrey is to be led away and will not be seen again. This final, or rather penultimate, phase in the conspiracy against him is taken quickly. Humphrey makes a brief greeting to the King and apologizes for his late appearance. Suffolk steps in, capping his words with 'Nay, Gloucester, know that thou art come too soon', and arrests him for high treason. But again the structure of what follows is varied from what happened in I. iii. Then Humphrey had left the stage without a word, returning only when his 'choler' had been 'overblown'; but now he takes his chance of defending himself. In the scene that now takes place the longest speeches are all his. His enemies too change their tune. They regard him as already condemned— indeed already dead—so that outright verbal assaults are no longer necessary. Their tone instead is one of contemptuous dismissal, as if Humphrey's indignant words were not worth getting excited about. So Beaufort says, with a temperance unusual for him: 'It serves you well, my lord to say so much'; so Margaret says, 'But I can give the loser leave to chide'. After Humphrey's longest speech Beaufort does not even deign to reply: he addresses the King, as if pained by the raving of a low criminal: 'My liege, his railing is intolerable'. And Buckingham takes up the same tone, a kind of sanctimonious impatience, as if social decorum were being violated in their having to witness Humphrey's unmannerly lunges: 'He'll wrest the sense, and hold us here all day'. The conspirators are content on the whole to play a subordinate part in this scene: the main part is 'the loser's'. This is the occasion for Humphrey's last formal statement, and he is given his say.

His first speeches are point-by-point rebuttals of the charges laid against him: he did not take bribes, or defraud the soldiers of their pay, etc. Now the King makes his single contribution: he hopes Humphrey will clear himself: 'My conscience tells me you are innocent'. This is the cue for Humphrey's longest reply, and stylistically this speech receives the heaviest rhetorical emphasis in the scene. Humphrey is in effect taking up the point made pro- leptically by York in his aside: England is at this moment at a parting of the ways; it is about to enter upon a scene of blood, and Humphrey's own death is the signal for it to begin:

> Ah, gracious lord, these days are dangerous!
> Virtue is chok'd with foul ambition,
> And charity chas'd hence by rancour's hand;
> Foul subornation is predominant,
> And equity exil'd your Highness' land.
> I know their complot is to have my life;
> And if my death might make this island happy
> And prove the period of their tyranny,
> I would expend it with all willingness.
> But mine is made the prologue to their play;
> For thousands more that yet suspect no peril
> Will not conclude their plotted tragedy.

Shakespeare is making use of the famous set piece from the *Metamorphoses:* the Age of Iron is about to come in, and all the virtues, Justice among them, fly away to Heaven. Humphrey has been speaking with a prophetic voice; but he now comes back to the present, to those in his presence, fixing each of his chief enemies with an incisive phrase:

> Beaufort's red sparkling eyes blab his heart's malice,
> And Suffolk's cloudy brow his stormy hate;
> Sharp Buckingham unburdens with his tongue
> The envious load that lies upon his heart;
> And dogged York, that reaches at the moon,
> Whose overweening arm I have pluck'd back,
> By false accuse doth level at my life.
> And you, my sovereign lady, with the rest,
> Causeless have laid disgraces on my head,
> And with your best endeavour have stirr'd up
> My liefest liege to be mine enemy;
> Ay, all of you have laid your heads together—
> Myself had notice of your conventicles—
> And all to make away my guiltless life.

The victimizers are, verbally at least, themselves pilloried. Each of the men named is hit off in a sharp vignette; the Queen herself is reproached for her part in the 'complot', though she is spared the humiliation of having her likeness caught. As far as the audience is concerned, Humphrey is recalling us to the essentials of the situation: the secret plots of a group of high-ranking, even august, hypocrites under a show of legality, and the moral reality of malice, hate, envy, and power-seeking. Where the centre of power should be—in the King—is only weakness. The King would help if he could, for he knows Humphrey is innocent, but he can do nothing but acquiesce. When Humphrey is duly led away, Henry collapses into a tearful lament, in the course of which Humphrey becomes almost sainted, a figure of pure virtue: 'Thou never didst them wrong, nor no man wrong'. He is a 'calf' led to the slaughter, but he, Henry, the 'dam', cannot help him.

The tragedy is nearly over. The conspirators make their last arrangements for the murder (the dialogue reaches an extreme point of callousness and blatancy) and, finally, about to leave for Ireland, York speaks a soliloquy, preparing us for the second part of the play (Jack Cade's rebellion and York's own bid for the crown). Humphrey's murder follows. At the beginning of III. ii a tableau shows the deed: '*Then the Curtaines being drawne, Duke* Humphrey *is discovered in his bed, and two men lying on his brest, and smothering him in his bed* (at least in the Quarto text; in the Folio the stage business is modified: '*Enter two or three running over the stage, from the murder of Duke* Humphrey').

The long Court scene that follows is almost entirely given to showing the impact of the news of the murder, first on the Court itself, and then on the country at large ('the commons'). Despite its very uneven execution (for example, Margaret's speech, 73 ff., which is much too long and seriously impedes the action at a point when things need to be kept briskly moving), the conception of this scene is in many ways impressive. A sense of profound shock is strongly established—indeed in some obscure way the crime is felt to be more than a murder, even a particularly heinous one: what has happened is more like some cataclysmic disturbance, an earthquake in the spiritual realm. (There are to be other violent deaths in the Henry VI plays and in *Richard III*, but none of them is greeted with such appalled wonderment.) All this is faithfully registered in the King's behaviour. Hearing of Humphrey's death, he swoons. Later, while he waits for Warwick to inspect the corpse, he prays aloud:

> O Thou that judgest all things, stay my thoughts.

Warwick reappears, exhibiting Humphrey's body, and gives his verdict:

> As surely as my soul intends to live
> With that dread King that took our state upon Him
> To free us from his Father's wrathful curse,
> I do believe that violent hands were laid
> Upon the life of this thrice-famed Duke.   (153–7)

The guilty Suffolk replies: 'A dreadful oath, sworn with a solemn tongue!' And Warwick's oath—which swells out without pause for three lines—is in fact quite exceptionally heightened even for this sonorously eloquent play. Within the world of the Henry VI trilogy nothing more serious than Warwick's oath can be said. And Henry's words, spoken just before it, when Warwick invites him to 'view this body', although less magniloquent, belong to the same order of seriousness:

> That is to see how deep my grave is made.

Looking back on this scene, we may feel that it hovers uncertainly between two different orders of effect. From one point of view it gives appropriate tragic expression to what was indeed a cataclysmic event, a turning point in England's history, when the dogs of war were about to be unleashed. Seen from another viewpoint, however, it may be felt to make an effect of wildly exaggerated clamour, as if heightened by the lurid colours of melodrama—something felt particularly in the elaborate protestations of the guilty ones. The question arises whether even the death of such a good man as Duke Humphrey could justify this degree of rhetorical amplification, this plethora of amazement, grief, and indignation. But whatever our critical judgement of the scene, there can be no doubt that its dramatic occasion is one of quite exceptional emotional stress. It brings to an unrestrainedly emphatic climax the tragedy of Duke Humphrey's fall.

I have tried to describe this tragic action so as to bring out its real structural lines, those effects which quicken an audience's response, focus attention, and arouse excitement. Two scenes stand out: those which isolate Humphrey and expose him to the hatred of a group. And in each case, for all the sadistic cruelty latent in the situation, there is an element of ceremoniousness in the way in which the attack is directed. With these considerations in mind, we can now turn to the mystery plays.

All four surviving mystery cycles trace the history of the world from the Creation to the Last Judgement; certain episodes are obligatory, others optional, but all four present a full and detailed dramatic narrative of the life of Christ. Indeed, from the incidents which illustrate Christ's ministry to the Last Supper, the arrest in the garden of Gethsemane, the trials before Pilate and Herod, the Crucifixion, the Resurrection, the appearance to the three Marys, and the supper at Emmaus, the impression made is of a tense, closely knit, tightly constructed sequence. Within that longer concatenation of scenes, the Passion sequence itself, from the Last Supper to the Crucifixion, stands out for its tragic or quasi-tragic impact. Now what will at once strike any reader new to these cycles is the way in which the dramatists develop the opposition to Christ in the persons of the High Priests Caiaphas and Annas. There are variations in the treatment of the Passion sequence in all the cycles, but this stress is common to all of them. We may take as an example the York Plays, perhaps the most vividly dramatic if not the most subtle. The sequence of plays is as follows:

xxvi	Conspiracy to take Jesus
xxvii	The last Supper
xxviii	The Agony and Betrayal
xxix	Peter denies Jesus: Jesus examined by Caiaphas
xxx	Dream of Pilate's Wife: Jesus before Pilate
xxxi	Trial before Herod
xxxii	Second accusation before Pilate: Remorse of Judas: Purchase of Field of Blood
xxxiii	Second trial continued: Judgement on Jesus
xxxiv	Christ led up to Calvary
xxxv	Crucifixion

What we have here is not a series of disjunct plays or scenes but a powerfully accumulative sequence; and essential to its effect of slowly gathering climax is the careful, leisurely, preparatory phase with which it opens, the scenes of conspiracy and

secret meetings, in which first Caiaphas and Annas approach
Pilate and his hall and then, outside, Judas tries, at first vainly, to
get past the porter and at last, having gained admission, broaches
his plan to betray Jesus. The sequence as a whole unfolds in
terms of three major phases : Conspiracy; Trials; Violent Death.
And it is important that these three clearly marked phases are kept
before us despite the wealth of episode and incident which the
sequence, closely following the New Testament narratives, also
manages to accommodate. So, alternating with the scenes involving Pilate, Herod, Caiaphas, and Annas, we have those
showing Jesus with his disciples and friends : the Last Supper,
the Agony in the Garden, Peter's Denial, The Lament of the
Virgin, etc. Everything proceeds with an effect of lifelike hap-
hazardness (the wealth of miscellaneous incident ensures that)
along with a quite other sense of inevitability : the formal addresses made by Jesus to the mystery play audience run counter to
the prevailing naturalism, appealing to our knowledge and the
doctrinal purposes of the entire dramatic undertaking.

There is admittedly in this cycle a good deal of tedious repetition and prolixity. The essential continuity is there, but each play
has to be introduced by its leading character in a monologue—
which does not make for economy—and in the five plays which
present a trial or an examination before a judge one too soon
comes to see the very limited number of topics at the author's
disposal : Caiaphas and Annas repeat their basic charges against
Jesus over and over again. In this respect the Chester playwright
has a distinct advantage in that he can include the entire Passion
sequence in a single play—from the first examination before
Caiaphas and Annas, after the arrest in the garden, right up to
the Deposition from the Cross. The result is an obvious gain in
economy and continuity; at the same time is also, one must admit,
probably less intensity, less opportunity for thrilling dramatic
emphasis.

The first thing to note about the York dramatist's treatment is
the almost obtrusive prominence given to the enemies of Jesus, the
High Priests Caiaphas and Annas. They, and not Pilate or Herod,
are the hero's antagonists, and it is they who supply the driving
power for the entire dramatic sequence. Indeed the York dramatist
goes further than any of the other cycles in building them up
into monsters of hate and malice. The role of Jesus, though of

course centrally placed in terms of stage action, is quite subordinate to theirs in terms of dialogue. In some scenes Jesus is completely silent, as in Herod's interrogation; in others he is given one or two brief replies. But whenever they are on stage the Priests, often called 'Bishops' and presumably dressed in an adaptation of contemporary ecclesiastical clothing, sustain the main burden of the dialogue. They keep up an unrelenting flow of verbal aggression. Pilate, by comparison, is a sympathetic figure, who frequently draws attention to their animus, their inequity, and their want of moderation. So, in the Cutlers Play ('The Conspiracy to take Jesus'), Pilate several times notes their spite and cruelty : 'I here wele ye hate hym' (35), 'Be-ware that ye wax noyt to wrothe' (40), 'Youre rankoure is raykand full rawe' (93), 'For sothe, ye are ouer cruell to knawe' (95). He is astonished at their malice ('Me meruellis ye malyngne o mys', xxx. 505), but despite his clear perception of their motives, he is pushed by the remorseless pair into setting the legal machinery in motion which grants Barrabas his freedom and crucifies Jesus with the two thieves.

Secondly, the conspiratorial element in the action, particularly in its earlier phases, is strong. The York editor names the Cutlers Play 'The Conspiracy to take Jesus', and, far more than in the Gospel narratives, we are made cognizant of a dark plot on the part of the Priests to trap Jesus, which makes headway only when Judas approaches them with the offer to sell his master. The dramatist works up a powerful sense here of evil being generated by human beings; at the same time, theatrical excitement is keen.

Thirdly, the appearance of legality is one which is carefully maintained. Although the Priests are only interested in disposing of Jesus as quickly as possible, by fair means or foul, they cannot act without Pilate's consent, and neither he nor in fact they themselves can openly contravene the law. Jesus finds himself in a political situation in which his enemies, Caiaphas and Annas, feel they must put him to death because they fear losing their power. That is the reality. But the appearance which they feel obliged to maintain (though in the York dramatist's treatment it is at times hardly even that) is one of the upholders of law and order virtuously suppressing the seditious activities of a trouble-maker.

As soon as he is arrested (this is the fourth consideration), Jesus is an isolated figure. He has friends and disciples, but they are helpless to protect him. What we see in the long series of scenes in which he is judicially examined is one man, for long periods silent or uttering only a few words, confronted—or rather sur-rounded—by a group or a whole crowd of adversaries, highly voluble, spiteful, malicious, scarcely containing their desire to wreak their hatred on him physically, and in some scenes of course not even doing that—Jesus is struck, pulled about, thumped, blindfolded, and in the penultimate stage of his ordeal formally whipped. In all these scenes Jesus is pre-eminently the Victim. But it is his apartness, his isolation, that is the present point: as soon as he enters upon his Passion—and dramatically this begins with his arrest—he is alone.

The York dramatist heavily stresses, indeed exaggerates, the roles of Christ's persecutors and tormentors; and in this he is followed by the author or authors of the Townley/Wakefield plays, whose work in some way derives from York's. The other two cycles, Chester and *Ludus Coventriae*, in keeping with their more flowingly continuative mode, are less given to repetition and exaggeration, and place correspondingly less stress on the malice of Christ's adversaries. However, granted local differences in treatment, it remains likely that a great deal in a mystery cycle would have been predictable; after reading four treatments of the Passion one discerns a strong family resemblance between them so that—to return to the point from which we set out—even if Shakespeare did not know any of our four cycles, but did know one or more others which have not survived, the likelihood is that he knew something very similar to what we have. He would have known, possibly in several forms, perhaps seen repeatedly over a number of years, a Passion sequence with (to resume the four features just listed) the roles of the malevolent priests given prominence, a strong conspiratorial element in the early phases, a stress on the legalistic nature of the process through which Jesus was ensnared, and finally a train of events which in due course completely isolated the hero. It seems likely, given the nature of the Gospel narratives and the way in which they were interpreted in the fourteenth and fifteenth centuries, that these features would have been present in any popular dramatization of the Passion.

It might be objected that any dramatization of the Passion would have to take much the same form as these plays. But this is not so. Passion Plays were written in the sixteenth and seventeenth centuries under the influence of humanism and sometimes for Protestant, not Catholic, ends. An example is the *Christus Patiens* (1607) of the Dutch humanist Grotius (which was translated into English by George Sandys). It shows neo-classicism at its most marmoreal, with the three unities, long retrospective narratives and declamations, messenger speeches, etc.; anything resembling liveliness is successfully eliminated. But any number of other ways of adapting the Passion to dramatic form are imaginable—there have been several attempts in our own time, including Pasolini's film of the St. Matthew Gospel as well as Anglo-American pop musicals: the tradition represented by our four mystery cycles is only one such possibility.

What we should envisage, I think, is Shakespeare's possibly knowing a number of these cycles, and, having seen one or more of them several times, reaching the kind of unthinking effortless familiarity with them that anyone in any historical period may arrive at with works of popular entertainment—especially when they have been experienced uncritically early in life (one might compare the way in which children until recently could become intimately familiar with the conventions of Western films). When in his twenties Shakespeare came to write plays of a historical or tragic kind, he would have had the Passion plays of his boyhood as a dramatic paradigm, carried lightly, perhaps half-consciously, at the back of his mind; it would have seemed a well-tried way of making a powerful tragic effect on an audience. Indeed if he saw the mystery cycles—and saw them on a number of occasions —before he became aware of more neo-classical ways of writing tragedy, those Passion plays may well have taken a position of absolute priority in his mind, seeming to him more moving, more natural, more fundamental, forms of tragic drama. And in any case the narrative of Christ's ministry and death was the supreme narrative, the prototype of all suffering and all tragic action. It was one of Shakespeare's distinctions as a tragic dramatist to remain imaginatively faithful to this tradition of his childhood.

At this point we can return to the fall of Duke Humphrey. In the foregoing descriptions of Shakespeare's early 'tragedy' and the typical mystery play treatment of the Passion I have tried to bring out, without forcing the evidence, a marked general resemblance in conception and structure. In making such a comparison we must, as far as possible, ignore the differences in status and morality between the persons concerned (Christ, Duke Humphrey), and consider simply the forms traced by the dramatic action. The four features I have distinguished in the typical Passion plot seem to recur in the action devised by Shakespeare to dramatize the chronicle account of Humphrey's fall: the stress on the enemies of the victim-protagonist, and on their virulent malice; the conspiratorial method of their undertaking against him: the legalistic procedure they find it expedient to adopt, with a consequential wide range of hypocritical speech-tones; and the progressive isolation of the hero, whose friends are powerless to help him. There seems to be no other dramatic source for an action shaped in this way than the mysteries: classical tragedy, for example, offers nothing as close. There is too a confidence in Shakespeare's handling of Humphrey's tragedy which perhaps suggests that he felt he was doing it in an approved, well-attested way—a way approved by audiences already accustomed to that kind of dramatic action.

This general resemblance is borne out by the choice of character types in 2 *Henry VI*. Among the court faction it is Margaret and Cardinal Beaufort, the most implacable of Humphrey's enemies, who most pointedly recall Caiaphas and Annas. Their affinities with the two priests are largely a matter of the way they are conceived as vocal personalities, speaking parts: the voices of all four are at times abrasively harsh, at others almost primly sanctimonious, but always in fact unrelentingly hard. The note is always one of pure hate unsatisfied until it destroys its object. Beaufort of course has a further likeness to Caiaphas and Annas: he too wears clerical vestments and is as little troubled by reminders of his holy office as they are. Henry VI, on the other hand, seems to combine in himself two roles. He recalls Pilate, the head of state, sympathetic to the hero-victim, yet powerless or without the will to help him. But he also has at least some of the qualities of the Virgin Mary. Henry swoons on hearing of Humphrey's death; in paintings of the Crucifixion, though not in the four extant play cycles, Mary too is often shown swooning. And, as we have seen, Henry compares Humphrey to a 'calf', himself to the 'dam', the wailing mother robbed of her 'darling'; in this extended simile (III. i. 210–20) the relative ages of Henry and Humphrey are quite ignored so as to bring out the maternal relationship felt by the King at this moment of loss. And, in the same speech, his line

> Thou never didst them wrong, nor no man wrong

can be matched by a characteristic one of Mary's (in the York *Mortificacio Christi*, 143):

> Allas! he did never trespasse.

In *2 Henry VI* the salient structural devices were the two scenes of baiting, the first exploding briefly, the second more extended and elaborated into a climax. Their dramatic antecedents seem to be those obligatory scenes in which Jesus is interrogated and ill treated by his assembled enemies. The number and duration of these scenes vary according to the cycle, although they always receive strong emphasis. With his rhetorically trained sense of economy and climax, Shakespeare reduced them to the minimum of two. We have therefore in the two baiting scenes an impression of a repeated series, in which we progress from the smaller to the greater; but there is no excess, no waste. Such scenes are planned with precision; their brevity increases their impact.

I remarked of the final scene of Humphrey's tragedy—the discovery of his body and the prolonged clamour that ensues— that there seemed to be something in the crime that was felt to be almost preternatural: it was not only a murder of an individual but a cataclysm in the entire order of nature. This is no doubt partly explained by the real importance of Humphrey's death in the setting of the incipient Civil Wars. But there may also be another dimension in Shakespeare's treatment, which can be accounted for by referring back to the Passion sequences. It is as if something of the uniquely heightened atmosphere of the Passion plays, their awe and horror, their unqualified seriousness, found an echo in this scene of violent death—as if the suggestion of ultimate climax, proper to depictions of the Crucifixion, had been carried over into the smaller-scaled secular tragedy of the fall and death (the 'passion') of the 'good' Duke.

At this point it may be wondered whether some kind of 'Christian' reading ought to be applied to *2 Henry VI* so that, if the resemblances just traced are accepted, Humphrey might be seen as a 'Christ figure', Henry as a 'Pilate figure' or even as a 'Pilate and Mary figure' combined. The answer seems to me clear.

There is nothing to warrant such a hunt for adumbrations of the Christian story. The resemblances in structure and conception, such as they are, between the tragedy of Humphrey and the typical mystery play Passion were not meant to be noticed, and as far as understanding the action of 2 *Henry VI* is concerned, nothing is gained by tracing any connection between them.

III. *The Passion Sequence: Later Tragedies*

Shakespeare made use of mystery play forms in a number of plays, late as well as early. The most interesting transformations come in the later tragedies, but one or two of the early histories show, like 2 *Henry VI*, the availability of the tradition.

Probably the outstanding tragic scene of *3 Henry VI* is that (i. iv) in which York is taken alive at the battle of Wakefield and is taunted by Margaret and Clifford before they stab him to death. Shakespeare's mention of a 'molehill'—'Come make him stand upon this molehill here', says Margaret—makes it clear that he was following Holinshed's, and not Hall's, account:

> Some write that the duke of Yorke was taken aliue, and in derision caused to stand vpon a molehill; on whose head they put a garland in steed of a crowne, which they had fashioned and made of sedges and bulrushes; and, hauing so crowned him with that garland, they kneeled down afore him (as the Iewes did vnto Christ) in scorne, saieng to him: 'Haile king without rule! haile king without heritage!' And at length, hauing thus scorned him with these and diuerse other despitefull words, they stroke off his head, which (as you haue heard) they presented to the queene.

Perhaps it was Holinshed's parenthesis that gave Shakespeare his cue, for the scene of York's death recalls more than one of the violent torture scenes in the mysteries (although, again, Shakespeare need not have known any of those extant). The last of the trial scenes in the York Plays ('The second Trial before Pilate continued; the Judgement of Jesus') shows Jesus whipped by the soldiers before being clothed in purple and pall, set on a seat, crowned with thorns and made to hold a reed for a sceptre. The soldiers then jeer at him:

> *i Mil.* Aue! riall roy and rex judeorum!
> Hayle! comely kyng, that no kyngdom has kende,

> Hayll! vndughty duke, thi dedis ere dom,
> Hayll! man, vnmyghty thi menye to mende.
>
> (XXXIII. 409–12)

and the other soldiers join in the 'hail' chorus. This anticipates in
a general way Margaret's long taunting speech to York, set on the
molehill, in the course of which she sets a paper crown on his
head. But another mystery play comes closer to the tone and
substance of what she says. This is *The Buffeting* (*Coliphizacio*) in
the Townley Plays. In this, Caiaphas indulges himself in a long
diatribe against Jesus, who keeps silent. Although in Shakespeare's
scene York is eventually given a chance, which he seizes, of
making a full reply to Margaret, during her long speech he too
keeps silent—thus making an effect, while it lasts, comparable to
that of the silent Christ. The whole of Caiaphas's speech (127–80)
is relevant, but the following lines are especially so:

> How durst thou the call / aythere emperoure or kyng?
>   I do fy the!
> what the dwill doyst thou here?
> Thi dedys will do the dere;
> Com nar and rowne in myn eeyr,
>   Or I shall ascry the.   (130–5)

> The dwill gif the shame / that euer I knew the!
> Nather blynde ne lame / will none persew the;
> Therfor I shall the name / that euer shall rew the,
> kyng copyn in oure game / thus shall I indew the,
>   ffor a fatur.   (163–7)

(Jesus is King Coppin: King Empty-Skein). So Margaret jeers at
York:

> What, was it you that would be England's king?
> Was't you that revell'd in our parliament
> And made a preachment of your high descent?

And the jeering is on the same topic: how dare you call yourself a
king! It is no doubt possible that Shakespeare was merely recalling
the Gospel narratives, without having the mystery plays in mind
here. But in view of the prominence given in the mysteries to the
malice of Christ's accusers—their long insulting diatribes and the
various ways in which Christ's physical sufferings and humiliations
were protracted on the stage—it seems likely that something of

this ritual of torment was carried over into Margaret's role in this scene.

In *3 Henry VI* the mystery play influence is apparently confined to this one scene. Among the English history plays *Richard II* is entirely about the fall and death of a king, and the comparisons which Richard himself makes between his own situation and Christ's are obviously of interest here. Indeed A. P. Rossiter suggested the influence of what he called 'the staged spectacle of a sacrificial king of sorrows before his judges' which, as he says, were familiar to Elizabethans from the mystery cycles; but he did no more than make the suggestion.[1] The impression I have, however, is that the scene in which Richard is deposed (IV. i) is very unlike the scenes of trial and torment in the mysteries, and indeed the fact that Richard compares himself to Christ may be a symptom of radical difference, not likeness. When Richard says

> Yet you Pilates
> Have here deliver'd me to my sour cross,
> And water cannot wash away your sin

the effect is to draw our attention to his bold and startling figure of speech, and, far from making us see Richard as another Christ, we are perhaps surprised into noticing the differences between them—Richard is, among other things, a man who finds such comparisons appropriate. But quite apart from the personal differences between the protagonists, there is a more fundamental difference in dramatic method. There is nothing in *Richard II* like the two baiting scenes in *2 Henry VI*: Richard is not subjected to virulent group-hostility, nor is he enmeshed by a conspiracy conceived by legalistically minded hypocrites. It would be rash to conclude that there is no mystery play influence, but if it is there it seems a remote and indirect one, for the play seems founded on a different idea of drama from the one we have been considering.

Shakespeare had available a number of basic structural models, any one or more of which he could use for a new play. Whether he was at all conscious of the process, he seems to have reverted to the Passion paradigm for only some of his histories and tragedies, using only those parts of it which were relevant to his new project. But he also wrote other tragedies that owed little or

[1] *Durham University Journal*, vol. 33, 1941, p. 136.

nothing to the old Passion plays: these would include *Titus Andronicus*, *Romeo and Juliet*, *Hamlet*, and *Othello*—although even in these ideas for particular scenes might be traced back to the mysteries. The plays which I shall discuss now, however, all have a large resonance of a kind which seems hardly explicable unless we refer back to the Passion plays. In these cases the basic shaping of each play seems to have owed something crucial to them, as if at a very early stage of its conception Shakespeare's mind went back to what were after all the oldest of English tragedies.

The first of these is *King Lear*.[1] Whatever weight we give to Lear's folly in the opening scene, from his first clash with Goneril (I. iv) to his discovery of Poor Tom on the heath (III. iv) he undergoes a series of shocks which constitute a prolonged ordeal. In two scenes (I. iv and II. iv) he is humiliated by the hostility shown him by his now powerful daughters. He is at first incredulous and then outraged, but nothing in what he says—his curses and protestations and threats—can disguise his utter incapacity to do anything about it. Both scenes are in effect heightened occasions in which the King is baited, first by Oswald and Goneril, and secondly by Regan and Cornwall, who are then abetted by Goneril. Structually the two scenes are variations on the two in which Duke Humphrey is baited: there is the same progression from a smaller to a grander occasion, from a brief explosion of animus to a more prolonged and ceremonious stripping of authority and expulsion from the group. In the first of the two there is even the same scenic device whereby the protagonist, overcome by passion, abruptly leaves the stage only to re-enter almost at once. Lear's adversaries too have qualities which give them a marked family resemblance not only to Margaret, Beaufort and the rest in *2 Henry VI* but to the typical Caiaphases and Annases of the Passion plays. Goneril and Regan—and their supporter Cornwall—are more economically drawn than those; there is in fact no prolixity or excess at all—they are entirely without the loud shrill vehemence of those earlier roles—yet the ferocity, though verbally restrained, is there, as well as the capacity for physical violence.

At the end of the York Play 'The Second Trial before Pilate continued; the Judgment of Jesus' (XXXIII) a moment occurs

---

[1] Maynard Mack has explored the affinities of *King Lear* with the morality play and medieval romance in *King Lear in Our Time* (Berkeley, 1965).

which may seem to a reader of Shakespeare pointedly to anticipate one in *Lear*. This is when Pilate has at last succumbed to the pressures put on him by Caiaphas and Annas and has sentenced Jesus to death. We are nearly at the end of a very long sequence of trials and examinations; the Crucifixion is imminent. Pilate gives sentence:

> Here the jugement of Jesu, all Jewes in this stede,
> Crucifie hym on a crosse and on Caluerye hym kill,
> I dampne hym to-day to dy this same dede,
> Therfore hyngis hym on hight vppon that high hill.
> And on aythir side hym I will,
> That a harlott ye hyng in this hast,
> Me thynkith it both reasoune and skill
> Emyddis, sen his malice is mast,
> > Ye hyng hym.
> Then hym turmente, som tene for to tast;
> Mo wordis I will not nowe wast,
> > But blynne not to dede to ye bryng hym.

> > (450–61)

After all the verbal and physical violence of this scene—Jesus has just been flogged and has fainted under it—Caiaphas' next speech, his last in this play, comes with an effect of pronounced moderation:

> Sir, vs emys in oure sight that ye sadly has saide

(Purvis translates: 'Sir, it seems in our sight that is soberly said').[1] Caiaphas' words show sadism lurking under a cover of judicious restraint, the tone of which is oddly like Regan's words spoken near the end of II. iv, the scene in front of Gloucester's castle, just after Lear has departed for the heath. The point is exactly comparable in its place in the dramatic sequence: the baiting of Lear, like the tormenting of Jesus, is now over, while the scenes on the heath correspond to the Crucifixion play that follows. She says:

> O sir, to wilful men
> The injuries that they themselves procure
> Must be their schoolmasters. Shut up your doors.
> He is attended with a desperate train;
> And what they may incense him to, being apt
> To have his ear abus'd, wisdom bids fear.

> [1] J. S. Purvis, *The York Cycle of Mystery Plays*, 1957.

Now that they have achieved their purpose, both Caiaphas and Regan speak with a demure quietness that is very disturbing.

It would be wrong to press very far the structural affinities of *Lear* with the typical Passion play: *Lear* is to some extent an outgrowth from several of Shakespeare's earlier plays (*2* and *3 Henry VI*, *King John*, *As You Like It*, and others) and it makes extensive use of morality play features. But in its first three acts, in the process through which Lear is resisted and humiliated and cast out from the group, the play seems to hold within itself memories of Passion sequences which Shakespeare had seen. And in a way comparable with what was said earlier about the possible 'exaggeration' of the scene of Humphrey's murder, Lear's experience on the heath is given an immensely emphatic treatment: it too seems a cataclysmic event, an upheaval in the spiritual sphere.[1]

The two other tragedies to be considered here are *Coriolanus* and *Timon of Athens*. It may at first seem improbable that these plays should have any connection with the mysteries, since they are after all both classical in setting, while the hero of the first certainly, and of the second probably, has on the face of it little in common with the Christ of these Biblical plays. But, as before, we need to ignore the personal qualities of the heroes and fix attention on the course of the tragic action, the process of suffering and deprivation endured by Coriolanus and Timon.

The first thing to note about *Coriolanus* is the prominence given to the two tribunes Sicinius and Brutus. They, rather than Aufidius, are the true antagonists of the hero. Their position is one of intransigent hostility to him. They are not of course unbelievable monsters of hate and rancour, yet, despite their real political grievances (which are made clear and are given due, or perhaps slightly less than due, value), they are small in stature and mean-spirited, without generosity and warmth. They are in fact very like priests of the old law, fearful of losing their power to the unconstitutional innovator; and in this they are probably the closest characters in Shakespeare to the Caiaphases and Annases of the mysteries. Shakespeare extends the duration of their roles throughout the play, from the opening scene to the penultimate

---

[1] In *The Story of the Night*, 1961, John Holloway searchingly examines Shakespeare's tragedies in the light of classical anthropology. But he fails to notice the more immediate relevance of the earlier Christian drama.

one, whereas in Plutarch their appearance is limited to that part of the narrative which corresponds to Shakespeare's third act (the sequence which leads immediately to the hero's banishment). This extension of their roles allows Shakespeare to build them up into figures who, like Caiaphas and Annas, oppose the hero at each stage of his tragedy.

Plutarch's *Life of Martius Coriolanus* at several points throws out strange echoes of the Gospel narratives—or rather, to a prospective dramatist who obscurely associated Christ's Passion with the writing of tragedy, that is what they might seem. After Martius' outburst against the people, for example, Plutarch writes:

> Whereupon Sicinius, the cruellest and stoutest of the Tribunes, after he had whispered a little with his companions, did openly pronounce, in the face of all the people, Martius as condemned by the Tribunes to die. Then presently he commanded the Aediles to apprehend him and carry him straight to the rock Tarpeian, and to cast him headlong down the same.

An affray ensues, and

> the tumult and hurly-burly was so great, until such time as the Tribunes' own friends and kinsmen, weighing with themselves the impossibleness to convey Martius to execution without great slaughter and murder of the nobility, did persuade and advise not to proceed in so violent and extraordinary a sort as to put a man to death without lawful process in law; but that they should refer the sentence of his death to the free voice of the people.
>
> Then Sicinius, bethinking himself a little, did ask the patricians for what cause they took Martius out of the officers' hands that went to do execution. The patricians asked him again why they would of themselves so cruelly and wickedly put to death so noble and valiant a Roman as Martius was, and that without law or justice.
>
> 'Well then,' said Sicinius, 'if that be the matter, let there be no more quarrel or dissension against the people; for they do grant your demand that his cause shall be heard according to the law.'

The day of the final session arrives, and sentence is duly passed:

> To conclude, when they came to tell the voices of the tribes, there were three voices odd which condemned him to be banished for life. After declaration of the sentence the people made such joy as they never rejoiced more for any battle they had won upon their enemies,

they were so brave and lively; and went home so jocundly from the assembly, for triumph of this sentence.[1]

There is enough here to recall the Passion story: the trial in front of the people; the eruptions of tumultous violence; and the two tribunes, who insist on process of law but are motivated by hate. Martius might even be seen as a Saviour of the People, who is expelled unjustly for the sins of others; in the last sentence quoted there is at least the suggestion that the people rejoiced in banishing the man who had done so much for them. With Plutarch's narrative, just quoted, St. Matthew's may be compared:

Pilate saith unto them, What shall I do then with Jesus which is called Christ? They all say unto him, Let him be crucified.

And the governor said, Why, what evil hath he done? But they cried out the more, saying, Let him be crucified.

When Pilate saw that he could prevail nothing, but that rather a tumult was made, he took water, and washed his hands before the multitude, saying, I am innocent of the blood of this just person: see you to it.

Then answered all the people, and said, His blood be on us, and on our children.

From one point of view, both these narratives, Plutarch's and St. Matthew's, can be seen as dealing with an episode of Roman history; and perhaps an Elizabethan author would have found it easier than one in a later period to make an easy transition from one to the other.

The whole of Shakespeare's third act seems to be a later variation on the structure we have already examined in *2 Henry VI* and, more briefly, in *Lear*: Martius is subjected to a process of humiliation and threat just as, for all their personal differences, Humphrey and Lear had been. The fact that Martius is a powerful soldier, well able to look after himself physically, and is also himself much given to vituperation, should not obscure the real resemblances between the action here and that of the two earlier plays. So, just as Humphrey and Lear were twice subjected to something that amounted to a formal ritual of group-hostility, so on two occasions Martius is also subjected to a situation which makes severe demands of him. The first is when, in II. iii, he is

[1] *Shakespeare's Plutarch*, ed. T. J. B. Spencer, Harmondsworth, 1964, pp. 327-9, 332.

required to stand in the 'gown of humility' and ask the citizens 'kindly' for their 'voices'. He finds it an ordeal for which his nature and previous training have ill qualified him. The second occasion is that in III. i, when he is confronted and openly braved by the tribunes and is exasperated to such a pitch that— after a long and ominous silence (178–223), during which the tumult is carried to a climax by all the others—he draws his sword against them. Both scenes are essentially tests of his self-control in a situation which is almost intolerable to him. And on both occasions he feels as if he were the victim of an act of aggression. The actual scene of his banishment (III. iii) is briefly dispatched; it is a foregone conclusion, like the murder of Humphrey; the tribunes have no more doubt as to what is to happen than Suffolk and Beaufort did. So the tribunes rehearse their tactics, not doubting the outcome:

> *Sicinius.* Assemble presently the people hither;
> And when they hear me say 'It shall be so
> I'th' right and strength o'th' commons' be it either
> For death, for fine, or banishment, then let them,
> If I say fine, cry 'Fine!'—if death, cry 'Death!'
> Insisting on the old prerogative
> And power i'th'truth o'th'cause . . .
> *Brutus.* And when such time they have begun to cry,
> Let them not cease, but with a din confus'd
> Enforce the present execution
> Of what we chance to sentence.   (III. iii. 12–22)

For they are not only Martius' adversaries but his judges. In the course of the ensuing commotion Menenius and Comminius appeal vainly for conciliation—in their pacific intents they match one side of Pilate—but sentence is pronounced:

> *Sicinius.* . . . in the name o'th' people,
> And in the power of us the tribunes, we,
> Ev'n from this instant, banish him our city,
> In peril of precipitation
> From off the rock Tarpeian, never more
> To enter our Rome gates. I'th' people's name,
> I say it shall be so

—lines which correspond with Pilate's speech, already quoted, sentencing Christ to death. Like Martius' previous clash with the tribunes in III. i, this scene is in effect a kind of trial scene, in which the tribunes are determined that the accused shall be found guilty: the judgement is to be a choice—depending on the 'chance' or 'hap' (22, 24) of what ensues—between death and banishment. If Martius is seen therefore to be in effect on trial throughout this sequence, his situation becomes more clearly comparable with Christ's. For his helpless intransigence makes him as vulnerable to the manipulations of the unscrupulous as, in a worldly sense, Christ is in the hands of the priests and the violent soldiers who are their agents.

Martius is banished, and is accompanied to the gates by his mourning womenfolk. We are next shown, in a brief scene, Volumnia denouncing the tribunes, and the first major movement of the play comes to an end. The next scene (IV. iii) initiates the second movement: '*Enter a* Roman *and a* Volsce, *meeting*'. (Editors generally place the scene on a 'highway' between Rome and Antium.) They exchange news, the Roman telling the Volscian of the banishment of Coriolanus:

> *Vols.* Coriolanus banish'd!
> *Rom.* Banish'd, sir.

The entire exchange recapitulates the tumultuous proceedings of the previous part of the play, but from the viewpoint of an outsider, one interested and sympathetic but removed from the Roman scene. It ends on a friendly convivial note:

> *Vols.* I am most fortunate thus accidentally to encounter you; you have ended my business, and I will merrily accompany you home.
> *Rom.* I shall between this and supper tell you most strange things from Rome. . . . So, sir, heartily well met, and most glad of your company.

This odd little scene is often cut in performance but, quite apart from its explicit content, it helps prepare for Martius' appearance in the next scene: in this respect, its function is to effect a change of tone—to one quiet, meditative, even contemplative. We view the action as if from a distance, and with full sympathy for 'that worthy Coriolanus' (21). The scene takes a backward glance over the whole play up to that point, before the second movement is properly set going in the next scene.

It seems possible that Shakespeare's mind is still running, no doubt unconsciously, on the Passion sequence, and that this scene recalls a play which seems to have been obligatory in mystery cycles—that in which two travellers on the road to Emmaus meet Jesus after his resurrection. (A play on this subject occurs in all four of the English cycles.) In the York cycle (XL), two pilgrims meet on the road between Jerusalem and Emmaus. They tell over, lamenting while they do, the recent events in the city—the arrest of Christ, his trial, suffering and death. A stranger then appears—he is the risen Christ—and they repeat their story to him. He reproaches them for their lack of faith, and they beg him to stay the night with them at the castle of Emmaus. He agrees, and eats supper with them before vanishing. If the encounter with the Stranger is omitted, what we have in IV. iii of *Coriolanus* is remarkably close to the occasion dramatized in the Road to Emmaus plays. In both, two travellers meet on a highway and discuss events just past in the city; both scenes end with a promise of supper. But it is not only its substance and its occasion which is so like the typical *Peregrini* play: also important is its position in the dramatic sequence. It is essentially a kind of epilogue to the main tragic events of the play, or rather a retrospective prologue to the final movement of the sequence—and there is, moreover, no suggestion for it in Plutarch.

The appearance of the 'Stranger' has no equivalent in IV. iii of *Coriolanus*. The next scene, however, opens as follows: '*Enter* Coriolanus *in mean apparel, disguis'd and muffled.*' This brief sequence—up to the self-revelation of Martius to Aufidius—is remarkably suggestive and imaginative. Martius in disguise has become a mysterious figure—and a suggestion of mystery is something the play *Coriolanus* on the whole lacks. When he encounters first the Citizen, and then Aufidius' servants, and is left waiting outside the hall while the feast goes on within, it is as if we have descended to a more primitive mythical level than that on which the earlier part of the play took place: this is a world of primitive epic or folklore, of disguised heroes and unrecognizing servants— not unlike the world of Ulysses in the *Odyssey*. (Plutarch actually refers to Homer's Ulysses in his account of these events.) Martius himself is a different person from what he was when we saw him last: an immense change has come over him. He is now silent, withdrawn, quietly sardonic. We are made to feel that he has been alone for a long time, communing with himself and brooding over the events that have brought him to his present state of 'vagabond exile'. In these new surroundings Martius is not only a stranger, he is also a strange man. His strangeness is stressed (Shakespeare perhaps took up the word from Plutarch: 'the strange disguising of this man'):

3 Serv. What fellow's this?
1 Serv. A strange one as ever I look'd on . . .
3 Serv. Prithee tell my master what a strange guest he has here.

(IV. V. 19–35)

The events dramatized in this short sequence are all in Plutarch, yet I want to suggest, in keeping with what I said earlier, that the new changed Coriolanus we meet in these scenes is an enigmatic ghostlike presence, and in this he is, if only fleetingly, like the Stranger met by Lucas and Cleophas on the road to Emmaus: a stranger in the land of the living. For this effect to be conveyed in performance it is essential that he should be as heavily disguised as the stage direction indicates: '*in mean apparel, disguis'd and muffled*'. The effect ought to be a little eerie.

The most visually striking scene in *Coriolanus* is that in the last act in which the women of the hero's own family appeal to him to spare the city. In Plutarch the whole narrative might be said to lead up to it, while for Shakespeare it was crucial, showing as it does the final—and for the hero, tragic—triumph of 'Nature' over the dehumanizing military ethic of Rome: '*Enter, in mourning habits,* Virgilia, Volumnia, Valeria, *young* Marcius, *with Attendants.*' Three women go to seek out the hero. The circumstances could hardly be more different, but they are not enough to obscure a resemblance in theatrical effect to an obligatory episode in the mystery plays (perhaps the earliest Gospel incident ever to be dramatized): the visit of the three Marys to Christ's tomb.

The perception or recognition of arcane parallels or analogies is not, on the face of it, a familiar habit of the modern mind (although there is a good deal like it in Freudian thinking); but that it was an ingrained habit of the late medieval mind, indeed a cultivated skill, is well attested. In the following passage, for example, the author is discussing the way in which the mystery cycles are careful to include what he calls 'foreshadowings and prophecies of the central incident, the redemption of mankind on the cross':

Summaries of preceding action abound, always with the emphasis on the scheme of salvation. Thus, God reviews man's creation, temptation, and fall as a prologue to the play of the Deluge, because it was man's sin that required the deluge as punishment. The Abraham and Isaac play is preceded by a similar summary, this time by Abraham, and there is another, by God again, as a prologue to the Annunciation. Here it serves as an introduction to the beginning of man's redemption, and it is reinforced with one of the parallels with which the devotional literature of the Middle Ages abounds. As there were three things in the fall, God says, a man (Adam), a maid (Eve), and a tree (of knowledge); so there will be three things in the redemption, a man (Jesus), a maid (Mary), and a tree (the cross).[1]

The capacity to find such parallels or analogies had certainly not been lost by the second half of the sixteenth century: the rhetorical procedure for 'inventing' matter suitable for a theme often involved seeking out parallels, sometimes remote and oblique, as we often find in poetic imagery, in panegyrical writing, as well as in the contriving of multiple plots for plays. The capacity for discovering such parallels went with an equal capacity for ignoring whatever was irrelevant to the comparison. So the fact that the 'maid' was a wife in the Fall but a mother in the Redemption is not considered in any way damaging to the parallel. What I am suggesting here is not that Shakespeare's three Roman women adumbrate the three Marys of the Gospel, but that this possible point of comparison—three women go to seek out the man who has been (1) crucified, (2) banished—may have encouraged Shakespeare to develop his new tragic subject in terms of the Passion sequences (to which in any case other features of the story of Coriolanus as told by Plutarch also pointed). Shakespeare's imagination was intensely theatrical: he was well practised in seeing potential subjects in visual stage terms; and it may have been enough to have imagined the three Roman women going out to see Coriolanus for him to have associated it with the theatrically comparable effect of the three Marys going to visit Christ's tomb.

The other late tragedy relevant here is *Timon of Athens*, which in the general direction of its movement has certain obvious affinities with *Coriolanus*. The first part of *Timon* takes place in the City, as does most of the first three acts of *Coriolanus*. The crisis comes in Act Three, as a result of which both heroes leave for the country outside; neither returns to the city of his birth. These similarities support the notion that what was true of the genesis

[1] Arnold Williams, *The Drama of Medieval England*, 1961, pp. 112–13.

of one play may also be true of the other. Both have a relation with the Passion paradigm.

Within the likeness, however, there are important differences. If we apply the fourfold test applied earlier to *2 Henry VI*—the prominence given to the hero's adversaries and their malice; their conspiratorial method; their legalism; and the progressive isolation of the hero—then it becomes clear that, while all four find some form in *Coriolanus*, even if much modified or given little stress, they are not all present in *Timon*. The feature most obviously missing is the second: the conspiratorial methods of the hero's adversaries. No one can be said to conspire Timon's downfall. The action of the play does not run in that direction. But of the remaining three features, all are well represented. However, the adversaries of the hero are not presented explicitly as such: there is instead a whole society of beneficiaries, all those who have 'tasted' of Timon's prodigal bounty. At first indeed we are not aware that there is any opposition, or potential hostility, between Timon and his apparent friends. Only in the second act, with the disclosure made about the state of Timon's finances, does a rift become apparent. What then emerges is the grouping, no longer of bountiful host and guests, but of the bankrupt and his predatory creditors. Timon's former friends are now definitely his adversaries, as is made clear in the series of short encounters between Timon's servants and Lucullus, Lucius, and Sempronius (III. i, ii, iii). It seems clear, then, that although none of these characters is given much individuality—they are presented frankly as types—taken together they form a group equivalent in function to the more sharply delineated adversaries of the plays earlier considered: Margaret, Beaufort, and the rest; Goneril, Regan, and Cornwall; and the tribunes. Secondly, although they do not proceed against the hero in a conspiratorial way, they share with those other adversaries something of their hypocritical legalism: they insist on recovering their debts or invent excuses for not lending Timon money although they have all in the past benefited from his generosity. (A recent editor of *Timon* refers to the displacement of 'the bond of loyalty and service' by 'the cash-book and by a cold impersonal legalism'; and in the scene between Alcibiades and the Senate he finds in the Senators 'an unrelenting application of the letter of the law'.[1]) But although there is no

[1] New Penguin *Timon of Athens*. Harmondsworth, 1970, ed. G. R. Hibbard, p. 35.

conspiracy against Timon, nevertheless the fact that he is himself in ignorance of his true financial state makes his position, as far as the action of the play is concerned, comparable with that of someone who is being plotted against. The true state of things dawns on him only when he experiences the changed behaviour of others. Finally, the isolation of the hero is so obviously present in this play that it needs only to be mentioned.

Timon's adversaries cannot be located in two or three named individuals; they are rather to be found in an entire society. It is therefore of some interest that—despite the (as it might at first seem) unpromising or recalcitrant nature of his material—Shakespeare should have devised two scenes in which the hero undergoes startlingly violent treatment. They can be called baiting scenes, without stretching the term too much, and they closely correspond to those in the plays earlier discussed. Both scenes are quite short: a reader of the play might be forgiven for altogether overlooking their existence. Yet they can be shown to have exactly the same kind of ritualistic force exerted by those other scenes in which the victim-hero is subjected to a hostile onslaught, not precisely physical in its terms, yet with a suggestion that physical violence is imminent. Both are scenes in which Timon is assailed by creditors.

The first (II. ii) opens with Flavius, Timon's steward, '*with many bills in his hand*' waiting for Timon to return from hunting: he means to have a showdown with him. Three servants enter, all sent by their masters to reclaim debts: we have just been shown, in the previous scene, a Senator instructing his servant Caphis not to be put off by mild words, but to press home his master's need for payment. The scene develops as follows:

Enter Timon *with his Train, with* Alcibiades.

Tim. So soon as dinner's done we'll forth again,
    My Alcibiades.—With me? What is your will?
Caph. My lord, here is a note of certain dues.
Tim. Dues! Whence are you?
Caph. Of Athens here, my lord.
Tim. Go to my steward.
Caph. Please it your lordship, he hath put me off
    To the succession of new days this month.
    My master is awak'd by great occasion
    To call upon his own, and humbly prays you

That with your other noble parts you'll suit
  In giving him his right.
Tim.   Mine honest friend,
  I prithee but repair to me next morning.
Caph. Nay, good my lord—
Tim.   Contain thyself, good friend.
Var. Serv. One Varro's servant, my good lord—
Isid. Serv. From Isidore: he humbly prays your speedy payment—
Caph. If you did know, my lord, my master's wants—
Var. Serv. 'Twas due on forfeiture, my lord, six weeks and past.
Isid. Serv. Your steward puts me off, my lord; and I am sent expressly
  to your lordship.
Tim. Give me breath.
  I do beseech you, good my lords, keep on;
  I'll wait upon you instantly.

(Exeunt Alcibiades and Lords)

The scene is in a way very slight; it is all over in a minute or so.
But the two-fold suggestion—of complete surprise on Timon's
part and of overwhelming concerted action on the parts of the
servants—is very telling. It falls into two carefully gradated
stages. First, Caphis importunes Timon for payment. He grows
more vehement, so that Timon tries to pacify him: 'Contain thyself, good friend.' But his words have the opposite effect to what
he intends. For the other two servants join in (this is the second
phase) and overcome Timon with their reiterated demands.
Timon's reply shows the physical effect on him of this 'tongue-
battery':

Give me breath.

The line stops abruptly. Timon is for a moment overcome, but
recovers sufficiently to make sure that his friends move on and
witness no more of his confusion.

The other scene (III. iv) repeats the effect, but on a larger scale
(like each of the second baiting scenes in *2 Henry VI*, *Lear* and
Coriolanus). The opening stage direction sets the scene: '*Enter
two of Varro's* Men, *meeting Lucius'* Servant, *and* Others, *all being
servants of Timon's creditors, to wait for his coming out. Then enter
Titus and* Hortensius.' There is presumably a crowd of servants,
as many as the acting company can muster. But the crowd are
kept waiting. First, Flaminius, one of Timon's servants, appears,
and goes into the house. Then '*Enter Flavius, in a cloak, muffled.*'

He too pushes his way past the servants ('You do yourselves but wrong to stir me up; / Let me pass quietly') and he too goes into Timon's house. At last a cry is heard from *'within'*—it is Flaminius crying 'Servilius, help! My lord! my lord!'—and Timon makes his appearance.

> *Enter* Timon, *in a rage*, Flaminius following.

Tim. What, are my doors oppos'd against my passage?
  Have I been ever free, and must my house
  Be my retentive enemy, my gaol?
  The place which I have feasted, does it now,
  Like all mankind, show me an iron heart?
Luc. Serv. Put in now, Titus.
Tit. My lord, here is my bill.
Luc. Serv. Here's mine.
Hor. And mine, my lord.
Both Var. Serv. And ours, my lord.
Phi. All our bills.
Tim. Knock me down with 'em; cleave me to the girdle.
Luc. Serv. Alas, my lord—
Tim. Cut my heart in sums.
Tit. Mine, fifty talents.
Tim. Tell out my blood.
Luc. Serv. Five thousand crowns, my lord.
Tim. Five thousand drops pays that.
  What yours? and yours?
1 Var. Serv. My lord—
2 Var. Serv. My lord—
Tim. Tear me, take me, and the gods fall upon you! (*Exit*)
Hor. Faith, I perceive our masters may throw their caps at their
  money. These debts may well be call'd desperate ones, for a
  madman owes 'em. (*Exeunt.*)
> *Re-enter* Timon *and* Flavinius.
Tim. They have e'en put my breath from me, the slaves.
  Creditors? Devils!

This is certainly a scene of 'passion' (in the senses imputed earlier to Humphrey). Timon enters 'in a rage' even before the servants get in their bills. He rushes away abruptly, but then as suddenly returns. He is a man off-balance, in a state of shock. (As we have seen, Humphrey and Lear betrayed themselves with similar unstable movements in the first of their baiting scenes.) The suggestion of physical violence is clearly greater here than in the earlier scene. The paper 'bills' brandished by the servants are figuratively transformed into the steel blades of halberds ('steel bills')—'cleave me to the girdle', 'Cut my heart', 'Tear me'. Timon is finally affected as before—by a loss of 'breath':

They have e'en put my breath from me, the slaves.

Since breath is life, robbing him of his breath is a token killing. As the servants 'put in' their bills, so that Timon is surrounded by assailants, one is reminded of the assassination of Julius Caesar, as Shakespeare had staged it. Though so brief, the scene is perhaps the most nakedly violent of all Shakespeare's baiting scenes. For although the occasion is one (merely) of a bankrupt man being besieged by creditors, the stage effect is of a mob tearing a man to pieces (again, as in *Julius Caesar*, when the mob kill Cinna the poet).

Shakespeare's sources for *Timon* offered very little in episode or incident, unlike the source for *Coriolanus*, which supplied a good deal. The gap between sources and play is therefore unusually large, for Shakespeare was obliged to invent most of his plot. What the finished product (or unfinished, as some scholars would say) unquestionably possesses is an immense resonance, an impressive power of suggestion, to which Wilson Knight has responded with least inhibition. He finds the play 'conceived on a scale even more tremendous than that of *Macbeth* and *King Lear*', while for him its 'universal tragic significance is of all most clearly apparent'.[1] Few perhaps have been wholly persuaded by his argument: *Timon* is still neglected, by readers as well as in the theatre. Yet the grandeur of its conception ought surely not to be a matter of dispute, even if one may grant, as Wilson Knight does, 'certain roughnesses due probably . . . to lack of revision'.[2] Indeed the thinness or lack of rich detail with which the play's world is established, the meagreness of its characterization, and the paucity of powerfully developed scenic occasions serve to throw attention on to its conceptual magnificence. Alone among Shakespeare's heroes Timon has no binding family relationships: his only bonds are voluntary ones, those with other members of

[1] 'The Pilgrimage of Hate: An Essay on *Timon of Athens*', in *The Wheel of Fire*, 1960 rep., p. 207.
[2] Ibid., p. 239.

society and with his own servants. This in itself—his personal
freedom—helps to raise the discourse enacted by the play to a
more abstract philosophical plane. As many have remarked, the
play is like a parable; the circumstances of the story are not
particularized with much care: indeed a certain deliberate perfunctoriness is one of *Timon*'s distinguishing characteristics. A
few incidents are lightly sketched in (like the generosity of Timon
to Ventidius, imprisoned for debt, and to the servant who is a
suitor to the old Athenian's daughter), but usually, as in these
instances, they seem brought in to illustrate a theme rather than
occurring as necessary details in a narrative. As editors have often
perplexedly noted, we are not told who the friend of Alcibiades
is, for whom he pleads before the Senate in III. v: but this with-
holding of specific detail, more deliberate than careless, is wholly
characteristic of the play. What we are made imaginatively to
entertain is the grand idea of Timon, the lover and hater of
mankind, *as* an idea, rather than be involved in the imitation of a
tragic action. And what the idea is—or one part of it—is suggested
by some of Wilson Knight's formulations: 'He is a thing apart,
a choice soul crucified . . . a principle of the human soul, a possibility, a symbol of mankind's aspiration.' For Wilson Knight he is
unqualifiedly 'Christlike': 'when Timon's servants part to wander
abroad separated, they are as disciples of the Christ meeting after
the crucifixion'.[1] And he quotes as a Gospel allusion the First
Stranger's lines

> Who can call him his friend
> That dips in the same dish?

(III. ii. 64–5)

The question arises whether these comparisons of Timon with
Christ are not absurdly extravagant, whether they are relevant in
any way. A firm answer is not, I think, easy to arrive at. Wilson
Knight is right, it seems to me, in saying that we are reminded of
the Passion at several points of *Timon*. But it is hard to know
what to make of these apparent analogies. The Passion seems both
relevant and irrelevant; it obtrudes itself occasionally on the
mind, yet with no very illuminating effect. One might make a
comparison with the forms of prosody. A poet may both evoke
the regular beat of an iambic line and at the same time thwart it

---

[1] 'The Pilgrimage of Hate: An Essay on *Timon of Athens*', in *The Wheel of Fire*,
1960 rep., p. 235.

in the variations he makes on it. In a comparable way, though hardly consciously, the Passion paradigm is evoked only to be dismissed; a comparison is made only to be rejected. Timon is not a 'Christ figure', but without the Gospel narratives of Christ's Passion and perhaps the plays that gave the Passion a dramatic form it is unlikely that the simple, perhaps too simple, but reverberant conception of *Timon of Athens* could have come into being. Those speeches which have been taken as allusions to the Gospels seem to work in a similar way: such a remark as 'Who can call him his friend / That dips in the same dish?' seems certainly to recall Judas at the Last Supper, but the result of the comparison is oddly unilluminating. A relation is made between the story of Timon and the story of Christ—but one of contrast as much as similarity.

One scene especially recalls the Gospel story. This is IV. ii, in which Flavius, Timon's steward, and his other servants share the last of their money and separate. Wilson Knight's comparison with the disciples of Christ meeting after the crucifixion has just been quoted. More to our purpose is the fact that this occasion was dramatized in the mystery cycles. In the Chester Plays, for example, it occurs at the beginning of 'The Sending of the Holy Ghost' (XXI), where Peter speaks 'ad condiscipulos':

> My deer Brethren, every one,
> you know well, both all and one,
> how our lord is from us gone
> to Bliss that lasteth aye.

> Comfort now we have none,
> save his Behest to leeve uppon;
> therfore lyve we in this wonne,
> that never one wend away. . . .

> Therfore lenge we all right here,
> this faythfull fellowship in fear,
> till our lord, as he can us leere,
> send us of heauen light.

(L. 16)

The play goes on to show the election of Matthew and the sending of the Holy Ghost, but the occasion with which it starts—the coming together of the disciples after the catastrophe—is closely paralleled in Shakespeare's scene. There is nothing to suggest the scene in Shakespeare's sources, and moreover, though very effective and well written in itself, it is not prepared for in the preceding action: it could be thought of as almost an excrescence (it might be cut without the audience noticing anything amiss), which might be taken as a sign that Shakespeare was in some way remembering an effective dramatic sequence from his youth. For a few moments Timon's servants are almost like disciples (the word 'fellows' is repeated, and 'fellows' and 'fellowship' occur in the Chester Play just quoted). And when Flavius urges them to remember Timon—

> Wherever we shall meet, for Timon's sake,
> Let's yet be fellows. . . .

—he makes it seem as if the act of remembrance will have (to put it no more strongly) its own solemn formality.

IV. *Judas and Herod*

An obvious difficulty in trying to trace the influence on Shakespeare of the mystery plays is that in certain areas it will be impossible to distinguish it from the direct influence of the Bible and of Christian teaching more generally. In *Antony and Cleopatra*, for example, the scene (IV. ii) in which Antony asks his servants to wait on him at supper for the last time reminded Middleton Murry of Christ eating supper for the last time with his disciples.[1] But Murry was certainly thinking of the Gospels here, not of the mystery plays, and—if there is anything in his comparison—he was probably right. I have borne in mind this possible objection in the present section in which I propose that Shakespeare made use of two distinct mystery play scenes without taking over the shaping of the Passion sequence as a whole. The plays concerned are *Othello* and *Macbeth*.

The second scene of *Othello* shows a meeting at night between Othello and Brabantio. Brabantio has just discovered Desdemona's elopement and has been worked up into a rage by Iago, who hopes to bring about a violent clash. This is Othello's first appearance in the play: he enters in conversation with Iago. But despite Iago's attempt to enflame him into a mood of angry resentment, Othello remains calm, and when Brabantio and the

---

[1] *Shakespeare*, 1936, pp. 361-4.

Officers arrive he again refuses the offer of violence, this time with the pacific words

Keep up your bright swords, for the dew will rust them.

Iago's schemes come to nothing: there is no clash of swords. Othello leaves for the Duke and Senators with the others.

Such a summary gives little sense of the scene's qualities in performance: its alternations of calmness and quiet and of noisy violence, and its romantic visual appeal to the eye. The scene is a nocturnal one, and the Folio stage directions three times call for torches: 'Enter Othello, Iago, Attendants, with Torches, 'Enter Cassio, with Torches', 'Enter Brabantio, Roderigo, with Officers, and Torches'. The effect of swords glinting in the flickering torchlight is thus ensured.

The occasion for this scene might be called Brabantio's projected arrest of Othello—a project which is thwarted. But the term arrest serves to indicate what was, I propose, its ultimate theatrical source in the mystery cycles: the arrest of Jesus in the garden of Gethsemane, a scene which occurs in all the surviving cycles. There is no narrative or dramatic source for this narrowly averted clash at night between Othello and Brabantio. For many of the scenes in Othello, Shakespeare adapted scenic inventions from his own earlier plays, but there is apparently nothing in them which could have supplied the germ for this present scene, which becomes for a few moments a secular version of the Betrayal. Just as Jesus is forcibly led away from the scene of his arrest to be tried before Pilate, so Othello leaves the scene of his thwarted arrest for the Senate where in I. iii he undergoes a kind of trial when he defends his marriage before the Duke and Senators.

I have just stressed the strictly theatrical qualities of Shakespeare's scene: the way in which darkness is evoked by means of torches, so that we have a number of lively contrasts: light and darkness; violence and noise on one side, dignity and calm (in the person of Othello) on the other. This set of contrasts is exactly matched in all versions of the arrest of Jesus. I shall quote from the Ludus Coventriae text: this cycle has by far the fullest stage directions, so that the comparison I am making—which turns on stage effect—can be best supported. The earlier part of the Gethsemane sequence has been hushed and still: the disciples have fallen asleep, Jesus prays, and '*An Aungel descendyth to jhesus* and *bryngyth to hym A chalys with An host ther in*.' The angel ascends, Jesus awakens the disciples, and at this point the scene abruptly changes its tempo. The following stage direction is the important one for my comparison:

here jhesus with his dyscipulis goth in-to the place and *ther xal come in A x personys weyl be-seen in white Arneys* and *breganderys* and *some dysgysed in odyr garmentys with swerdys gleyvys* and *other straunge wepons as cressettys with feyr* and *lanternys* and *torchis lyth* and *judas formest of Al conveyng hem to jhesu be contenawns.*[1]

We have here the collocation of night, torches, and armed men arriving with the intention of arresting one who is the 'hero' of the play. In the *Ludus Coventriae* text this exchange immediately follows:

> *Jhesus.* Serys in your way ye haue gret hast
> To seke hym that wyl not fle
> Of yow I am ryth nowth A-gast
> Tell me serys whom seke ye.
>
> *Leyon.* Whom we seke here I telle the now
> A tretour is worthy to suffer deth
> We know he is here A-mong yow
> His name is jhesus of nazareth.
>
> *Jhesus.* Serys I am here that wyl not fle
> Do to me all that ye kan
> For sothe I telle yow I am he
> Jhesus of nazareth that same man.

A few moments later Judas kisses Jesus, and Peter draws his sword and cuts off Malchus' ear. Jesus replaces the ear ('*cryst blyssyth it* and *tys hol*'), saying:

> Put thy swerd in the shede fayr and wel
> Ffor he that smyth with swerd with swerd xal be smete.

The opponents of Jesus proceed to place him under arrest, Leyon saying:

> Let me leyn hand on hym in heye
> On to his deth I xal hym bryng
> Shewe forth thi wyche-crafte and nygramansye
> What helpyth the now Al thi fals werkyng.

[1] *Ludus Coventriae*, p. 264.

Jesus mildly remonstrates on his rough treatment:

> Ffrendys take hede ye don vn-ryth
> So vn-kendely with cordys to bynd me here
> And thus to falle on me be nyth
> As thow I were A thervys fere.

But he is violently haled away:

> *here the jewys lede cryst outh of th*e *place wit*h *gret cry* and *noyse some*
> *drawyng cryst forward* and *some backwarde* and *so ledyng forth with here*
> *weponys A-lofte* and *lytys brennyng*. . . .

There are several points of likeness between this scene and i. ii
of *Othello*. In both the hero behaves with dignified calm: he does
not prevaricate or try to evade the issue; he declares himself
instantly, meeting his destiny full-on. So Jesus twice repeats the
phrase 'that will not fle', and in a speech not quoted above he
says yet again:

> I told you now with wordys meke
> Be-forn you All that it was I.

Othello too refuses flight or evasion. First Iago counsels
caution:

> Those are the raised father and his friends.
> You were best go in.

But Othello replies:

> Not I; I must be found.
> My parts, my title, and my perfect soul
> Shall manifest me rightly.

Secondly, both Jesus and Othello act the part of peace-makers.
Each has to restrain the overenthusiasm of his followers, Jesus
miraculously undoing the violence of Peter. Even their words on
this occasion may be compared:

> Put thy swerd in the shede fayre and wel.

> Keep up your bright swords, for the dew will rust them.

(The York version is slightly closer to Shakespeare here: 'For-thy
putte vppe thi swerde / Full goodely agayne'.) Thirdly, Jesus is
accused of witchcraft and necromancy and treated as if he

were a thief. So too is Othello. Brabantio's first words to him
are these:

> O thou foul thief, where hast thou stow'd my daughter?
> Damn'd as thou art, thou has enchanted her;
> For I'll refer me to all things of sense,
> If she in chains of magic were not bound . . .
> Judge me the world, if 'tis not gross in sense,
> That thou hast practis'd on her with foul charms,
> Abus'd her delicate youth with drugs or minerals
> That weakens motion.

The comparison I am making is strictly a theatrical one. (I am
not suggesting that Othello is a 'Christ-figure'.) It seems likely
that the scene of the Betrayal formed a big and effective set-piece
in the mystery plays—certainly in the *Ludus Coventriae* it makes a
vivid stage action—and it may well have made a strong impression
on anyone who saw it. The scene in *Othello*, to which I have
compared it is usually (in my experience) the most brilliant visual
moment in the play: it frames Othello's first entry, and its swords
and torches and chiaroscuro effects ('Dusk faces with white
silken turbans wreath'd') make it, despite its brevity and rapidity,
intensely memorable and beautiful.

The association proposed here may perhaps be accounted for
in terms of Iago's character. He may have suggested the link
between Othello and Christ. For in the opening sequence of the
play (I. i, ii) Iago plays the part of Judas. Indeed his words at
I. i. 555–8 are distinctly evocative of Judas' kiss of betrayal:

> Though I do hate him as I do hell pains
> Yet, for necessity of present life,
> I must show out a flag and sign of love,
> Which is indeed but sign.

Shakespeare more than once in other plays refers to Judas' kiss,
as in *3 Henry VI* (v. vii. 33–4), when Richard Gloucester hypocritically kisses King Edward's new-born son:

> To say the truth, so Judas kiss'd his master,
> And cried 'All hail!' when as he meant all harm.

Iago's plotting in this opening scene and his rousing of Brabantio
against Othello can then be taken as in a way analogous to Judas'
secret dealings with the High Priests: both men betray their

masters. And there may be one further slight point of contact between the two betrayers. Judas sold Jesus for thirty pieces of silver, and his preoccupation with money accords with the fact that he acted as the treasurer for Jesus and his disciples: he was their purse-bearer. (The Geneva Bible version of John 12: 12 has 'Now he said this, not that he cared for the poore, but because he was a thefe, and had the bagge, and bare that which was given.' The headnote for this page is 'Iudas the purs bearer'.) The mystery plays sometimes make something of this fact, as the York dramatist does in the scene of Judas' despair (xxxii):

> The purse with his spens aboute I bare,
> Ther was none trowed so wele as I,
> Of me he triste no man mare,
> And I be-trayed hym traytourly.

If Judas in his traditional role as arch-villain deceiver-betrayer contributed something to Iago, as he did to Richard Gloucester, then the opening words of *Othello*, spoken to Iago by Roderigo, may take on a further sinister implication:

> Tush, never tell me; I take it much unkindly
> That you, Iago, who has had my purse
> As if the strings were thine, shouldst know of this.

This makes Iago, like Judas, a purse-holder. Whether an audience would, unprompted, pick up the allusion, if it is there, is another matter.

In the context of *Othello* as a whole, this scene of Othello's thwarted arrest is a minor one; but the scene that I now want to consider from *Macbeth* is in itself of much greater importance. This is the banquet scene (III. iv), one of the play's climactic scenes, which in some ways could be taken as a distillation of the entire action. I have already suggested Suetonius' Life of Claudius as a major narrative source. The only other source that has been proposed is De Loier's *Treatise of Spectres* (1605), where King Thierry 'on an evening as he sat at supper' is haunted by the ghost of a man he has slain.[1] Among dramatic analogues in earlier Shakespearian plays are the scene in *Richard III* (II. i) in which Richard Gloucester suddenly announces the death of Clarence, so shattering the harmony just achieved at Court by

---

[1] H. N. Paul, *The Royal Play of 'Macbeth'*, New York, 1950, pp. 58–9.

King Edward, and two scenes from *Hamlet*, the first ghost scene
and the play scene.[1] These three scenes did, I think, decisively
influence the shaping of the banquet scene, but they do not
supply us with its main dramatic model. They may offer close
parallels for such things as the timing of the Ghost's two entries,
for the histrionic nature of Macbeth's behaviour, and for the
over-all shaping of the episode—the way it narrows to a final
duologue between Macbeth and his wife. What they do not
account for is something obscurer, less easily accessible: the
source of the scene's extraordinary power, which seems to be
located at the heart of the *occasion* which underlies its more
consciously wrought artistry. It is, again, only in the mystery
plays that we shall find anything like an adequate explanation for
the primitive power which is generally agreed to be exerted by
this famous scene.

Essential to the banquet scene is the idea of the conviviality
of the feast curdled by something utterly incongruous with it:
violent death. Death at the feast—that is the basic point, the
underlying contradiction. One of the extant mystery plays
happens to illustrate this theme perfectly, and it is this play—
not necessarily this particular text, but a play on the same subject
—which may have given Shakespeare his essential idea. The play
occurs in the *Ludus Coventriae* cycle and is made up of two
episodes: 'The Massacre of the Innocents' and 'The Death of
Herod'. Of these episodes, the first is by no means irrelevant to
Macbeth, and I shall return to it later. But it is the second, 'The
Death of Herod', that seems to have furnished Shakespeare,
whether directly or not, with the model for the banquet scene.
It can be briefly summarized. Herod has arranged for all the
male infants of his land to be slaughtered. When his knights
report that his orders have been carried out, he joyfully proclaims
a feast; he need no longer fear for his throne: 'Ffor now my fo is
dead'. But while Herod is celebrating his victory—

> I was nevyr meryer here be-forn
> Sythe that I was fyrst born

—Mors (Death) enters and introduces himself in a monologue.
No one notices Mors, and the feast goes on:

[1] Emrys Jones, *Scenic Form in Shakespeare*, pp. 217–19.

> Therfore menstrell rownd a-bowte
> blowe up a mery fytt.

The stage direction describes what happens next: *Hic dum buccinant mors interfeciat herodem et duos milites subito et diabolus recipiat eos.*[1] To the sound of his own trumpets Herod is dragged away to hell.

The scene is not particularly well managed; it is the conception that matters. Death makes his appearance in Herod's banqueting-hall as unobtrusively as Banquo's Ghost, and stands there unnoticed while the revelry continues. When the feast is at its height, Death suddenly strikes, and the two worlds—the apparently self-sufficient realm of the tyrant and the actual all-enclosing world of God (and Death, as he tells us, is 'goddys masangere')—come into collision, Herod's inevitably collapsing. The conception is simple, but powerful, even alarming. It has its own Gothic quality of terror. It must have existed in several versions, dramatic and undramatic, and despite the very different circumstances of Macbeth's situation it can be felt as persisting into Shakespeare's tragedy, its accidents new, its essence unchanged.

The connection between the two scenes can be clarified by looking at the situations of Herod and Macbeth in a larger context. In the *Ludus Coventriae* Herod appears in two plays: the one just described, and an earlier one, 'The Adoration of the Magi'. In this Herod meets the three kings who are on their way to pay homage to the new-born Child; as the first king says:

> He is born of a mayd ȝynge
> he xal be kynge ouer every kynge
> We go to seke that louely thinge
> to hym ffayn wolde I lowth.

$$(155-8)$$

They promise to return to Herod's court when they have found him. But as soon as they have left, Herod rages, swearing to raise up 'A derke devyll' when he learns where the child is to be found. The rest of the play shows the kings at Bethlehem, and later being warned by an angel not to return to Herod's court but to go home by another way. The second Herod play opens where the first left off: Herod is still waiting to hear from the

---

[1] *Ludus Coventriae*, p. 176.

kings, his rage increasing when he realizes that they have eluded him. But he fears the prophecies they mentioned, that the new-born child will become a king of kings, and he puts into operation his plan for killing all male infants under two years. But, again, warned by an angel, Mary and Joseph take the infant Jesus into Egypt and so escape.

I have recalled the familiar story in order to bring out the elements it has in common with the story of Macbeth as told by Shakespeare. Herod and Macbeth are both confronted by prophecies which seem to entail their own displacement from their throne. Both lash out violently in a vain attempt to escape their destiny. Herod is a killer of innocent children, and so— later in the play—is Macbeth. Indeed Banquo's son Fleance is also presented as a child and he is included in Macbeth's murderous plans (he corresponds, one might say, to the infant Jesus). But just as the one child Herod must kill escapes, so the one child Macbeth must kill also escapes:

> *Macb.* Yet he is good that did the like for Fleance.
>   If thou didst it, thou art the nonpareil.
> *Murd.* Most royal sir—Fleance is 'scap'd.

Further than this, despite all the obvious circumstantial differences, there is a moment in 'The Adoration of the Magi' when a reader will be struck by something that seems to anticipate Shakespeare's play. This is when, hearing from the three kings of the purpose of their journey and of the prophecies which have made them undertake it, Herod dissembles his real feelings, revealing them only when they have left. The verbal and dramatic medium is simple and unsubtle, but a complex psychological situation is faintly adumbrated which can be said to point towards the scene (I. iii) in which Macbeth is confronted by the Weird Sisters, hears their prophecies, and is thrown into mental turmoil. Like Herod, he dissembles. And in terms of stage grouping there is another point: Herod, dismayed by the three Kings who stand in front of him speaking of prophecies, is matched by Macbeth, dismayed by the three Weird Sisters who stand in front of him speaking prophetically.

Herod is certainly the chief prototype of Macbeth in the mystery plays, and these similarities between their situations make it the more likely that it was some sort of memory of a play about

Herod's death at his own feast which inspired Shakespeare to conceive Macbeth's banquet. At another point in the play, however, there is a detail clearly intended to link Macbeth with the other New Testament character who for Christians was the prototypical human malefactor: Judas. While Duncan takes supper at Inverness, his host Macbeth communes with himself on whether he can bring himself to murder him:

> If it were done when 'tis done, then 'twere well
> It were done quickly.

So, while Duncan is in fact eating his 'last supper', Macbeth plays Judas, for to Judas Jesus at the Last Supper said: 'That thou doest, do quickly' (John 13 : 27). Thus Macbeth's opening words make plain that he is a latter-day Judas. (He is a Judas to Duncan, a Herod to his later victims.) I am not suggesting that this Judas-touch has any necessary connection with the mystery plays, since there is nothing especially scenic or theatrical in question; although the words 'Quod facis fac cicius' are in fact quoted thus in Latin in the York play 'The Last Supper'.

V. *From Mystery to Tragedy*

In a well-known passage in his book on Marlowe's plays, F. P. Wilson ventured the opinion that Shakespeare's early history plays were possibly the earliest that we have. We are often referred back, he said, to Shakespeare's predecessors in the genre, but when we look for these pre-Armada chronicle plays, where are they?[1] I am not questioning the justice of Wilson's position: the Henry VI plays are, as far as we know, the earliest plays in English closely based on the chronicles and giving, for all their dramatic distortions, a more or less responsible account of what historically happened. It would, however, be possible to formulate another answer to Wilson's question and say that—somewhat enlarging the meaning of the term—it is the mystery plays that are our first history plays. Quite as much as Shakespeare's English and Roman histories they are dramatizations of historical documents—the Biblical narratives— and they render the sense of these narratives very faithfully. Again and again one finds that details which may at first seem

[1] *Marlowe and the Early Shakespeare*, Oxford, 1951, p. 105.

freely introduced for imaginative purposes are in fact accounted for by the Biblical source. But Shakespeare takes over not only their fidelity to history: as I have tried to show, some of his tragedies, late as well as early, can be seen as secular passion plays. Conversely, the mysteries can be seen as sacred history plays. When all due qualifications have been made, there would seem to be considerable continuity between the two bodies of drama. Since Shakespeare's later tragedies are among the greatest literary works we have, this continuity is a cultural phenomenon of the first importance.

Secondly, I want to suggest that what the Passion paradigm essentially contributed to Shakespearian tragedy was a dramatic sense of *value*. It helped Shakespeare to give an immense emphasis to the hero's fall and death, a suggestion of spiritual greatness overwhelming in its resonance. However much Shakespeare owed the humanists in literary terms, it may be that the great imaginative power of the Shakespearian hero derives not so much from 'Renaissance' ideals as from the native late-medieval conception of the God-man hero. In the course of the sixteenth century the religious power which centred on the figure of Christ was liberated or transferred to secular figures in a drama fashioned ostensibly for secular ends. But at this point an antithesis formed on the terms 'religious' and 'secular' becomes misleading and indeed unnecessary. One might prefer to say that a certain residue of religious feeling persists into Shakespeare's tragic writing, and that when in the seventeenth century the drama lost contact with those medieval forms of feeling it quickly declined into triviality.[1]

[1] The influence of the medieval saint's play on Elizabethan drama is a different, though closely linked, question. So few English saint's plays have survived that little beyond speculation seems possible. But F. D. Hoeniger has related *Pericles* to that genre in an illuminating way (New Arden *Pericles*, 1963, pp. lxxxviii-xci), and it is likely that other plays might be similarly clarified. *Henry V*, for example, has been seen as drawing on the powers of the saint's play genre, as O. B. Hardison, Jr. has suggested: 'a clear example of the use of ritual form for a secular subject' (*Christian Rite and Christian Drama in the Middle Ages*, p. 290). Romeo and Juliet can also be regarded as latter-day saints—but saints of erotic love. H. A. Mason remarks of the balcony scene: 'My . . . impression is the predominance in this scene of the *sacred*' (*Shakespeare's Tragedies of Love*, 1970, p. 46). Antony and Cleopatra is another tragedy which might be related to the saint's play tradition.

3. Shakespeare and Euripides (I): Tragic Passion

AFTER being more or less denied Shakespearian authorship for two hundred years, *Titus Andronicus* is now firmly back within the canon. With varying degrees of enthusiasm, or regret, most scholars now accept it as Shakespearian. And for many playgoers the production in 1955 at Stratford and London helped to confirm the scholarly swing towards reinstating it: the play works in the theatre even today or rather, if done with imagination and conviction (and preferably genius) it *can* work—so as to make its popular success on the Elizabethan stage comprehensible as never before. Even the late Professor Dover Wilson, who in his edition of *Titus* put forward the view that it was a sort of barbarous burlesque, changed his mind when he saw Peter Brook's production and Olivier's performance.

The play is altogether less perplexing than it was. A number of critics have looked at it unflinchingly and found much that they could positively admire if not candidly like. In particular Hereward Price has approached it with a refreshing freedom from the usual prejudices and shown that some of its rhetorical and dramaturgical skills are superior to anything in Marlowe, Kyd, Peele, and Greene, and in his opinion stamp it as authentically Shakespearian.[1] Others have described the play's literary style (or styles), and especially its cultivation of Ovidian manner.[2] The study of its sources has made comparable advances: as well as Seneca and Ovid, the play draws on Plutarch.[3] But the biggest step forward in this field was Ralph Sargent's discovery of the chap-book which probably contains a version of the chief

---

[1] Hereward T. Price, 'The Structure of *Titus Andronicus*', *Journal of English and Germanic Philology*, vol. 42, 1943.

[2] M. C. Bradbrook, *Shakespeare and Elizabethan Poetry*, 1951, pp. 104–10. For Ovid, see Eugene M. Waith, 'The Metamorphosis of Violence in *Titus Andronicus*', *Shakespeare Survey*, 10, 1957.

[3] R. A. Law, 'The Roman Background of *Titus Andronicus*', *Studies in Philology*, vol. 40, 1948.

narrative source: a short tale called *The Tragical History of Titus Andronicus*.[1] The tale throws valuable light on Shakespeare's aims and methods in this early tragedy: it also helps to free the play from the Senecan label which has traditionally and somewhat misleadingly been attached to it. The most obviously 'Senecan' feature of the play has always seemed the cannibalistic banquet with which it ends. But this feature is present in the chap-book, not taken direct from *Thyestes* as was usually assumed before the chap-book was found. Of course there are undeniable 'Senecan' elements in *Titus Andronicus*—some quotations (or misquotations)—and the banquet itself may well have been considered Senecan even though its source was not. But we cannot get very far by attempting to explain the play with reference to the author of *Thyestes*.

In recent years a few critics have gone further than any before them in finding *Titus Andronicus* not only historically interesting but important for our understanding of Shakespeare. One of them says, 'It foreshadows the later tragedies because it is their archetype. Instead of being dismissed as an immature tragedy written for its age, it deserves to be approached as a central and seminal play in the canon of Shakespeare's works.'[2] While another, comparing it with *Lear*, remarks: 'they have more in common with each other probably than either has with any other of Shakespeare's plays.' He goes on: 'There is, in fact, a tremendous inventiveness and intelligence active in this often despised play.'[3] Both these critics seem to me to be right—though we need not think the play a living, or even a dormant, classic: it is not that, and no amount of historical interpretation will make it one. It is, for Shakespeare, too academic, too bookish; though never dull, it is altogether too far removed from English life. But as Shakespeare's earliest attempt at a formal tragedy, it is of unique historical interest. This is what Shakespeare, at the age of (as I take it) twenty-five or twenty-six, was capable of in the most exacting of dramatic kinds.

But if *Titus Andronicus* is less perplexing than it was, there is still

---

[1] Ralph M. Sargent, 'The Source of *Titus Andronicus*', *Studies in Philology*, vol. 46, 1949. I have used the text reprinted in *Narrative and Dramatic Sources of Shakespeare*, ed. G. Bullough, vol. vi. The priority of the chap-book tale to Shakespeare's play has been challenged by Marco Mincoff, 'The Source of *Titus Andronicus*', *Notes and Queries*, vol. 216, 1971, pp. 131-4.

[2] A. C. Hamilton, *The Early Shakespeare*, San Marino, 1967, p. 67.

[3] Nicholas Brooke, *Shakespeare's Early Tragedies*, 1968, pp. 4, 47.

something mysterious about it. Scholars have traced the derivation of many of its details of plot and character and diction, but they have not asked where Shakespeare's over-all conception of tragic form came from: the fundamental shape of the play's action. I can best frame the question by first describing the play's basic dramatic procedure and then asking some further questions about Shakespeare's intentions.

I

At a performance of *Titus Andronicus* it will be found, I think, that the play falls into two clearly marked movements, the first of which occupies the first three acts, the second the last two. And each act is itself given to a clearly marked phase in the action. The first act is an elaborate and very resourcefully dramatized expository movement, which ends with all the characters in position for the main action. Titus has already turned Tamora, Queen of the Goths, into an implacable enemy by ritually sacrificing her eldest son, and followed that up by antagonizing the new emperor Saturninus. In the second act Tamora and Aaron the Moor plot the downfall of Titus' family: his son-in-law is murdered, his two sons are accused of the crime, and his daughter Lavinia is raped and mutilated. In the third act the threads are all brought together, and we are shown, in a single scene, the acuteness of Titus' sufferings. Lavinia is brought to him; he vainly tries to save the lives of his two condemned sons, losing a hand in the process; and his last remaining son Lucius is banished from Rome. If we allow for the ramifications of intrigue and the various stressing of episode, during these first three acts we witness a persistent decline in the fortunes of the hero—from his triumphal return home to Rome at the beginning, through his brief phase of folly and crime (his choice of Saturninus for the Emperorship, his sacrifice of Tamora's son, and his slaying of his own son Mutius) into a longer drawn-out series of stages marked by increasing pain and suffering. This last phase of suffering fills the third act, which forms the climax of the play's first movement. This is not the place to analyse the passion scene (III. i), with its carefully gradated ascent to the climax of feeling with Titus' hysterical laughter.[1] But what must be observed is

---

[1] I have discussed this scene in *Scenic Form in Shakespeare*, pp. 8–13.

the way we are prepared for the play's massive change of direction.
The Messenger has just shown Titus the heads of his two sons
and his own severed hand, and Titus is silent, in a state of deep
emotional shock. His brother Marcus remonstrates with him:

> *Marcus.* Now is the time to storm; why art thou still?
> *Titus.* Ha, ha, ha!
> *Marcus.* Why dost thou laugh? It fits not with this hour.
> *Titus.* Why, I have not another tear to shed;
>   Besides, this sorrow is an enemy,
>   And would usurp upon my wat'ry eyes
>   And make them blind with tributary tears.
>   Then which way shall I find Revenge's cave?
>
> (III. i. 264–71)

This is the first emphatic announcement by Titus of his new
preoccupation: revenge. He goes off with Marcus and Lavinia,
leaving Lucius, now a banished man, alone. Lucius' short soliloquy brings this first movement of the play to a close. He too ends
with the thought of revenge:

> Now will I to the Goths, and raise a pow'r
> To be reveng'd on Rome and Saturnine.

Revenge is the chief concern of Acts Four and Five, the play's
second movement. Saturninus, Tamora, and her two sons blindly
deliver themselves into Titus' hands, thinking him harmless;
his project is successful, and he duly takes his revenge. So the
play's main change of direction is one from passivity and passion
to purposeful waiting and sudden action, from acute suffering
to actively planned and executed revenge.

This fundamental change in the nature of the hero's emotional
experience—and consequently in the emotion generated in the
audience—is perhaps one which critics concerned only with
reading the play as a literary text will not find much to say about;
possibly it will escape their attention altogether, or seem too
obvious to be worth mentioning. But in a performance of the
play—in a successful one, at any rate—the audience will find
itself harassed by succeeding waves of anxiety during the second
and third acts and finally driven to an almost intolerable pitch
of feeling with Titus' desperate attempts to save his sons' lives.
And the undertones of barbarous farce, with Aaron watching his
victim writhe merely for the fun of it, will serve only to intensify

the audience's response: one's feelings will have an ambiguous, hysterical quality—laughter is very close. It is at this point, with a sure command of audience emotion, that Shakespeare makes Titus first of all speak the single line, his only verbal response to the sight of his sons' heads—

When will this fearful slumber have an end?

—and then, in reply to Marcus' attempts to make him vent his grief in lament, break out into laughter. Titus' feelings can go no further in that direction—helpless acceptance of bad news, ghastly pain, frightful grief. Such emotion must be converted into something else; relief of some sort must be found. What Titus does is first to withdraw into an equivocal state of apparent insanity, itself a partial relief, and then having failed to secure justice from the gods to proceed with his own satisfyingly horrible revenge. The emotions experienced by the audience, however, though dependent on Titus', will of course be of a rather different nature. Whereas Titus withdraws into a kind of insanity, the audience withdraws into a measure of emotional detachment, a state of mind which does not preclude feelings of excitement and suspense, though far less intense than those aroused by the passion scene of Act Three. In that scene Titus aroused close sympathy; but in the last two acts of the play he becomes more and more of a monster, until the Thyestean feast removes him into a ghastly realm of lunatic ingenuity and insensibility. A member of the theatre audience during this final scene will no doubt experience feelings of horror and a kind of wonder, and his viewpoint will imperceptibly merge with that of Lucius, who has returned from the outside world into the madhouse of Rome. It is with Lucius that we finally view the horrid spectacle, pity mingling with an intellectual understanding of the events which led up to it.

In retrospect, if we trace the course of our feelings during a performance of *Titus Andronicus* we shall, I think, be aware of something like the swing of a huge pendulum, first moving in one direction—the direction of tragic grief—and then turning on itself to swing back, first slowly, then with increasing momentum, until finally the relief-giving pleasure of revenge is savoured by the hero and, with altogether more moderate intensity, indeed with increasing detachment as it emerges from the spell of the action, by the audience. To speak in these terms is to address oneself only to the fundamental layer of the theatrical experience; of course the drama engages and stimulates the mind in a wide variety of other ways. Nevertheless this two-part movement of feeling, however we choose to describe it, this intensification of tragic grief until it is converted into the ferociously gleeful pleasure of wrath spending itself in a hated victim, constitutes the essential dramatic experience afforded by *Titus Andronicus*. This is the basic form of the play, a grand powerful structure, containing parts various and complex in themselves, but as a whole making an impact elemental in its simplicity.

What I want to stress, since my argument is going to be conducted very largely in structural terms, is the clarity and decisiveness with which the emotional stages of the action are articulated, and particularly the rapid yet convincing transition from the first movement to the second, from grief to revenge. Immature though we must of course consider the play, this basic form seems remarkably effective and assured.

II

The following is (or was) a famous story from the history of Troy. During the Trojan war Priam and Hecuba sent their young son Polydorus into the protection of the Thracian king Polymestor; a heap of gold was sent with him to secure him from want if Troy should fall. After the city's capture, while the Greek army was waiting to set sail for home, the ghost of Achilles appeared, demanding that Polyxena, the daughter of Priam and Hecuba, should be sacrificed to him. And despite the pleas of Hecuba, who was now a captive in the Greek camp, Polyxena was sacrificed. While still in a state of extreme grief, Hecuba was preparing to wash her daughter's body before burying it, and sent her attendants to the sea-shore for water. They discover a corpse floating at the water's edge. When Hecuba sees it she recognizes it as her last remaining son Polydorus. He has been murdered by his protector Polymestor for the gold. Hecuba now feels astonishment and rage rather than grief and can think of nothing but how to revenge herself on her son's murderer. She sends word to Polymestor that he should come to her tent where he will find something to his advantage. He arrives with his two sons and is invited by Hecuba into her tent. There he is

set upon by her women; his sons are put to death, while Polymestor's eyes are gouged out with brooches. In his blindness
Polymestor foretells that Hecuba will be metamorphosed into a
howling glaring dog.

This story was dramatized by Euripides in his tragedy *Hecuba*,
which I wish to propose as Shakespeare's chief dramatic model
for *Titus Andronicus*.

It has so often been denied that Shakespeare shows any knowledge of Greek tragedy that the case for it will have to be argued
afresh. Virgil K. Whitaker states summarily that 'there is no
evidence that Shakespeare knew a single Greek play even in
translation',[1] and Whitaker's position is the orthodox one. No
item of unimpeachable objective evidence has apparently come
to light since Whitaker wrote his book; what evidence exists was
probably known to him as to other authorities on the subject.
If I differ from them it is because the evidence can be interpreted
in more than one way: connections can be made which have
not been made. Our opinion of the opportunities open to
Shakespeare will depend on our conception of Tudor literary
culture.

All the extant Greek tragedies were made available in editions
and in Latin translations during the sixteenth century, so there is
no question but that they would have been accessible to anyone
with not much more than a moderate reading ability in Latin.
This last is something which not all scholars have been willing
to allow Shakespeare; but the following remark from F. P. Wilson's essay, 'Shakespeare's Reading', gives temperate and indeed
cautious expression to a view which is probably now widely
accepted:

Few who have read through T. W. Baldwin's treatise on *William
Shakspere's Small Latine & Lesse Greeke* will have the strength to
deny that Shakespeare acquired the grammar-school training of his
day in grammar, logic, and rhetoric; that he could and did read in
the originals some Terence and Plautus, some Ovid and Virgil; that
possessing a reading knowledge of Latin all those short-cuts to learning in florilegia and compendia were at his service if he cared to avail
himself of them; and that he read Latin not in the spirit of a scholar
but a poet.[2]

[1] *Shakespeare's Use of Learning*, San Marino, 1953, p. 165.
[2] *Shakespearian and other studies*, pp. 131–2.

But if it can be assumed that Shakespeare might have got through, with more or less fluency, the relatively easy Latin of the sixteenth-century translations, it does not follow that he would have directed himself to those tragedies which modern judgement and taste have especially favoured. On the evidence of frequency of translation and imitation Euripides was, of the three Greek tragic dramatists, by far the most congenial to sixteenth-century taste—no doubt for many reasons, including his choice of subjects, his style, and his prominent use of rhetorical argument and debate. Even so some of the Euripidean tragedies most highly valued today seem to have been ignored in the sixteenth century (e.g. *The Bacchae*, which may have seemed incomprehensibly or uninterestingly remote). In the case of some other of his plays, like *Medea* and *Hippolytus*, Euripides may have been neglected in favour of Seneca, who had written his own versions of these Euripidean themes. On the other hand, some plays which are commonly given a low place today were much admired in the sixteenth century. Among these were *Hecuba* and *Phoenissae*. But both these plays, it should be noted, were highly popular in late antiquity and both kept their place as reading texts in the Byzantine schools.[1] The sixteenth century was not being eccentric in admiring them; on the contrary, it was being faithfully traditional. It is only in more recent times that these two plays have fallen out of critical favour.

In his survey *Euripides and his Influence*, F. L. Lucas noted the exceptional popularity (if that is the word) of *Hecuba* in the sixteenth century, judging from the number of translations into Latin, Italian, French, and Spanish. But to Lucas this preference for *Hecuba* was a sign of the bad taste of the age, and he tried to explain it by referring to the play's physical atrocities: 'Horrors in particular . . . were in the age of the Borgias an essential tragic convention'.[2] But this explanation is superficial and quite unconvincing. *The Bacchae* is quite as 'atrocious' as *Hecuba*, but seems to have made no appeal to 'the age of the Borgias'. In any case *Hecuba* is not verbally stimulating or titillating: there is nothing to compare, in the account of the killing of the two boys and the blinding of Polymestor, with the revolting descriptions

[1] *Hecuba*, ed. W. S. Hadley, 1894, p. xvi: 'With the *Phoenissae* and *Orestes*, [*Hecuba*] formed the favourite reading book in the Byzantine schools.'

[2] *Euripides and his Influence*, 1923, p. 93.

of Seneca's *Thyestes*. What Lucas oddly failed to recognize is that *Hecuba* had been admired for centuries, so that by the time it came down to the sixteenth century it was accepted as being quite obviously one of the chief masterpieces of Euripides. According to Stiblinus, who edited him, Euripides was 'princeps tragicorum', while *Hecuba* held the principal place among his tragedies ('principem locum tenet').[1] The critical tradition which thus extolled the play may be itself open to criticism, but *Hecuba*'s vogue in the sixteenth century has nothing to do with a depraved taste for horrors.

In *The Senecan Tradition in Renaissance Tragedy* H. B. Charlton learnedly argued that Greek influence on Renaissance tragedy was so slight as to be negligible. If Greek themes percolate through by way of translations they are, according to him, inevitably 'Senecanized'. But, in passing, he too noted the prominent place taken by *Hecuba* in translations from the Greek, although the Senecan explanation is again put to use:

And although the already noted greater familiarity with Euripides is marked by the publication before 1541 of ten editions of Latin translations of two of his plays and three of one, it is significant that all the thirteen editions confine themselves to the *Hecuba* and *Iphigenia in Aulis*; it is more significant for our purposes, too, to note that whereas both plays occur in ten editions, the *Hecuba* is the one chosen for issue in all three of the editions of one play only; for the *Hecuba* by the atrocity of its theme, the signal proportion of set lamentations, and the simplicity as opposed to Aristotle's complexity of plot, is the most Senecan of Euripides' plays.[2]

I have quoted this sentence for the evidence it incidentally supplies for the frequency with which *Hecuba* was reprinted during the sixteenth century, although Charlton's explanation of its popularity seems to me as unacceptable as Lucas's. No convincing reasons are given for describing it as 'the most Senecan of Euripides' plays'. As I have said, other plays are at least as given to atrocities, some surely more so. Indeed if *Hecuba* really is the most 'Senecan' of the plays, it is odd that Seneca himself was not as attracted to it as he was to *Heracles* and *Medea*, in each of which a parent personally kills his or her children. Like Lucas's, Charlton's explanation of *Hecuba*'s appeal to scholars and scholarly

---

[1] *Euripides*, Basel, 1562, p. 38.   [2] 1946 rep., p. 33.

minded dramatists on the grounds of its one scene of off-stage physical atrocity is more than a little absurd.

It is more relevant to recall that Hecuba had been considered for centuries as the supreme example of tragic grief.[1] Chaucer thinks of her in this light; so do the authors of *Gorboduc*; and so does Hamlet. In *Titus Andronicus* itself Young Lucius says:

> For I have heard my grandsire say full oft,
> Extremity of grief would make men mad;
> And I have read that Hecuba of Troy
> Ran made for sorrow.

> (IV. i. 18–21)

Hecuba could be seen as the heroine of the tragic tale of Troy; and mythical-minded Britons (or Italians or Frenchmen) who thought of themselves as being ultimately of Trojan stock would have had something of a proprietary interest in her. All this should be recalled, quite apart from the fact that Euripides' tragedy is after all one of considerable power. Commentators on the play agree that the episode of the willing self-sacrifice of Polyxena is an inspiringly noble one, and the prologue, spoken by the Ghost of Polydorus, is delicate and poignant. Lucas and Charlton allude to the scene in which Polymestor is blinded and his sons murdered as if Euripides were pandering to a crude appetite in his audience. The scene is certainly horrifying, but the physical violence is used in a far more responsible way than it ever is in Seneca (indeed there is no comparison). The scene comes immediately after that in which Hecuba has persuaded her new master Agamemnon to allow her to avenge herself on the Thracian tyrant, who—as she has just discovered—has treacherously murdered her last remaining son. Agamemnon is already feeling guilty that he has made the priestess Cassandra his concubine, and he agrees to let Hecuba do as she wishes, provided that his army is not let into the secret. The context of the atrocity is therefore characteristically Euripidean in its harsh irony, and the familiar Euripidean themes are sounded: the aftermath of war in which all, victors and defeated, are degraded; the shabby, conniving

---

[1] Cf. Lily B. Campbell, *Shakespeare's Tragic Heroes*, Cambridge, 1930, p. 131. Also C. O. McDonald, *The Rhetoric of Tragedy*, University of Massachusetts, 1966, on Aphthonius's use of Hecuba as an example of 'passive' *ethopeia*. McDonald calls Hecuba 'the *cliché* exemplar of tragic emotionality' (p. 86).

compromises of those in authority; and the power of suffering to destroy the personality. The tragedy of *Hecuba* is far from being a piece of *grand guignol*; in performance it can be moving and morally interesting as well as theatrically exciting. It was a powerful performance of *Hecuba* that brought out for me not only the play's own quality but also its profound kinship in emotional progression to *Titus Andronicus*.[1]

Scholars have established the currency of *Hecuba* in the sixteenth century by referring to the number of editions and translations; but it can also be demonstrated from the critical writings of the period. It is noteworthy, and for my argument significant, that Scaliger, Minturno, and Sidney all illustrate their theories by referring to it. In his *Poetices* Scaliger has the following passage; he is discussing tragic actions:

> Argumentum ergo brevissimum accipiendum est: idque maxime varium multiplexque faciundum. Exempli gratia, Hecuba in Thracia, prohibente reditum Achille. Polydorus iam interfectus est. Caedes Polyxenae. Exoculatio Polymestoris. Quoniam vero mortui non possunt introduci, eorum phantasmata, sive idola, sive spectra subveniunt: ut Polydori, ut Darii apud Aeschylum, quod & supra dicebamus.[2]

Scaliger's subject is plot construction in tragedies; he is arguing that the plot should be as brief as possible yet at the same time 'varied and multiplex'. *Hecuba* serves as an example, since its plot can be reduced to two events—the sacrifice of Polyxena and the blinding of Polymestor—with the Ghost of Polydorus relating the events that led up to the opening of the drama. In his *Apology for Poetry* Sidney follows Scaliger in taking *Hecuba* as his example when he is discussing how to construct a dramatic plot:

> Lastly, if they will represent an history, they must not (as Horace saith) begin *ab ovo*, but they must come to the principal point of that one action which they will represent. By example this will be best expressed. I have a story of young Polydorus, delivered for safety's sake, with great riches, by his father Priam to Polymnestor, king of Thrace, in the Trojan war time. He, after some years, hearing the overthrow of Priam, for to make the treasure his own, murdereth the

---

[1] By the Greek National Theatre in London in 1966, with Katina Paxinou.
[2] *Poetices*, 1581, Book 3, chap. 97, p. 386.

child. The body of the child is taken up by Hecuba. She, the same day, findeth a sleight to be revenged most cruelly of the tyrant. Where now would one of our tragedy writers begin, but with the delivery of the child? Then should he sail over into Thrace, and so spend I know not how many years, and travel numbers of places. But where doth Euripides? Even with the finding of the body, leaving the rest to be told by the spirit of Polydorus. This need no further to be enlarged; the dullest wit may conceive it.[1]

Sidney's concern is with unity of time; it is not to his purpose to consider the crucial function of the Polyxena episode which, combined with Polydorus' death, breaks Hecuba's spirit. He does not therefore really clarify the play's structure. Even so it is of interest that *Hecuba* should have figured in this context—how to construct a dramatic plot—for although the *Apology* was written about 1581–3 and not printed until 1595, presumably a few years after *Titus Andronicus* was written, Shakespeare may have had access to it in manuscript. But we need not assume that Shakespeare was directed to *Hecuba* by reading Sidney; it simply happens to be of interest that the play should be given such detailed treatment in Sidney's discussion—no other classical play detains him for so long. The other contemporary Italian critic to whom Sidney was indebted, Minturno, also has a discussion of the action of *Hecuba*, as to whether it is 'simple' or 'complex'.[2] Since I shall be arguing that *Hecuba* served Shakespeare as a structural model, it is worth pointing out here that all three critics, Scaliger, Minturno, and Sidney, discuss *Hecuba* from a structural point of view—the aspect most useful perhaps to a practising playwright.

I have kept until now one fact which is of the utmost importance for the case I am arguing. This is that a translation into Latin of *Hecuba* and *Iphigenia in Aulis* had been made by Erasmus. The fact is important because of Erasmus' unique position as the presiding genius of Tudor school education. Indeed it is hardly too much to say that Tudor literary culture until the third quarter of the sixteenth century is overwhelmingly Erasmian in inspiration. His influence is everywhere. (One of his proverbs is quoted in the last scene of *Titus Andronicus*.[3]) His Euripides translations had

---

[1] *Apology for Poetry*, ed. G. Shepherd, 1965, p. 135.
[2] *L'Arte Poetica*, 1563, pp. 85–8.
[3] *Titus Andronicus*, v. iii. 118: 'For when no friends are by, men praise themselves.' This appears near the opening of *The Praise of Folly*: 'I follow that well-worn

besides a special English connection: they were dedicated to William Warham, Archbishop of Canterbury, and the small 1507 volume containing the two plays ends with a poem by Erasmus whose title runs: *Erasmi Roterodami de laudibus Britanniae, Regisque Henrici Septimi ac regiorum liberorum* . . . These Latin versions of Euripides were reprinted throughout the century, sometimes bound up with other Latin translations from the Greek (I have already quoted Charlton's reference to ten editions of both plays and thirteen of *Hecuba* before 1541). Evidence is lacking that the two plays were studied in Tudor schools or universities, but Lodge mentions them in his *Defence of Poetry* (1579) in an allusive way which suggests that they were well known: 'What made Erasmus labor in Euripides tragedies? Did he indevour by painting them out of Greeke into Latine to manifest sinne unto us? or to confirme us in goodness?'[1] We can, I think, assume that with Erasmus' imprimatur on them both his *Hecuba* and his *Iphigenia* would have stood a strong chance of being widely read for educational purposes (particularly perhaps in the middle decades of the sixteenth century, when his influence was especially strong). This needs to be stressed, since historians of the Elizabethan drama have never made any connection between Erasmus' translations and the rise of Shakespearian tragedy, nor has *Hecuba* ever figured in discussions of the Elizabethan revenge play.[2]

III

I have said that *Titus Andronicus* consists of two movements of feeling, the first dominated by passionate suffering, the second by purposeful revenge. It is in such a simple dynamic form as this

popular proverb which says that a man does right to praise himself if he can't find any one else to praise him' (tr. Betty Radice, Harmondsworth, 1971, p. 66). A. H. T. Levi notes that the proverb is also included in the *Adagia*. In his *Rambler* 193, Dr. Johnson quotes the proverb in Latin and English and attributes it to Erasmus.

[1] *Elizabethan Critical Essays*, ed. Gregory Smith, vol. 1, p. 68. For the possibility of school performances of *Hecuba*, see F. S. Boas, *University Drama in the Tudor Age*, Oxford, 1914: 'Melanchthon's scholars . . . acted the *Hecuba* of Euripides, but in the Latin translation by Erasmus' (p. 16). Also J. P. Mahaffy, *Euripides*, 1870: 'The *Hecuba* has always been a favourite play, and has not only been frequently imitated, but edited ever since Erasmus' time for school use' (p. 76).

[2] It goes unmentioned, for example, in Fredson Bowers's *Elizabethan Revenge Tragedy*.

that the play is likely to be felt by a member of an audience: suffering intensified to an intolerable pitch, followed by the relief of aggressive action.

It is in this context that *Hecuba* becomes relevant. The structural divisions of *Hecuba* are very clearly marked: they will be apparent even to a careless reader, and to the playgoer they will be inescapable. This is because the play falls into two clear parts, and so clear is this division that the question of the play's unity has been repeatedly raised by commentators. A modern critic's description of *Hecuba* as 'a loose play of two independent actions' is representative of a whole critical tradition.[1] In his study of Euripides, G. M. A. Grube meets the traditional charge by examining the sequence of episodes and finds that, unlike for example the *Andromache*, *Hecuba* possesses 'dramatic and emotional unity'. He begins his discussion:

The play does fall into two parts; the first is concerned with the sacrifice of Polyxena upon the tomb of Achilles, the second with vengeance on Polymestor for killing Polydorus. Some formal connexion, at least, there obviously is between the two events: the ghost of Polydorus speaks the introductory monologue, and he mentions the fate of Polyxena; his body is later found upon the beach by the attendants whom Hecuba sends to wash raiment for the funeral of Polyxena; the two bodies are buried together at the end. These, however, are mere technical devices, and, unless they correspond to a real dramatic connexion, they are of little value.

Grube goes on to argue that there is a true dramatic development, not an arbitrary succession of episodes:

The growing of sorrow into hatred and of lamentation into a desire for vengeance is a theme that attracted Euripides. It is the story of Medea, of Phaedra and Alcmene. But whereas in Medea we have the gradual development from one to the other, here the change is abrupt; (from 750 on, all Hecuba's thoughts are of vengeance).

He then goes on to show how the arrangement of the play's episodes helps to express the meaning of the tragedy as a whole: the order of events as we have seen it in *Hecuba* is, he argues, far more effective dramatically than it would have been if Euripides had placed the discovery of Polydorus' body *before* the sacrifice of Polyxena:

---

[1] Madeleine Doran, *Endeavors of Art*, University of Wisconsin, 1954, p. 278.

we see Hecuba first as the suffering queen; after Polyxena has gone, all her hopes are concentrated upon the life of her last son: and he has been foully murdered. Then something snaps. She loses all dignity and nobility in her thirst for vengeance and is to become, as is foretold at the end, a hound of hell baying upon the plains of Troy. Euripides took that tale in its crude form and turned it into a great play. As in *The Trojan Women* he depicts the deterioration of the conquerors themselves and puts a new meaning into the old formula of insolence and punishment, so here we have the moral degradation of the conquered and the close connexion between sorrow and vengeance, two elements that appear in all his plays on war and conquest. The first part of *Hecuba* is dominated by sorrow and the second by vengeance. Both together give us the complete picture of the so pitiful and yet so terrible queen upon whom the greatest burden has fallen: she has right on her side, but, because she has suffered more than human nature can bear, she becomes less, not more, than human.[1]

Grube's account brings out clearly the basic form of *Hecuba* as well as the strong appeal the tragedy can exert for a sympathetic reader. What also emerges for a reader of Shakespeare is the close resemblance of its form to that of *Titus*, both having an action divisible into two parts, the first dominated by grief, the second by revenge, in both the transition from first to second part being similarly rapid and decisive. Moreover, the *relation* between the two parts is also very similar, for the Euripidean theme of 'the growing of sorrow into hatred and of lamentation into a desire for revenge' finds a strong echo in Shakespeare.

A close look at the central sequence of each play will show that they are both constructed with a view to a comparable effect: in each case we witness the emotional collapse of a heroically powerful character. Hecuba has two chief maternal interests: Polydorus and Polyxena. Euripides might have told his story in the form of a loose series: first Polyxena, then Polydorus, finally Polymestor. But the form he chose, as far as the two children are concerned, is more like a chiasmus, a criss-cross arrangement: a, b, B, A. That is: (1) the announcement of Polydorus' death (told by the Ghost in the Prologue); (2) the announcement of Polyxena's death; (3) Polyxena's death; (4) Polydorus' death. This arrangement sees to it that the deaths of both children are broken to Hecuba one after the other. And it is the close proximity of the two blows that precipitates her into madness (if madness

[1] G. M. A. Grube, *The Drama of Euripides*, 1941, pp. 82–4.

it is). In his second and third acts, Shakespeare shows a similar desire to expose Titus to a rapid succession of calamities which will also have the effect of precipitating him into a vengeful insanity. In the source tale the crucial events are strung out in a loose sequence. In Chapter Three the prince (i.e. Bassianus) is murdered; in Chapter Four Titus' sons are arrested for the murder, they are executed, and Titus' hand is cut off; in Chapter Five Lavinia is raped and mutilated. What Shakespeare does is to weave these separate events into a complex sequence, so that Lavinia's rape (for example) comes before the two sons are arrested. By doing this he prepares for the great passion scene of III. i in which Titus endures one appalling event after another. Although the narrative circumstances of the plays are widely different, the psychological and emotional processes involved are closely similar.

The moment of change, during which Hecuba and Titus make the decisive move from passivity to activity, is dramatized in each case by a short interval of silent self-communing and withdrawal. Hecuba speaks to herself in a long aside, during which Agamemnon tries to make her answer him; but she is entirely self-absorbed, conceiving her plan of revenge. Titus is similarly withdrawn, silent for a few moments until he bursts into laughter. Moreover the drying-up of Titus' grief ('Why, I have not another tear to shed') is not unlike Hecuba's reply to Agamemnon:

Agamemnon. Poor Hecabe! What boundless suffering you have borne!
Hecabe. My heart is dead now; there is no heart left to suffer.[1]

The context of these remarks in both plays is one of exhausted near-calm, after the passions and laments of the first part, and before the action has moved into the second movement with its quest for revenge.

There is finally another feature in the situation of Euripides' Hecuba which finds a close parallel in *Titus* and throws light on Shakespeare's conception of his hero. When she discovers Polydorus' body, Hecuba reaches an extreme point, a kind of *ne plus ultra*, of grief in that she has now lost the last of her fifty sons. And it is this—the loss of her last son—following on the loss of Polyxena, that transforms her into a savage revenger.

[1] *Medea and Other Plays*, tr. Philip Vellacott, Harmondsworth, 1963, pp. 86–7.

The loss of Polydorus is the last in a long series of griefs; now she has lost everything. This heaped-up, peculiarly desperate, intensity of grief is matched, on an admittedly smaller scale, in Shakespeare's presentation of Titus. If Hecuba, supreme in grief, had fifty sons and lost them all, Titus had twenty-five, of whom only Lucius (Shakespeare's addition to the chap-book tale) survives. Titus himself draws the parallel in his first speech, not it is true with Hecuba, but with Priam:

> Romans, of five and twenty valiant sons,
> Half of the number that King Priam had,
> Behold the poor remains, alive and dead!

The comparison is with the father of the Trojan royal family— Shakespeare's grizzled warrior hero could hardly compare himself with the aged mother-queen of legend. But in his accumulated griefs which later culminate in dry-eyed insensibility and a single-minded desire for revenge he is to follow the pattern set by Hecuba (as Young Lucius serves to remind us). We shall not properly appreciate the play unless we see that Shakespeare's Titus is in essence nothing else than a male Hecuba.

The story of Titus Andronicus as told in the chap-book version is in itself not only repellent but quite unimpressive. Any reader will wonder what it was that attracted Shakespeare to it. The clue is in the long summarizing title which begins: 'The History of Titus Andronicus, The Renowned Roman General. Who, after he had saved *Rome* by his Valour from being destroyed by the barbarous *Goths*, and lost two-and-twenty of his valiant Sons in ten Years War . . .' Titus had twenty-five sons in all; the remaining three are beheaded in the course of the story. (There is no one corresponding to Shakespeare's Mutius or his Lucius.) The number of Titus' sons and the reference to a ten years' war would surely have reminded Shakespeare of the Trojan story; indeed it seems clear that the author of the tale had incorporated some of the legendary features of the tale of Troy and adapted them to his new hero Titus Andronicus. The prose narrative is rough and loose; as we have seen, the sequence of events is different from Shakespeare's, although the main incidents are already present. Nor is the disposition of material suggestive of dramatic or theatrical form. There is no dialogue, and the narrative is not laid out in scenes; Shakespeare had to work up his central passion scene from a very dispersed and unfocused narrative sequence. He must have brought to it an idea of tragic structure to which the contents of the tale would be made to conform. *Hecuba* supplied that fundamental structure, while the tale gave Shakespeare his Hecuba-like hero.

IV

In the thirteenth Book of his *Metamorphoses* Ovid had retold the story of Hecuba, Polyxena, Polydorus, and Polymestor, clearly using Euripides. Shakespeare's knowledge of the *Metamorphoses* is quite certain: the poem is actually named in *Titus Andronicus* (IV. i. 42), and in the same scene Young Lucius makes his reference to 'Hecuba of Troy'. This reference, together with that a little later to Ovid's 'tragic tale of Philomel', makes it look as if Ovid is the author borne in mind for the whole of this scene. (In fact the phrase Ovid uses of Polymestor when Hecuba goes to him—'vadit ad artificem dirae, Polymestora, caedis', 'she went to the contriver of the vile murder, Polymestor'—is taken over by Titus in this scene; 'till the heavens reveal / The damn'd contriver of this deed'; IV. i. 36).[1] It might therefore be argued that the presence of Ovid makes the Euripidean hypothesis unnecessary.

In the first place we are not faced with a choice between Euripides and Ovid, since no one denies Ovidian influence. The choice is between Ovid alone and Ovid together with Euripides.[2] Study of Shakespeare's source materials for his other plays has taught us that he habitually used multiple sources: they made for complexity and richness; perhaps he thought they made for truthfulness. The same, I think, applies here. The main reason for supposing Shakespeare to have made use of Euripides is that Euripides could give him what he could perhaps find

[1] See also J. C. Maxwell's note on III. i. 263: 'Now is a time to storm; why art thou still?' (New Arden *Titus Andronicus*, 1953.) He refers to E. Wolff's comparison of the line with Ovid's Hecuba: 'Troades exclamant, obmutuit illa dolore' (*Met.* XIII, 538).

[2] If Shakespeare had access to an edition of the *Metamorphoses* with notes by Raphael Regius (as T. W. Baldwin believed), he would have found himself directed to Euripides. On the opening lines of the Hecuba episode, Regius remarks: 'Haec autem de Euripidis Hecuba ab Ovidio sumpta esse vident.' (*Metamorphoses*, Venice, 1540.)

nowhere else: a famous, highly esteemed tragedy with a successful stage history, whose structure was of a kind which could be
imitated and adapted to a modern theatre.[1] The structure of
Ovid's episode, on the other hand, is one proper to narrative
poetry, not drama. The tale reads very much like a summary of
Euripides: Ovid skims rapidly over the main points of the story
(it takes only 146 lines), jumping from one key point to another,
giving emphasis to Polyxena's last speech before her death and
Hecuba's long lament, but foreshortening the final stages of the
revenge on Polymestor. At the very end the narrative movingly
opens out with Hecuba's metamorphosis and the pity felt for her
by everyone—Trojans, Greeks, gods, even Juno. But despite
good moments, the episode as a whole is not a particularly
strong specimen of Ovid's art. It seems one of those places
in the *Metamorphoses* where the existence of a previous work of
high quality has had the effect of inhibiting Ovid's inventiveness;
it reduces him to a kind of brisk second-hand perfunctoriness,
with only one or two touches of his characteristic power and
pathos. However that may be, reading what he makes of the
story is a very different matter from reading Euripides' *Hecuba*
(or seeing it performed). The difference is not only a matter of
length (the fact that the play is over ten times as long as Ovid's
tale), though that has something to do with it; it is rather a
matter of the posture which Hecuba assumes as the protagonist
of a drama, free-standing before us, and of the degree of identi-
fication she elicits from us. And there is finally the superb swing
of the action which Euripides—after all a great master of dramatic
construction—devised for his play and which Shakespeare seems
to have imitated. It is this which more than anything else per-
suades me that Euripides probably had a place in the composition
of *Titus Andronicus*.

A small detail remains which needs mentioning. In the first
act of *Titus* Tamora pleads for the life of her eldest son, but he is
led away to be sacrificed. One of her two remaining sons, Demetrius, offers her comfort:

[1] The method Shakespeare used for working up his sources into the complex and
diversified action required for the Elizabethan stage is suggested by a remark of
Rymer's in *The Tragedies of the Last Age* (1677): 'If the *English Theatre* requires more
intrigue, an Author may multiply the *Incidents*, may add *Episods*, and *thicken* the *Plot*,
as he sees occasion; provided that all the *lines* tend to the same *center*' (ed. C. A.
Zimansky, p. 26).

Then, madam, stand resolv'd, but hope withal
The self-same gods that arm'd the Queen of Troy
With opportunity of sharp revenge
Upon the Thracian tyrant in his tent
May favour Tamora, the queen of Goths—
When Goths were Goths and Tamora was queen—
To quit the bloody wrongs upon her foes.

(I. i. 135–41)

J. A. K. Thomson comments on these lines: 'The reference is to
a scene in the *Hecuba* of Euripides in which the eyes of Polymestor, a Thracian tyrant, are destroyed by Hecuba the Trojan
queen. The story is related by Ovid . . . and one would have little
hesitation in saying that the source of the English poet here is
Ovid, were it not for the addition of the words "in his tent".
Ovid says nothing about a tent, but it is in his tent that Polymestor is blinded in Euripides.'[1] In fact Polymestor is blinded in
Hecuba's tent, not his own. The phrase 'in his tent' may be either
a slip on Shakespeare's part or—much more probably—a calculated distortion of the story: he changed the tent from Hecuba's
to Polymestor's in order to invent a new parallel between Hecuba
and Tamora. Just as Hecuba, says Demetrius, revenged herself
upon Polymestor in *his* tent, so Tamora will revenge herself
upon the 'barbarous' Roman Titus in *his* home city. One might
compare another deliberate distortion of history for poetic
purposes at III. i. 295–8: Lucius is prophesying his revenge on
Saturninus:

If Lucius live, he will requite your wrongs,
And make proud Saturnine and his emperess
Beg at the gates like Tarquin and his Queen.

Here Tarquin's queen seems invented only to complete the parallel
with 'Saturnine and his emperess'. However, the detail of the tent
is interesting in that it points towards Euripides, though in itself
it is hardly conclusive: Shakespeare might have picked up the
detail from some other place (such as a mythological handbook or
dictionary). Dramatically, the passing comparison of the wicked
Tamora with Hecuba shows Shakespeare's usual firm grasp on
the ethical principle of reciprocity. Tamora at this moment is

[1] *Shakespeare and the Classics*, 1952, pp. 57–8.

to Titus what Titus is later to be to her. Later—indeed for most
of the play—it will be his turn to play Hecuba.[1]

V

It is not my purpose to prove beyond doubt that Shakespeare
made use of Euripides in writing *Titus Andronicus*: conclusive
evidence does not exist. It is enough if a case has been formulated.
It may be that he had never read *Hecuba*; he may have chanced
to see it, or a version of it, acted. We know that Peele translated an
Iphigenia while he was still at Oxford, which was acted with success
at Christ Church.[2] Some Shakespearian scholars persist in seeing
traces of Peele's authorship in *Titus Andronicus*, and it may be
that it was through Peele that Shakespeare was introduced to
Hecuba. But all this is mere conjecture. We are on firmer ground
in saying that we have assented too uncritically to the notion that
the violence and ferocity of certain Elizabethan tragedies can be
sufficiently described as 'Senecan'; the dramatic influence of
Seneca's tragedies, while perfectly real, has been exaggerated.
Ascham's opinion in *The Schoolmaster* (1570) is well known:
'. . . the Grecians Sophocles and Euripides far over match our
Seneca in Latin, namely in *Oikonomia et Decoro*, although Senecaes
elocution and verse be verie commendable for his time'.[3] It
need not be supposed that Ascham, who was himself an influence
to be reckoned with, was alone in thinking so. In Shakespeare's
case it may be that we have not had enough faith in his reading
ability in Latin—though it is not clear why Shakespeare, whose
genius was above all linguistic, should have been daunted by the
relatively easy Latin used by the translators of his own century.

One of H. B. Charlton's arguments against Greek influence in
Renaissance tragedy was that translators into Latin or the ver-
naculars invariably 'Senecanized' their Greek subjects. It is
admittedly true that if we look at the only Elizabethan version of
a Greek play published in the sixteenth century, the result does
at first seem obviously 'Senecan'. This is the play called *Jocasta*

---

[1] Shakespeare's later revenge tragedy is comparable in this respect. After he
kills Polonius, Hamlet is to Laertes what Claudius was to Hamlet at the beginning of
the play: his father's killer.

[2] David H. Horne, *The Life and Minor Works of George Peele*, New Haven, 1952,
pp. 41–6.

[3] *Elizabethan Critical Essays*, ed. Gregory Smith, i. 19.

by Kinwelmersh and Gascoigne, which was based on Dolce's Italian version of the *Phoenissae* of Euripides (in turn based on a Latin version). But it does not follow that if it seems 'Senecan' to us, it also seemed 'Senecan' to its first audiences and readers. They may well have taken for granted the qualities we call 'Senecan', but have been all the more alert to those other qualities which were unfamiliar to them—the 'Greek' ones. It seems unlikely that those who saw *Jocasta* performed were quite unconscious of its Euripidean qualities. They would presumably have believed that they were seeing a Greek play, and—despite the many departures from the original text—they would have been right: they would have been seeing something essentially Euripidean; they may even have been closer to the spirit of the original play than we can be. Charlton's argument falters perhaps through a failure to grant the sixteenth century the chance of making its own leaps into the past despite what a modern classical scholar might consider the crudity of its means.

Titus Andronicus is similarly a classical play whose Greek qualities may not have been as imperceptible to its contemporaries as they have been to modern readers. Despite its stylistic use of Latin idiom, its references to Roman history and myth, and the quite exceptional number of times it mentions Rome, it is not a Roman tragedy in the sense usually implied of Shakespeare's later three Plutarchian plays. It is not committed, as they are, to a disciplined interpretation of a single historical period. This is one reason perhaps for supposing it to precede the Henry VI trilogy: it was written before the invention of the Shakespearian history play with its responsible historical presuppositions. As Professor Terence Spencer observed of it: 'The play does not assume a political situation known to history; it is, rather, a summary of Roman politics. It is not so much that any particular set of political institutions is assumed in *Titus*, but rather that it includes *all* the political institutions that Rome ever had. The author seems anxious, not to get it all right, but to get it all in.'[1] Furthermore, although a Roman play in this looser compendious sense, *Titus* is often Greek in feeling—if we take 'Greek' in one of the ways Elizabethans might have understood the term. Its setting is Roman, but the story it tells is one of Thracian violence—for in Greek mythology Thrace was a land of wild

---

[1] 'Shakespeare and the Elizabethan Romans', *Shakespeare Survey*, 10, 1957, p. 32.

passions and fierce inhuman cruelty. Shakespeare must have seen in the chap-book narrative of *Titus* a fusion of two stories each involved with Thrace: the rape of Philomel by the Thracian tyrant Tereus and the revenge of Hecuba on another Thracian tyrant Polymestor. In keeping with this Thracian pattern, Shakespeare worked in a reference to 'the Thracian poet' Orpheus (II. iv. 51) as well as giving the Moor the name Aaron, probably by a link with Marlowe's villainous Ithamore in *The Jew of Malta*: according to Num. 4: 28, 'Ithamar' was 'the son of Aaron the priest',[1] and Marlowe's Ithamore is said to have been born in Thrace.

The play's first act of barbaric violence is Titus' own—his sacrifice of Alarbus, son of Tamora. This act of human sacrifice, an addition to the source, is itself not Roman but Greek.[2] Shakespeare is probably thinking of Greek stories of human sacrifice such as he could have found in the *Hecuba* of Euripides, or in Seneca's adaptation in *Troades*, or in Ovid's episode of Hecuba. The 'lopping' of Alarbus' limbs in order to 'appease the groaning shadows' of the dead, is placed emphatically near the beginning of the play. It distances the subsequent action into a barbaric and alien world, wholly in accord with the ambitiously classical aims of Shakespeare's first attempt at tragedy.

Some further support for the notion that Euripides played a part in the writing of *Titus* comes from an unexpected quarter— and where the evidence is so incomplete any corroborative facts seem worth taking into account. In my next chapter I shall therefore turn aside from Shakespeare's early plays to a point later in his career when that influence seems to emerge again: this time in a scene in *Julius Caesar*. Though these two plays— Shakespeare's earliest Roman tragedies—are in most ways very remote from each other, they have (or so I shall argue) at least this Euripidean influence in common, even if it now manifests itself in a different form. We move, in short, from tragic passion to tragic sentiment.

---

[1] *Narrative and Dramatic Sources*, ed. G. Bullough, vi. 20.

[2] Aeneas admittedly sacrifices prisoners (*Aeneid*, x. 517 ff.) but, as W. A. Camps remarks, 'human sacrifice was barbaric to authors such as Cicero and Livy, and Virgil's presentation of Aeneas here remains extraordinary' (*An Introduction to Virgil's Aeneid*, 1969, p. 29).

4. *Shakespeare and Euripides (II):*
Tragic Sentiment

In his later tragedies Shakespeare very often derived ideas for scenes from his early tragedies and histories. The earliest of the mature tragedies, *Julius Caesar*, illustrates this process very fully (a process which may well have been wholly or largely unconscious). Thus although Plutarch's Lives of Brutus and Julius Caesar gave Shakespeare most of his historical material, it was from his own earlier play *2 Henry VI* that he took over what amounted to the basic form of *Julius Caesar*: a conspiratorial assassination followed by a civil war. But other history plays, notably *Richard III* and *1 Henry IV*, contributed a number of ideas which, combined and developed, were made to serve quite different ends in the new context of Shakespeare's Roman tragedy. So, for example, the form assumed by the episode of Hastings's decision to go to the Tower (*Richard III*, III. ii, iv) was put to further use in the scenes dealing with Caesar's comparable decision to go to the Capitol where he, like Hastings, was to meet sudden death; like Hastings too, Caesar was warned through the dreams of another person. The idea for one important scene seems to have come not from his own plays but from a contemporary's.[1] This was I. ii, the occasion of the Lupercalia, in which Caesar's train crosses the stage on its way to the Capitol, leaving Brutus and Cassius alone together. For this scene he seems to have recalled Greene's *James IV* in which the King is tempted by Ateukin just as Brutus is tempted by Cassius. The process is complicated by the fact that Shakespeare seems also to have adapted I. iii of his own *1 Henry IV*, in which Hotspur is drawn into the first stages of conspiracy by his uncle Worcester, who in this corresponds to Cassius; while in the earlier part of this scene Henry IV's hostility to Worcester—he dismisses him from his presence—foreshadows Caesar's mistrust of Cassius. So both scenes—the one in *James IV* and the one in *1 Henry IV*—became

---

[1] Emrys Jones, *Scenic Form in Shakespeare*, pp. 21-3.

structural sources for the powerfully conceived Lupercalia scene in *Julius Caesar*.

Most of the major scenic ideas of *Julius Caesar* can in this way be shown to be developments from scenes in earlier Shakespearian plays. The famous quarrel scene (IV. iii), however, is an exception. This scene, in which Brutus and Cassius first quarrel and are then reconciled, is one of the remarkable set-pieces of the play and has always been much admired. It seems to have made a special appeal to the classically minded critics of the seventeenth century, for it is specified in the earliest dramatic criticism of Shakespeare that we have. But, unlike the others, it is not anticipated by anything in Shakespeare's earlier dramatic practice.

The narrative source for this part of *Julius Caesar* was Plutarch's *Life of Marcus Brutus*. For this period of Brutus' life (after his departure from Rome and before the decisive battle at Philippi), Plutarch tells of a process of fluctuating relationship between the two friends. He describes several occasions on which differences occurred between them—it is not a matter of a single clash of wills but of several. In constructing the quarrel scene, therefore, Shakespeare brought together in one continuous action what in Plutarch were several disparate incidents. Nevertheless there is one passage in Plutarch which must have served as the germ for the scene, although exactly what it was that the friends said to each other is not disclosed. The passage runs as follows:

About that time Brutus sent to pray Cassius to come to the city of Sardis; and so he did. Brutus, understanding of his coming, went to meet him with all his friends. There, both their armies being armed, they called them both emperors. Now as it commonly happeneth in great affairs between two persons, both of them having many friends and so many captains under them, there ran tales and complaints betwixt them. Therefore before they fell in hand with any other matter, they went into a little chamber together, and bade every man avoid, and did shut the doors to them. Then they began to pour out their complaints one to the other, and grew hot and loud, earnestly accusing one another, and at length fell both a-weeping. Their friends that were without the chamber hearing them loud within and angry between themselves, they were both amazed and afraid also lest it would grow to further matter. But yet they were commanded that no man should come to them.[1]

---

[1] *Shakespeare's Plutarch*, ed. T. J. B. Spencer, pp. 145–6.

Immediately after this passage Plutarch tells how one Faonius burst into the chamber and 'with a certain scoffing and mocking gesture which he counterfeited on purpose' quoted two lines of poetry with the aim of terminating the quarrel; he is pushed out of the room by Brutus. This incident is introduced into the quarrel scene at line 123. In the passage just quoted the only hint of the emotional course of the interview is the sentence beginning 'Then they began to pour out their complaints one to the other . . .', and this presumably suggested to Shakespeare that a big scene on the subject of a quarrel was possible. Other passages before and after this one supplied matter for the conversation, but otherwise Shakespeare was left to his own devices with regard to the scene's construction.

The quarrel scene is not necessary to the plot of *Julius Caesar*. It is quite possible to imagine the action of the play without it. It is not without its function: it is indeed crucial to the play's movement of feeling—it serves to swing the sympathies of the audience over to Brutus and Cassius, with whom they stay until the end. But nothing necessarily leads up to it, nor does it necessarily lead up to anything else. Its importance is emotional and sentimental. Shakespeare need not have invented it; and it remains in some ways curiously detachable from the rest of the play.

As with many other scenes, what happened, I imagine, was that Shakespeare brought to his narrative source, in this case Plutarch, a scenic idea latent in his mind which was then summoned into consciousness by a suggestive passage like the one just quoted. He had, I would conjecture, already encountered a highly effective scene which showed two close friends who first bitterly quarrel and then unexpectedly, but with a convincing naturalness, drop their antagonism and re-pledge their friendship. This was the scene between Agamemnon and Menelaus which occurs near the beginning of Euripides' *Iphigenia in Aulis*. In his book on Euripides, Gilbert Murray called it 'a masterly quarrel scene'.[1] There is no other scene like it in classical drama, Greek or Roman. This scene—or rather a scenic form abstracted from it—and the Plutarchian narrative were, I suggest, brought together to create the quarrel scene in *Julius Caesar*.

I have already argued that the basic form of *Titus Andronicus* was derived, either directly or mediately, from the *Hecuba* of Euri-

[1] *Euripides and His Age*, 1947 rep., p. 114.

pides. The present hypothesis is probably best considered in conjunction with that one; they may be felt to offer some mutual corroboration. Certainly, taken on its own, the notion that the quarrel scene was derived from a scene in Euripides would scarcely be taken seriously. There would of course be less of a problem if one of Shakespeare's contemporaries had recorded an impression that the two scenes had something in common; but no such useful note has survived. (I am thinking of the sort of note that John Manningham entered into his diary after seeing *Twelfth Night* in 1602: he found the play 'much like the *Commedy of Errores* or *Menechmi* in Plautus, but most like and neere to that in Italian called *Inganni*.[1]) The next best thing to contemporary evidence would be evidence occurring in a period shortly after Shakespeare's own. Here we are better served, for as it happens the earliest discussion we have of any scene in Shakespeare is one by Dryden in his Preface to *Troilus and Cressida*. The scene in question is the quarrel scene in *Julius Caesar*.

Dryden introduced into his adaptation of Shakespeare's *Troilus* (1679) what was regarded by some of his contemporaries as an imitation of the quarrel between Brutus and Cassius. The passage in which he discusses it needs to be quoted in full:

I will not weary my reader with the scenes which are added of Pandarus and the lovers, in the third act; and those of Thersites, which are wholly altered; but I cannot omit the last scene in it, which is almost half the act, betwixt Troilus and Hector. The occasion of raising it was hinted to me by Mr. Betterton: the contrivance and working of it was my own. They who think to do me an injury by saying that it is an imitation of the scene betwixt Brutus and Cassius, do me an honour by supposing I could imitate the incomparable Shakespeare; but let me add that if Shakespeare's scene, or the faulty copy of it in *Amintor and Melantius*, had never been, yet Euripides had furnished me with an excellent example in his *Iphigenia*, between Agamemnon and Menelaus; and from thence, indeed, the last turn of it is borrowed. The occasion which Shakespeare, Euripides, and Fletcher have all taken is the same; grounded upon friendship: and the quarrel of two virtuous men, raised by natural degrees to the extremity of passion, is conducted in all three to the declination of the same passion, and concludes with a warm renewing of their friendship. But the particular groundwork which Shakespeare has taken is incomparably the best; because he has not only chosen two of the greatest heroes of their

---

[1] *Narrative and Dramatic Sources*, ed. G. Bullough, i. 269.

age, but has likewise interested the liberty of Rome, and their own honours who were the redeemers of it, in this debate. And if he has made Brutus, who was naturally a patient man, to fly into excess at first, let it be remembered in his defence, that, just before, he has received the news of Portia's death; whom the poet, on purpose neglecting a little chronology, supposes to have died before Brutus, only to give him an occasion of being more easily exasperated. Add to this, that the injury he had received from Cassius had long been brooding in his mind; and that a melancholy man, upon consideration of an affront, especially from a friend, would be more eager in his passion than he who had given it, though naturally more choleric.

Euripides, whom I have followed, has raised the quarrel betwixt two brothers who were friends. The foundation of the scene was this: the Grecians were windbound at the port of Aulis, and the oracle had said that they could not sail, unless Agamemnon delivered up his daughter to be sacrificed: he refuses; his brother Menelaus urges the public safety; the father defends himself by arguments of natural affection, and hereupon they quarrel. Agamemnon is at last convinced, and promises to deliver up Iphigenia, but so passionately laments his loss that Menelaus is grieved to have been the occasion of it and, by a return of kindness, offers to intercede for him with the Grecians, that his daughter might not be sacrificed. But my friend Mr. Rymer has so largely, and with so much judgment, described this scene, in comparing it with that of Melantius and Amintor, that it is superfluous to say more of it; I only named the heads of it, that any reasonable man might judge it was from thence I modelled my scene betwixt Troilus and Hector.[1]

The critical essay of Rymer's to which Dryden refers was *The Tragedies of the Last Age*, which had appeared the previous year in 1678. Rymer had written a full critique of *The Maid's Tragedy*, and in the course of his adverse examination of Fletcher's quarrel scene had introduced a damaging comparison with Euripides:

But that I may never find a fault without shewing something better, —For a quarrel betwixt two friends, with the *turn* and *counter-turn*, let me commend that Scene in the *Iphigenia* in *Aulide*: Where *Agamemnon* having consented that his Daughter should be sacrific'd, and (that her Mother might let her come the more willingly) sent for her with a pretence that she was to be marri'd to *Achilles*, yet in a fit of Fatherly tenderness he privately despatches Letters to hinder her coming. *Menelaus* meets the Messenger going from *Agamemnon*, suspects the business, takes the Letters from him before *Agamemnon's*

---

[1] *Of Dramatic Poesy and Other Critical Essays*, ed. George Watson, 1962, i. 241–2.

face, and read[s] them; and now arose the contest: *Menelaus* was zealous for the publick good, the more because it agreed so much with his own interest, and *Agamemnon* had cause enough to stand up for his Daughter; but yet, at length, with weeping eyes and shame for his weakness and partiality, he yielded up the cause. But *Menelaus* now seeing the conflict of *Agamemnon*, the tears rowling down his cheeks, and his repentance, this sight melted the heart of him, and now he turns Advocate for *Iphigenia*: He will have *Hellen* and the concerns of *Greece* left to the mercy of Heaven rather than that his Brother, *Agamemnon*, should do so much violence to himself, and that so vertuous a young Princess be trapan'd to lose her life.

Here all the motions arise from occasions great and just, and this is matter for a *Scene* truly passionate and Tragical.[1]

These two passages are not only interesting in themselves as early specimens of English dramatic criticism: they also offer a useful lead into the present subject. In the first place, whereas *Iphigenia in Aulis* is no longer a particularly admired or much read tragedy, it would appear from both Rymer's and Dryden's accounts that it was one of those classical plays which were selected for study, whether at school or university, and that, as in the case of *Hecuba*, it had been approved by a well-established critical tradition. (Four years before Rymer's essay, in 1674, Racine had produced his *Iphigénie*, based on *Iphigenia in Aulis*, although not imitating its quarrel scene.)

What makes Dryden's remarks useful here is the mere fact that he should have found such a close similarity between Shakespeare's and Euripides' scenes. Indeed the further fact that he could have been thought to be imitating Shakespeare when he was actually imitating Euripides is in itself a strong argument for their likeness. Of course it does not occur to Dryden that Euripides might have been behind Shakespeare too: Shakespeare is already what he was to so many in the century following him—the great untaught genius who 'needed not the spectacles of books to read nature'.

It is worth insisting, however, that Euripides' quarrel scene is rather an exceptional scene in the larger context of Greek tragedy, just as Shakespeare's quarrel scene is rather exceptional in his own plays. When Dryden observes of all three quarrel scenes that they are 'grounded upon friendship: and the quarrel of two virtuous men, raised by natural degrees to the extremity of passion, . . .

[1] *Critical Essays of the Seventeenth Century*, ed. J. E. Spingarn, 1908, ii. 204-5.

concludes with a warm renewing of their friendship', he is saying something which is true of this scene and no other in Shakespeare. In Shakespeare's other rhetorically heightened scenes which are designed to arouse audience feeling, the emotional content has something violent or harsh about it: they are displays of virulent hatred or crazed grief—as in the scene of York's death in *3 Henry VI*, the passion scene in *Titus Andronicus*, or the last appearance of Constance in *King John*. In the quarrel scene, by contrast, we have something milder, less distressing: not passion so much as 'feeling' or even what a later age would call sentiment. Nor, if we extend the comparison further, is there anything much like the quarrel scene in the plays of Shakespeare's Elizabethan contemporaries, or in the tragedies of Seneca. In Seneca we are largely confined to the realm of criminal pathology: in such works as *Thyestes* or *Medea* or *Oedipus* there is little scope, outside the choruses, for anything approaching sentiment: few characters have either the chance or the wish to show kindness to each other. But the two quarrel scenes are pre-eminently displays of natural feeling: kindness, kinship, triumphs. And it triumphs through a display of weakness and inconsistency, qualities here made wholly sympathetic.

'Euripides', says Dryden, 'has raised the quarrel betwixt two brothers who were friends'; in each case the occasion is 'grounded upon friendship'. In *Iphigenia* it is the fraternal bond which is most stressed, although the duties of friendship are several times appealed to in the course of the scene, as in the following exchange:

> *Menelaus.* All's over, then. I'm in despair. I have no friends.
> *Agamemnon.* You have—if you'll stop trying to ruin your friend's lives.
> *Menelaus.* Did one father beget us both? Will you prove that?
> *Agamemnon.* I'll be your brother in fair dealing, not in crime.
> *Menelaus.* As a true friend, you ought to feel for my distress.
> *Agamemnon.* Use kindness, drop your malice; and then call on me.
> *Menelaus.* You mean, then, you won't help your country in her need?
> *Agamemnon.* Some god has struck my country, and you, with lunacy.
> *Menelaus.* Well, then: boast of your generalship; betray your brother.
>   I have other resources, and I have other friends.[1]

Shakespeare conceives Brutus and Cassius primarily as friends (instances of the noble-minded *amicitia* described by Cicero in his

---

[1] *Orestes and Other Plays*, tr. Philip Vellacott, Harmondsworth, 1972, pp. 381–2.

treatise on the subject). But he seizes on the fact, casually mentioned at one point by Plutarch, that Cassius had married Brutus' sister, and at several points in the play refers to them as 'brothers'. Most of these references cluster around the quarrel scene. Cassius broaches the subject of his grievance in IV. ii with the words 'Most noble brother, you have done me wrong'; during the quarrel itself he says he is 'brav'd by his brother', and when finally he parts from Brutus he calls him 'my dear brother'. Brutus replies, 'Good night, good brother', and twice more in the scene refers to 'my brother Cassius'. It does not of course necessarily follow from these fraternal references that Shakespeare was following Euripides, but the effect is to bring the two scenes more closely together.

The remarks of Dryden and Rymer throw light in other ways. The quarrel, says Dryden, is between 'two virtuous men'. The reasons for the quarrel between Brutus and Cassius are not at once apparent—they emerge only gradually and obliquely, and in such a way that we remain relatively detached about the issues involved. And our detachment is confirmed by the essential goodness of both men: we sympathize with both, seeing their weaknesses and faults, but attracted by their mere humanity. A remark of Rymer's a little earlier in his essay happens to be relevant: 'In *Epick Poetry* enemies are kill'd; and *Mezentius* must be a wicked Tyrant, the better to set off *Æneas's* piety. In Tragedy all the clashing is amongst friends; no *panegyrick* is design'd, nor ought intended but pitty and terror; and consequently no shadow of sense can be pretended for bringing any wicked persons on the Stage.'[1] So it is in *Julius Caesar* (if not in Rymer's despised *Othello*): 'all the clashing is amongst friends'. The entire point of the scene is the humanity of the two men, their relatedness or kindness. This too is very much the point in *Iphigenia*: Menelaus relents because he sees his own case in Agamemnon's grief. It is precisely because both men are vulnerable and inconsistent that the scene has human interest; if Menelaus were entirely politic and selfish it would not be so very different from many others in Euripides.

Another remark of Rymer's takes us further: 'For a quarrel betwixt two friends, with the *turn* and *counter-turn*, let me commend that Scene in the *Iphigenia in Aulide* . . .' The scene is in two parts,

[1] Spingarn, ii. 197.

separated by the appearance of the Messenger. In the first, Menelaus presses his advantage: he contemptuously attacks Agamemnon
for his duplicity and for his indifference to the public good.
In the second, however, Agamemnon's very weakness—his collapse into tears—has the effect of routing Menelaus, who changes
direction, withdraws his hostility, and protests his love and friendship. So we have what Rymer calls 'the *turn* and *counter-turn*': a
surprising, but convincing, change of movement, a kind of swerve
of line which produces its own pleasure. This kind of movement
or oscillation of feeling is an effect which became fairly common
in the heroic drama of the seventeenth century: we find it in
Beaumont and Fletcher as well as in Dryden. We might be
tempted to call it baroque: for there is something flamboyantly
dynamic in its conception which might justify the term. Shakespeare's scene is less overtly symmetrical than the terms '*turn* and
counter-turn' would imply, but the way it traces the unexpected
swerves of human feeling is comparable. Cassius accuses Brutus,
but is met by a steady pressure of even stronger counter-accusa-
tion; finally, overcome by Brutus' coldness, Cassius collapses into
a posture of utter dejection and offers him a dagger and his
naked breast. At this point Brutus himself is won round by his
friend's helplessness, and the quarrel is dissolved. After the
brief interruption by the 'Poet' and the others, nothing is
left for the two friends but the repledging of their love through
an informal but deeply felt ritual: they drink together a bowl
of wine.

Shakespeare's scene was clearly much admired during the
seventeenth century. Although they do not mention it specifically,
Leonard Digges's lines on Shakespeare in the First Folio sound
as if they might be alluding to the quarrel scene:

> Nor shall I e're beleeue, or thinke thee dead
> (Though mist) vntill our bankrout Stage be sped
> (Impossible) with some new straine t'out-do
> Passions of *Iuliet*, and her *Romeo*;
> Or till I heare a Scene more nobly take,
> Then when thy half-Sword parlying *Romans* spake.

The word 'nobly' here suggests that Digges had in mind a scene
of generous feeling, for which the quarrel scene would qualify
more than most. And in fact in the poem which Digges wrote for

the 1640 edition of Shakespeare's *Poems*, he expanded his earlier lines so as to make the allusion more explicit:

> So have I seene, when Cesar would appeare,
> And on the Stage at halfe-sword parley were,
> *Brutus* and *Cassius*: oh how the Audience
> Were ravished, with what wonder they went thence.[1]

Dryden imitated the scene, if not in *Troilus and Cressida*, at least in *All for Love* (1678), in the Preface to which he wrote, referring to Shakespeare, 'Yet I hope I may affirm, and without vanity, that by imitating him I have excelled myself throughout the play: and particularly that I prefer the scene betwixt Antony and Ventidius in the first act to anything which I have written in this kind.'[2] He has another imitation in *Don Sebastian*, in the scene between Sebastian and Dorax, though not so close. That the quarrel scene was so admired not only in Dryden's time but in Johnson's (who refers to 'the celebrated contention' in his general note on *Julius Caesar*) is in itself an interesting fact about it: it may tell us something about the nature of its rhetoric and its emotional appeal. (It may also suggest why the scene is perhaps not so much admired now as it has been.) If he was in some way imitating Euripides, Shakespeare was inaugurating a style that was not to be fully exploited until the seventeenth century—which would explain why the scene was singled out for approval and imitation in the way it was. It might also explain some qualities in the conduct of the quarrel which we may ourselves detect: a slightly thin, febrile emotionality together with a certain willed pressure in the lay-out of the scene. The moment of deepest feeling comes at the drinking of the wine, after the quarrel has been terminated, and this, as far as we know, is entirely Shakespeare's invention.

Dryden was almost certainly unaware of one important fact which I have already mentioned in connection with *Titus Andronicus*. This is that one of the tragedies of Euripides translated into Latin by Erasmus was *Iphigenia in Aulis*. The fact that Erasmus translated this play made it available within Tudor literary culture in ways which are very difficult to trace and which to some extent we can only guess at; but we need not doubt that his authority encouraged the diffusion of all his translations. In the middle

---

[1] Quoted by David L. Frost, *The School of Shakespeare*, Cambridge, 1968, pp. 4–5.
[2] *Of Dramatic Poesy*, ed. Watson, i. 321.

years of the sixteenth century Lady Lumley translated *Iphigenia in Aulis* into English prose (in a version which remained in manuscript until the twentieth century). Along with the *Jocasta* (*Phoenissae*) of Kinwelmersh and Gascoigne, it is the only extant Tudor English version of a Greek tragedy, and it is significant that she should have made use of Erasmus: she seems to have kept his Latin text alongside the Greek original while she translated.[1] It may also be important for the present argument that Peele translated an *Iphigenia* into English and that it was apparently successfully acted at Christ Church, Oxford, in the 1570s. The play has not survived, so that it is not certain whether it was *Iphigenia in Aulis* or *Iphigenia in Tauris*, but in view of Erasmus' version of the former one may guess that it was that play that Peele, like Lady Lumley, chose to translate. If it was *Iphigenia in Aulis*, then it may have been the means—either along with Erasmus' version or alone—of bringing the quarrel scene to Shakespeare's attention.

Finally, one further slight resemblance between the two quarrel scenes may be noted. In Plutarch the altercation between Brutus and Cassius takes place indoors: 'Therefore before they fell in hand with any other matter, they went into a little chamber together, and bade every man avoid, and did shut the doors to them.' In Shakespeare, however, the scene takes place in a military camp—the quarrel itself in Brutus' tent. The quarrel in *Iphigenia* also takes place in a camp, this time in front of Agamemnon's tent. The common location may seem an insignificant matter, but it is just the sort of circumstance which a dramatist might be expected to remember. It may be that Shakespeare's two generals in a tent with their armies all around them were in some way prompted by the two quarrelling generals of Euripides, also brothers, also in the midst of a military action, and also with their armies all around them.

---

[1] David H. Greene, 'Lady Lumley and Greek Tragedy', *Classical Journal*, vol. 36, 1941, pp. 537–47.

5. A Time of Crisis: the Early Histories

SHAKESPEARE'S early histories belong to the critical period of Elizabeth's reign, the three or four years which followed upon the Babington Plot (1586). The Plot brought to a blaze feelings of hostility against Mary Queen of Scots which had been smouldering ever since she had entered England in 1568. In the months leading up to her execution the Government saw to it that a stream of propaganda stirred up public feeling in favour of the impending event. Speeches were made, pamphlets written, imploring Elizabeth to rid the land of its mortal enemy. The themes chosen were the usual ones of the dangers of division in the state, and particularly the acute peril arising from the mere fact of there being two Queens on English soil. Historians of the drama have often in the past appealed to the defeat of the Armada as somehow effecting an imaginative release on a national scale. It seems much more likely that the immediately important events were the Babington Plot and the execution of Mary (1587). More than any other recent event, the Plot revived genuine fears of another civil war. The alarm over the threatened assassination of Elizabeth, and the long-standing but now rapidly growing fear of having two 'monarchs' in one monarchy would have given a topical edge only slightly delayed to such plays as the three Parts of *Henry VI*.

In a pamphlet published in 1586 called *The Peril of the State of the Realme*, the Speaker of the House of Commons, 'master sergeant Puckering', pleads with the Queen that she should hasten the execution of Mary. In the way usual at the time, analogies are raked up from the distant past: 'As the Lydians saide, *Unum Regem agnoscunt Lydi, duos autem tolerare non possunt:* So wee say, *Unicam Reginam Elizabetham agnoscunt Angli, duas tolerare non possunt*'. In the following year a pamphlet by M. Kyffin appeared called *A Defence of the Honorable Sentence and Execution of the Queene of Scots*. It makes the same points though with different materials: Mary, he argues, left her 'sovereignty' behind her in Scotland when she entered English territory: 'If the King of *Spaine* should come into *Fraunce*, although perhaps the French King mought take him for his brother, in the sence of the Poet (*fratrum concordia rara*) yǝt I doubt he would not take him there for his fellow, *omnisque potestas impatiens consortis erit:* there is no Kingdome that will abide a Copartner.' Such reiterated stress on the theme of two monarchs competing for sovereignty within one state must have given a contemporary urgency to such a heightened dramatic moment as this from the opening scene of *3 Henry VI*:

> *King Henry.* I am thy sovereign.
> *York.*   I am thine.

or to a line in Marlowe's *Edward II* which rings out like a slogan:

> Two Kings in England cannot reign at once.
>   (v. i. 58)

The thought was one which the English people had become accustomed to during the months before and after Mary's death at Fotheringay. In *3 Henry VI* the unthinkable situation was staged with astonishing boldness: the throne was claimed by two kings, each backed by an army, only Fortune determining the outcome. One may wonder whether there was some governmental impulse behind the Henry VI plays. They may have been felt to make a contribution to the official propaganda which continued after Mary's death, for in making vivid the horror of civil war they implicitly upheld the Council's decision to do away with the troublesome Scots Queen.

Fear of division in the state is the main political factor behind these plays, but another contemporary event may have given further point to the first play in the trilogy. In November 1590 George Talbot, sixth Earl of Shrewsbury, died. He had played a prominent part in public affairs. He had been married to the notorious virago 'Bess of Hardwick', with whom he had conducted a scandalous quarrel for several years. More important, he had been keeper to Mary Stuart during most of her English imprisonment. It was he who presided over her execution. In celebrating Talbot, first Earl of Shrewsbury, the actors playing *1 Henry VI* were inescapably paying a compliment to Talbot's Elizabethan successors. This would have given an extra force to the oddly brief scene in which Henry VI creates Talbot Earl of

Shrewsbury (III. iv). And there are further links between the play's Talbot and the sixth Earl. Each of the play's three women— Joan, the Countess of Auvergne, and Margaret—can be seen as dangerous French temptresses. Talbot encounters only the first two, and successfully resists them. But the sixth Earl had been keeper to the contemporary 'French' temptress, Mary Stuart (who in upbringing and manners was French rather than Scottish), and could therefore be said to have done in contemporary terms what his ancestor had done in fifteenth-century France. If Shakespeare was deferring to the Talbot family, this may explain a certain stiffness in his portrayal of Talbot: he was perhaps working under constraint, which shows in the writing in a certain lack of conviction.

The dangerous political situation of the late 1580s had other literary effects: books were published which Shakespeare read and which help to place the Henry VI plays in a more definite context than they are usually given. Some of these works were not newly written but only reprinted during these years. This did not prevent them from having as much influence as if they were new. But the fact that they were only reprints has perhaps led to their not being noticed as part of the literary situation immediately behind Shakespeare's plays. In one or two cases a work was reprinted with an obviously didactic or propagandistic motive—possibly a similar motive to that which prompted Shakespeare to embark on his history series.

In 1587 Holinshed's *Chronicles* were reprinted, with additions by Stow and others which brought them up to date—right up to the year of publication. This is known to be the edition that Shakespeare used. Near the beginning of his long chapter on Elizabeth's reign, Holinshed incorporates a full account of the City of London celebrations which in January 1559 inaugurated the Queen's reign. Her progress through the City was punctuated by pauses in front of triumphal arches, by the performance of brief masques and shows, and by the recitation of poems and laudatory addresses. At 'Gratious street', near the start of her journey, says Holinshed, 'the citie had erected a gorgeous and sumptuous arch. . . . A stage was made which extended from the one end of the street to the other, richlie vawted with battlements conteining three ports, and ouer the middlemost was aduaunced three seuerall stages in degrees.' His description needs quoting at length:

Upon the lowest stage was made one seat roiall, wherein were placed two personages, representing king Henrie the seventh, and Elizabeth his wife, daughter of king Edward the fourth; either of these two princes sitting under one cloth of estate in their seates, none otherwise divided, but that the one of them which was king Henrie the seventh, proceeding out of the house of Lancaster, was inclosed in a red rose, and the other which was queene Elizabeth, being heire to the house of Yorke, inclosed with a white rose. . . . Out of the which two roses sprang two branches gathered into one, which were directed upward to the second stage or degree, wherein was placed one representing the valiant and noble king Henrie the eight, which sproong out of the former stocke, crowned with a crowne imperiall, and by him sat one representing the right worthie ladie queene Anne, wife to the said king Henrie the eight, and mother to our most sovereigne ladie queen Elizabeth that now is. . . . From their seat also proceeded upwards one branch, directed to the third and uppermost stage or degree, wherein likewise was planted a seat roiall, in the which was set one representing the queenes most excellent majestie. . . . The two sides of the same were filled with lowd noises of musicke. And all emptie places thereof were furnished with sentences concerning unitie, and the whole pageant garnished with red roses and white. And in the fore front of the same pageant, in a faire wreath, was written the name and title of the same, which was; The uniting of the two houses of Lancaster and Yorke. This pageant was grounded upon the queenes majesties name. For like as the long warre betweene the two houses of Yorke and Lancaster then ended, when Elizabeth daughter to Edward the fourth matched in marriage with Henrie the seventh, heire to the house of Lancaster: so sith that the queenes majesties name was Elizabeth, and for somuch as she is the onelie heire of Henrie the eight, which came of both the houses, as the knitting up of concord: it was devised, that like as Elizabeth was the first occasion of concord, so she another Elizabeth, might mainteine the same among hir subjects, so that unitie was the end whereat the whole devise shot, as the queenes majesties name moved the first ground.[1]

If we are looking for something which might have given Shakespeare his cue for his civil war plays, we are unlikely to find anything more to hand than this description. The Roses were of course often used on ceremonious occasions. But the occasion described by Holinshed expressly linked the wars of the Roses with the accession of Elizabeth in a way which would have been particularly pertinent in the late eighties when the Queen's own

[1] Holinshed, *Chronicles*, 1808 rep., iv. 161.

supremacy was being so perilously challenged. Henry VI's reign was synonymous with the idea of division. The choice of his reign as the subject for a drama would therefore have made a powerful implied contrast with the 'concord' and 'unity' associated with Elizabeth.

The 1587 edition of Holinshed was brought up to date by other historians. Almost at the very end it includes the final stages leading to Mary's execution, printing Puckering's address to the Queen, as well as the proclamation announcing the decision to proceed with the sentence against Mary. There is a strong sense of timeliness here, as if the *Chronicles* had been brought out to exploit the current situation, as well as to give a full perspective to the Government's long-delayed action against the Queen of Scots.

Holinshed's history was certainly, for Shakespeare, the most important work to have been reprinted during the late eighties. But it is significant that three academic tragedies, all treating the subject of civil war, were also printed, or reprinted, during these years. Taken together, they help to form a more specifically dramatic context for Shakespeare's own civil war plays. In 1587 Gascoigne's literary works were given a second edition (the first appeared in 1575). This volume included two plays, the comedy *Supposes* (translated from Ariosto, and used by Shakespeare for the sub-plot of *The Taming of the Shrew*), and the tragedy *Jocasta*. This was a translation, by Gascoigne and Kinwelmersh, of Dolce's Italian tragedy, itself based on a Latin version of the *Phoenissae* of Euripides. Since its subject was the civil war between the brothers Eteocles and Polynices, it had an obvious bearing on the situation of the time—Elizabeth and Mary were 'kinswomen'. That the play's reappearance did not go unnoticed is shown by Marlowe's use of it in *2 Tamburlaine*. The famous tableau of Tamburlaine in his chariot drawn by two kings was based on the opening dumb-show of *Jocasta* in which Sesostris king of Egypt, representing Ambition, is drawn in a chariot by four kings.

In the following year, 1588, appeared another civil war tragedy, Thomas Hughes's *Misfortunes of Arthur*, which was performed before the Queen on 28 February. This is an original work of sorts, though much of it is no more than a *mélange* of close translations from Seneca and Lucan.[1] It was acted about a year after

---

[1] See J. C. Maxwell, *Notes and Queries*, vol. 192, 1947, pp. 521–2; O. A. W. Dilke, *Notes and Queries*, vol. 208, 1963, pp. 93–4; and George M. Logan, *Review of English*

Mary's execution, and was very possibly written with a view to justifying the Government's action. So Arthur shadows Elizabeth, and Mordred Mary.[1] Despite his utterly pedestrian sense of drama, Hughes had some literary ability (if not much), and Shakespeare (I believe) read him and remembered some of his phrases.

Finally, in 1590 *Gorboduc* (first acted in 1561) was reprinted, bound up with another work, Lydgate's prose tract *The Serpent of Division*, which had probably been written during the first year of Henry VI's reign and was printed in 1559, the first year of Elizabeth's reign. The reappearance of *Gorboduc* in 1590 is another sign that in these crisis years men were looking back to the beginning of the Queen's reign—just as Shakespeare did, or may have done, in reading Holinshed's account of the City's coronation celebrations with their theme of 'vnitie'. Both *Gorboduc* and Lydgate's tract warn England of the perils of division. Lydgate takes his main theme from the civil war between Julius Caesar and Pompey (Lucan's own subject). For Elizabethans its relevance was spelt out by the 1590 title-page:

> Three things brought ruine vnto Rome . . .
> England take hede, such chance to thee may come:
> Foelix quem faciunt aliena pericula cautum.

The Serpent of Division may have left a trace on the first of the Henry VI plays. When he makes his first appearance in III. i, Henry VI, still a child, tries to pacify his quarrelling seniors:

> Believe me, lords, my tender years can tell
> Civil dissension is a viperous worm
> That gnaws the bowels of the commonwealth.

He is speaking the 'moral' of the whole trilogy, and in doing so he is varying the phrase used by Lydgate for his title. *Gorboduc* too may have affected the Henry VI plays. Considered as a theatrical entity, *2 Henry VI* is a play with an open ending. It ends just after the beginning of open hostilities, but before the bloodiest atrocities of civil war—they are reserved for the next play. For this structural arrangement Shakespeare may have owed something

---

Studies, vol. 20, N.S., 1969, pp. 22–32. See also O. A. W. Dilke, 'Lucan and English Literature', in *Neronians and Flavians*, ed. D. R. Dudley, 1972. For Shakespeare and Lucan, see Appendix B below.

[1] See Gertrude Reese, 'Political Import of *The Misfortunes of Arthur*', *Review of English Studies*, vol. 21, 1945, pp. 81–91.

to *Gorboduc*, which also has an ending designedly inconclusive, leaving the audience with the burden of foreknowledge. *Gorboduc* ends with a formal 100-line oration by the good counsellor Eubulus. He foretells that the land will be devastated by far greater bloodshed than it has yet experienced:

> One kinsman shall bereaue an others life,
> The father shall vnwitting slay the sonne,
> The sonne shall slay the sire and know it not . . .

—which is exactly what happens in *3 Henry VI*, in the scene at Towton, when first enters 'a Son that hath kill'd his Father', and then 'a Father that hath kill'd his Son'.[1] Like *Gorboduc*, *2 Henry VI* ends with the collapse of the commonwealth.

Finally, given the age's neo-classical assumptions, it was almost inevitable that the late 1580s should have seen a revival of interest in Lucan, the supreme poet of civil war. There is plenty of evidence that he was studied for his political insight as well as admired for his literary qualities. There were many editions to choose from; one was published in London in 1589. The first book of the epic particularly, which focused on the rivalry between Caesar and Pompey, could be used as a source of political tags. The phrase already quoted from Kyffin's pamphlet (*'omnisque potestas impatiens consortis erit'*) comes from a much-studied passage near the beginning of the poem. Marlowe did an interesting blank-verse translation of the whole of Book One; his version of this passage is as follows (the poet is apostrophizing the two antagonists):

> O faintly ioyn'd friends with ambition blind,
> Why ioine you force to share the world betwixt you?
> While th' earth the sea, and ayre the earth sustaines;
> While *Titan* striues against the worlds swift course;
> Or *Cynthia* nights Queene waights vpon the day;
> Shall neuer faith be found in fellow kings.
> Dominion cannot suffer partnership;
> This need no forraine proofe, nor far fet story:
> Roomes infant walles were steept in brothers bloud;
> Nor then was land, or sea, to breed such hate,
> A towne with one poore church set them at oddes.

'Dominion cannot suffer partnership'—that was Lucan's message to Elizabethans.

---

[1] The resemblance in phrasing here was noted by Joan Rees, in *Notes and Queries*, vol. 199, 1954, pp. 195–6.

Marlowe's own civil war play may or may not have preceded Shakespeare's. *The Massacre at Paris* (*c*. 1589–92) brought to the stage the horrors of the wars still being fought out across the Channel. Unfortunately its garbled text makes it impossible to form a judgement of its effectiveness. No doubt other writers took up the theme, as did another of the University Wits, Thomas Lodge. He wrote a Roman history play on a subject parallel to Lucan's, the conflict of Marius and Sulla, and gave it a frankly admonitory title—*The Wounds of Civil War*—which invited an application to home affairs: 'England take hede . . .' Its date is not known; though printed in 1594, it probably belongs to the late eighties; if so, it provides another anticipation of the Henry VI plays.

It is sometimes felt to be surprising that, since Shakespeare's history plays cover a more or less continuous period from Richard II to Richard III, he should have taken the later part (Henry VI to Richard III) before the earlier (Richard II to Henry V). But if the civil war preoccupations of the 1580s are borne in mind, it becomes clear that only the events of Henry VI's reign could have furnished Shakespeare with a convincing parallel. The choice was made for him. He had to begin with 'our late Pharsalian fields in the time of Henry the Sixth'.[1]

---

[1] Burton, *Anatomy of Melancholy*, Everyman edn., 1932, i. 58.

6. An Elizabethan Trilogy

In the Henry VI plays and *Richard III* Shakespeare wrote four history plays which are obviously in sequence. We often refer casually to the first three as a trilogy or to all four as a tetralogy. But are such terms justified? There is no firm agreement on the question. Shakespeare may have conceived the whole sequence as a unity when he embarked on the earliest of them (whichever that was), or he may have been altogether more improvisatory, adding further plays when it became clear that the first ones were theatrically successful. The possibilities are numerous, and scholars have reached different conclusions. Some think the first three plays a trilogy, which ought properly to be detached from *Richard III*. Others think the last three plays the true trilogy, with *1 Henry VI* as the odd man out. Others again think all four plays a true tetralogy, conceived as such by Shakespeare before writing the first of them. The conclusion we reach will clearly affect the picture we have of the early Shakespeare. If he actually projected, designed, and executed a trilogy or a tetralogy, he was doing something exceptionally large in scope for his day. Unfortunately the whole question of the composition of the Henry VI plays is problematical and controversial.

Since Peter Alexander's fundamental work on the text of *1, 2,* and *3 Henry VI*, a movement has grown asserting the dramatic integrity of these plays. It reached a climax with A. S. Cairncross's New Arden edition (1957–64), the first to accept the implications of Alexander's textual work and to present the plays as written in the obvious order, with Part One first, and as intended from the beginning as parts of a tetralogy which included *Richard III*. Alexander's views had already won wide acceptance, though not by any means universal: the New Cambridge edition of the Henry VI plays by J. Dover Wilson (1952) maintained the older view that Shakespeare was reworking plays written by other men (Greene, Peele, etc.) and that Part One was written after Parts Two and Three. Nor have Cairncross's post-Wilsonian arguments converted all sceptics. It is possible for a subsequent editor of *2 Henry VI*, Arthur Freeman, to reject the argument that Part One was written first.[1] For Freeman, Part Two came first, then Part Three, and finally Part One, and he takes this position with full knowledge of Cairncross's work. Others still incline to the view that Part One was written by more than one man—and this too has possibly damaging implications for the idea that Shakespeare designed a play sequence of three or four Parts.[2] In this state of affairs it can hardly be thought unnecessary to ask whether Shakespeare really did set out to write a trilogy or a tetralogy.

These plays are, I believe, not part of a tetralogy, as Cairncross has it, nor a two-part play with *1 Henry VI* and *Richard III* subsequently added, nor (as Freeman suggests) a trilogy composed of *2* and *3 Henry VI* and *Richard III*, with *1 Henry VI* as an independent play, but what after all the First Folio presents them as being—a three-part sequence and a separate play, *Richard III*, obviously a sequel to the others, but far more able to stand on its own (as its stage history abundantly confirms). However useful 'tetralogy' may be as a handy descriptive term, it is not quite accurate. The term 'trilogy', though slightly portentous, and though not used in Elizabethan English (it seems to be first recorded in the late seventeenth century), is the appropriate one here.

It may be objected that, as an Elizabethan dramatist and even perhaps a Tudor apologist, Shakespeare could not have embarked on a Henry VI series without intending to complete the story at Bosworth. According to this view, a Henry VI trilogy is a radically improbable notion: only a Henry VI–Richard III tetralogy makes historical sense. But this view contains several questionable assumptions which are worth bringing into the open.

There is in the first place a difference between Shakespeare's work as it was in the writing and as it now appears to us some centuries later. Looking back over his career, we now find it natural to say that he wrote a tetralogy. But whether he did so prospectively—intentionally—is quite different matter. The very notion of a tetralogy is possibly our own retrospective simplification of what happened. Marlowe, for example, in *Tamburlaine* wrote the first Elizabethan two-part play, yet it is known that he did not plan a two-part play. In what we now call Part One he

---

[1] *2 Henry VI*, Signet edn., New York and London, 1967.
[2] e.g. Kenneth Muir, 'Image and Symbol in the Histories', in *Shakespeare the Professional*, 1973, pp. 71–2.

wrote a complete play on the rise to power of a hero, and only later in response to the play's extraordinary success added a sequel. It may be inevitable for us to call the result a two-part play, but we should resist thinking it that in conception—to do so would blur the lines of Part One, which for a short time was complete in itself. Similarly with *Richard III*, considered as the last part of a tetralogy: although the historical materials of the Henry VI sequence might seem to us to 'demand' completion in a Bosworth-ended play, the writing of *Richard III* may well have been an afterthought which occurred to Shakespeare either at some point during the writing of *Henry VI* or after its completion.

One reason for supposing that he embarked on a set of three plays, not four, is that for Elizabethans (and for a long time after) the most natural and obvious historical division was according to the reign of a king. The history of England was marked by reigns, and when dramatists took to writing history plays they usually chose as a subject either a whole reign or a part of one, but not several. In the Henry VI plays Shakespeare may have been doing something extraordinarily ambitious and original for the popular stage, but there would have been no doubt as to what gave the three plays their unity of subject. It was quite simply the reign of Henry VI. The first play opens with Henry V's funeral, while the penultimate scene of the third shows Henry VI's death. The final scene arranges a perfunctory tableau for Edward IV's court and gives Edward the last word. The harmony he announces is admittedly precarious and hollow—'For here, I hope, begins our lasting joy'—for Gloucester's soliloquies and asides have prompted us to look ahead to the historical outcome. None the less the trilogy ends here; and dramatically there is a considerable hiatus between the end of *3 Henry VI* and the beginning of *Richard III*. The opening of *Richard III* makes a new start. Though it assumes a knowledge of what historically preceded the events it dramatizes, it creates its own autonomous dramatic system—we never feel, when we see it performed, that we are seeing an incomplete play. The three Parts of *Henry VI*, on the other hand, are much less able to stand on their own as individual plays—at least for audiences no longer familiar (as Shakespeare's were) with fifteenth-century history.

Even so, each of the Henry VI plays must have been self-subsistent in terms of performance. Shakespeare could not have

expected an identical audience for each of the three plays. A man
might drop in for *3 Henry VI* on one day and return for *1 Henry VI*
a few days later and on each occasion expect to find what he did
find—a more or less unified theatrical experience that certainly
referred outwards to a larger mass of historical information but
which he did not expect to find represented within his afternoon's
entertainment. Something like this must have been a common
experience in the older mystery play performances: an audience
might often see performed only part of the entire cycle; the rest it
would see, if at all, some other time. Knowing the whole, it would
accept a part. What applies to individual plays, however, also
applies to the entire Henry VI trilogy. No more than a single
play does the trilogy have to take us to the end of the story in
Bosworth: it too can dismiss its audience at an intermediate
stopping-place; and this the third play does with the death of
Henry.

Since each of these highly rhetorical plays was intended for a
distinct theatrical occasion, it would be a mistake to look for the
kind of detailed consistency that we would expect in a modern
sequence of naturalistic novels. But one should not, as Dover
Wilson and others do, jump to the conclusion that (for example)
apparent inconsistencies between *1* and *2 Henry VI* necessarily
prove the chronological priority of the latter. One should rather
pause to consider the peculiar conventions of the play-sequence
as practised by Shakespeare. Nor, on the other hand, should one
ignore these inconsistencies, as opponents of Dover Wilson sometimes do, since by trying to make sense of them something useful
may emerge about the play's dramatic procedure. One needs to
maintain a properly flexible tension between the sometimes way-
ward autonomy of each play and the over-all design of the sequence.
There is much in each play that is not strictly necessary to the
trilogy scheme; the local abundance of each play is self-justifying.
But at the same time a concern for the ultimate effect, the long-
distance continuity, periodically makes itself felt; and, as Cairncross
and others have shown, the concluding scenes (corresponding
roughly to the fifth acts) of the first two plays are strongly continuative: expectation is thrown forward to the play's successor. However, the use made of the fifth act in each play provides a further
argument for the integrity of *1, 2,* and *3 Henry VI* as a trilogy.
Unlike the fifth acts of the first two plays, the fifth act of *3 Henry*

VI does not initiate a fresh subject, which is then made the main subject of the following play; it simply completes the business set going earlier in the same play. The effect made by the last act of *3 Henry VI* is that the action is drawing to a more spacious conclusion than was possible at the end of the earlier two Parts.

It remains true that not until the ending of *Richard III* is the action allowed to rest on a note of absolute closed finality. To say therefore that the Henry VI plays are marked off from *Richard III* and yet at the same time require it to bring the sequence to a full conclusion might seem self-contradictory. But no self-contradiction is involved. Admittedly the close of *3 Henry VI* does not let us feel that the *historical* process has reached a point of rest: that was possible only with Richmond's victory at Bosworth. But it has its own more limited *dramatic* conclusiveness: its fifth act sees the fall of the House of Lancaster. One after another its leaders are disposed of: first Warwick, then Margaret and Prince Edward, and finally Henry VI himself. The trilogy ends with Lancaster in eclipse and York ascendant. Naturally, as any Elizabethan would know, the Yorkist victory was not, historically speaking, a real conclusion. But Henry's life has come to an end, and so completes the business of the three plays: the reign of Henry VI.

One set of details, small in themselves but significant, supports this argument. The three Parts are deliberately linked in their final and opening speeches: Suffolk closes *1 Henry VI* and opens *2 Henry VI*, while Warwick closes *2 Henry VI* and opens *3 Henry VI*. There is no such precise link between *3 Henry VI* and *Richard III*. Shakespeare could easily have given the last speech of *3 Henry VI* to Richard Gloucester, who opens the following play, but he chose not to. Moreover these speech-links acquire further point by being given to someone other than the king: the fact that (for example) Henry IV closes *Richard II* and opens *1 Henry IV* is not felt to be as significant as that Suffolk closes *1* and opens *2 Henry VI*. In this case, as with Warwick, a real continuativeness is suggested.

Such details as these are one kind of sign that these plays were designed as a set of three. No one doubts that *2* and *3 Henry VI* form a sequence: the real stumbling-block is Part One. For evidently the belief that these plays make a trilogy entails believing that Part One came first in the sequence and not as an afterthought. The problem can be approached by considering the case as stated

by the opposition. Arthur Freeman, for example, takes up the
following position: 'Despite the consecutive titles provided by
the Folio editors for *Henry VI*, Parts One, Two and Three, it is
probable that Parts Two and Three originally constituted a two-
part play, and that Part One had an independent conception and
existence in the contemporary repertory.' He goes on:

> Scholarly opinion, however, is divided on the question of prece-
> dence: did the composition proceed chronologically, with Part One
> first, followed by a double play on subsequent events, or was Part
> One, with its emphasis on action and adventure, worked up *after*
> Parts Two–Three, to capitalize upon their evident popularity?
> Certain inconsistencies of plot and characterization suggest, if any-
> thing, the latter alternative . . . but all we can be moderately sure of is
> that the three parts did not constitute an intentional trilogy.[1]

Freeman's points clearly owe something to Dover Wilson's fuller
arguments. Both find the action of Part One different in kind from
that of the other two Parts. As Dover Wilson put it: 'it differs from
the rest of the cycle in one striking particular: while they are
concerned entirely with domestic affairs, i.e. with the dynastic
struggles of the fifteenth century, the centre of its interest is the
fighting in France. No fewer than twenty out of the twenty-seven
scenes take place across the Channel, whereas the three plays that
follow contain only one French scene between them.'[2] In reply to
this one must begin by agreeing that there is indeed this difference.
But when one reads the whole of Hall's long chapter on Henry
VI—and not just brief excerpts from it—one has exactly the same
impression: most of the Joan–Talbot business does in fact come
earlier, and is undeniably different in kind from the later civil
disturbances in England. But Shakespeare was following what he
found in the chronicles: French fighting first, civil war at home
later. He could hardly escape this sequence except by abandoning
his relatively close, though selective, fidelity to history. And if
this is so, Dover Wilson's point is without any force. Freeman's
phrase for the play—'its emphasis on action and adventure'—
seems a gratuitous distortion, as if Part One were merely a blood-
and-thunder pot-boiler and as if it can be discussed adequately
in his crudely reductive commercial terms. It must be stressed
that in reading through Hall's long account one experiences a
change of subject-matter entirely comparable with the change

---

[1] Signet edn., p. 165.   [2] New Cambridge *1 Henry VI*, 1952, p. xi.

felt in passing from *1* to *2* and *3 Henry VI*. Theories of chronology cannot be based on this felt change.

One of the incidental uses to Shakespeare of the overseas Talbot material was that it helped to traverse that early part of Henry VI's life which could not be dramatized directly. When Henry V died, the new king of England was a baby of nine months. In *1 Henry VI*, therefore, there is an expressive value in the fact that the king does not appear at all for the first two acts. It is as if he is being given time, behind the scenes, to grow from a baby to a youth. In the last three acts Henry appears in five scenes, and it is noteworthy that in each of them he calls attention to his youthfulness. It is clear in fact that in Part One his role was designed for a boy actor. In his first speech (in which he speaks the 'moral' of the entire trilogy) he uses a special diction proper to childhood's innocence and ignorance which Dover Wilson, who calls it 'empty, trite, diffuse', misunderstands:

> Believe me, lords, my tender years can tell
> Civil dissension is a viperous worm
> That gnaws the bowels of the commonwealth.
>
> (III. i. 71–3)

The king is here still a child, without personal authority, in the midst of his uncles; and although a king, he does not speak until late in the scene—that is, he occupies a subordinate position. When he appeals to his uncles to be reconciled, Warwick reminds us of his youth: 'Sweet King! . . . What, shall a child instruct you what to do?' In later scenes the verbal references are similarly sustained, as in 'When I was young, as yet I am not old' (III. iv. 17: here he is made to remember his father speaking, an impossibility invented for the context). Even in the last act, when Gloucester broaches the question of marriage, Henry's youth is insisted on: 'Marriage uncle! Alas, my years are young!' (v. i. 21). And in the closing moments of the play we leave him experiencing love-longing for the first time: Henry has reached adolescence. In his final speech he speaks of the unfamiliarity of his erotic feelings: whether (he says) it is Suffolk's description of Margaret

> . . . or for that
> My tender youth was never yet attaint
> With any passion of enflaming love,
> I cannot tell . . .

The diction is quasi-pastoral, with its stress on the speaker's inexperience; it anticipates the Young Shepherd's song in Jonson's *Sad Shepherd*:

> Though I am young and cannot tell
> Either what death or love is well . . .

Such references, carefully placed on each of Henry's appearances, run through the play so as to ensure that, concurrently with the political action, we are kept mindful of the growing-up of the king. In *2* and *3 Henry VI*, the king being now an adult, his age or time of life is immaterial: it receives no attention. He is now characterized not in terms of age but of weakness, folly, saintliness —the attributes of a grown man. It seems highly unlikely that Shakespeare would have gone back, after the later two plays, to show the youth of Henry—as he would have had to do if Dover Wilson and the rest were right. In the more natural and plausible order we have, first, in Acts One and Two of *1 Henry VI* an off-stage infancy and childhood, next in Acts Three to Five youth, and then in *2* and *3 Henry VI* the manhood and later age of the king, ending with his murder. The arc described by the king's life is traced continuously through the three plays: youth in Part One; incompetent and unhappy involvement in the world in Part Two; increasing withdrawal from the world in Part Three. All this strongly suggests a single governing conception, though one adapted to the serial presentation of a play-sequence.

As part of his case for the chronological priority of Part Two over Part One, Dover Wilson makes the following observation: 'What does surprise us is to find the writer or writers of *2* and *3 Henry VI* three times informing the audience that Henry had been only nine months old when he ascended the throne . . . So forgetful of the earlier play if it was earlier, and so unnecessary, since some phrase about boyhood would have served equally well!'[1] The reply to this is that Shakespeare had not forgotten that in *1 Henry VI* he had shown Henry as a youth rather than as a baby: on the contrary, it is a sign of the dramatist's tact in the care he has for the illusion he is creating of time passing, that he should not refer to the king's being a baby of nine months until *2 Henry VI*. There is nowhere in *1 Henry VI* any such reference to the precise age of the baby king because that would have violated the

---

[1] New Cambridge *1 Henry VI*, 1952, p. xii.

delicately vague sense we have of historical time passing with different rates of speed in different parts of the play. As we have seen, as far as Henry is concerned, the play opens with him as a mere baby and ends with him on the verge of marriage. But in the Talbot–Joan scenes the duration of the action seems much more circumscribed: it might be weeks, months, or a couple of years— hardly more. In order to blend these differing time-rhythms into one complex, but seamless, dramatic illusion, Shakespeare had to avoid any of the over-recalcitrant particulars of history. Consequently we find that, in the first two acts when Henry is still only an off-stage infant, the only two references to him are studiously indistinct: these occur at the end of the first scene when Gloucester exits saying 'And then I will proclaim young Henry king', and Exeter follows with 'To Eltham will I, where the young King is.' There is no reference to his being a baby: 'young' serves as a dramatic euphemism. Only in the next play can the notion of a baby king, made in retrospect, be allowed to obtrude on the audience's attention.

The second point made by Dover Wilson in favour of the priority of Part Two concerns the characterization of Duke Humphrey. Wilson declares that he appears as 'two different men' in each Part. In Part Two he is 'a noble gentleman', the 'good Duke Humphrey', while in Part One he is not much better than his enemy Winchester: 'he shows neither dignity nor self-control, but conducts himself like a common brawler, who outbids Winchester in sacrilegious abuse . . .' The author of Part Two, argues Wilson, could not have drawn this 'roaring-boy'.[1] The answer to this must be sought by recalling what might be termed the qualified autonomy of each of the Henry VI plays. I have just argued that the presentation of Henry VI himself is coherent throughout the three plays; it is at any rate not conspicuously at odds with itself. This argument does not apply to Gloucester. The Gloucester of both Parts needs to be seen within the particular strategy adopted by the dramatist for each occasion. It is in this case unrealistic to look for an organically coherent, gradually unfolding character portrayal. In the first play (until the fifth act), Gloucester is seen entirely within the setting of England's quarrelling peers. He is never given any special personal stature, but is always seen either as one of a group of peers (as in the first scene, where he is

---

[1] Ibid., pp. xii-xiii.

one of a quartet) or as the antagonist of Winchester. He is also
the King's Protector, but only in his last two scenes (v. i, v) does
he begin to take on the lineaments of the conscientious upholder
of law and the commonwealth that he becomes entirely in Part
Two. But even in Part Two (in II. i) he keeps up his undignified
feud with Winchester (a fact which Dover Wilson passes over).
In this second play, however, Gloucester's chief role is that of
tragic hero. In the first movement of *2 Henry VI*, therefore, his
role is structurally dominant: it is *his* 'passion' that is at the centre
of the stage. And this explains what appear to Dover Wilson and
others as 'inconsistencies of characterization'. But again, from
these differences of presentation nothing concerning the chronological order of the two plays can properly be inferred.

 Dover Wilson winds up his case by playing what he evidently
regarded as his trump card:

 I conclude this section by asking any who may still believe *1* and *2*
Henry VI to have been written in that order to answer the following
question. How comes it that Talbot, the hero of Part I, is never once
mentioned in Part II? True, by that time 'the sweet war-man' is
dramatically, though not historically, 'dead and rotten'. But in the
first scene of Part II Gloucester gives a list of those who had shed
their blood in France to preserve what Henry V had won, and over-
looks the name of Talbot altogether. Is that not very strange?[1]

A reply to this question, which is an interesting one, must again
appeal to the peculiar blend of continuity and discontinuity which
we find in these plays. It is again a question of the dramatist's
tact, his concern to seize the audience's attention, guide it in the
appropriate channels, and not offer it any disruptive distractions.
The speech referred to by Wilson is that spoken by Gloucester to
the assembled peers. The humiliating terms of the King's marriage
treaty have been read; the King, his new Queen, and Suffolk have
just left; and Gloucester's grief for England bursts out. Through
Gloucester's speech, Shakespeare is establishing the outlines—
the guidelines, one might say—of the opening situation in a new
play. What has gone before in this scene (up to the King's exit)
serves as recapitulation—it reminds us where we are in the story
—but it is quietly pitched and briskly dispatched. The new action
proper starts here with Gloucester's speech—'Brave peers of

---

[1] New Cambridge *1 Henry VI*, 1952, p. xiii.

England, pillars of the state'—and it is essentially a new rhetorical
situation. The speech is really a formal oration, whose function
is to set in a new order the main personages of this new drama:

> What! did my brother Henry spend his youth,
> His valour, coin, and people, in the wars? . . .
> Have you yourselves, Somerset, Buckingham,
> Brave York, Salisbury, and victorious Warwick,
> Receiv'd deep scars in France and Normandy?
> Or hath mine uncle Beaufort and myself,
> With all the learned Council of the realm,
> Studied so long . . . debating to and fro
> How France and Frenchmen might be kept in awe?
>
> (I. i. 73–87)

Gloucester is speaking passionately, rhetorically, and tenden-
tiously. What he says inevitably involves simplification and omis
sion. It is useless to look in his speech for a fair summary of what
we have seen happening in Part One. Gloucester (or Shakespeare)
is addressing himself to the *present* situation and what follows from
it. It suits Gloucester to assume that York and Somerset were
heroes of the French wars: the fact that in Part One they had
helped to seal Talbot's doom is not relevant here; it is certainly
inconvenient to remember it. For they are present and Talbot
is not. It is even to Gloucester's purpose to pay tribute to Winchester, his inveterate enemy, simply because the whole tendency
of the speech is to assert the heroic solidarity of the English lords
which is now being shamefully undermined by Suffolk. As Dover
Wilson says, it is strange that Talbot finds no place in this list—
until one sees that there might be a good reason for leaving him
out. And there is one. Shakespeare's usual procedure, especially
in his opening scenes, is to throw the attention *forward*, excite
anticipation, engage interest in what is happening *now* between
the persons on stage. It would run entirely counter to this forward
movement if we were to be thrown back to 'brave Talbot' and
the previous play. Talbot would bring with him too many com-
plications, the disloyalty of York and Somerset among them. So
neither Talbot nor Joan nor any of the other French warriors
are mentioned. Far from proving that Part Two was written
before Part One, the omission of Talbot's name here helps to
prove the opposite. Dover Wilson ignores the fact that Talbot
figures prominently in the chronicles: the author of Part Two did

not have to rely on Part One to know about him. The omission—
suppression, rather—of Talbot from this list can therefore be
taken as implying the pre-existence of Part One, since it was in
order to avoid calling on the audience's memory of the earlier
play that he was passed over.

Even if such objections as Dover Wilson's to the priority of
Part One can be shown to be without much substance, it still
needs to be asked why so many competent judges seem predis-
posed to be sceptical about an 'intentional trilogy'. It is as if they
find something inherently implausible in the notion. An important
factor is that, consciously or not, they want to fit Shakespeare
into an intelligible post-Marlovian theatrical situation. Since the
impact of the two-part *Tamburlaine* was so great, there seems to be
a kind of logic in assuming that, like others, Shakespeare too
must have been prompted to write a two-part play—hence the
persistence of the idea that he did in fact write one in *2* and *3*
Henry VI. For even if one grants the originality and audacity of the
young Shakespeare, it seems too much to suppose that he invented
or—as far as modern drama is concerned—reinvented the trilogy.
According to this way of thinking, there seems something too
improbably singular about such an undertaking.

When we look for a possible model for Shakespeare's trilogy in
the English drama of his time, we are, it is true, driven to admit
that there is nothing close at hand—or nothing extant—which
could have served him. The only other previous English trilogy
seems to be John Bale's three Protestant moralities, all of them
short, and probably acted in a single day. But there is no likelihood
that Shakespeare knew them and they are so different from the
Henry VI plays as to be unilluminating. (There is also a set of
three Cornish mystery plays which were acted on separate days;
but they were translated only in the nineteenth century). One
should certainly not underestimate the possible influence of the
mystery plays on Shakespeare's dramatic sequence and on the
expectations of Elizabethan audiences: there may have been
mystery play performances spread over three days. Chambers
records a performance in 1384 lasting five days, another in
1391 four days, and another in 1409 eight days: such extended
performances would no doubt have disposed audiences who
remembered them to respond sympathetically to a three-part
history play. Yet despite the importance to Shakespeare of the

mysteries, there seems nothing in them which might have prompted him to embark specifically on a historical trilogy.[1]

There is, however, one trilogy close at hand which offers itself as a likely candidate for being Shakespeare's model. This is *Richardus Tertius*, written in Latin by Thomas Legge, Cambridge Professor of Civil Law and Master of Caius College. It has been studied as a possible source for Shakespeare's *Richard III*, although nothing conclusive has emerged. But oddly enough, it has apparently never been considered in connection with the Henry VI plays. Until fairly recently, perhaps, the notion that Shakespeare designed a trilogy was so seldom seriously entertained that no investigation into its antecedents was thought necessary. Probably too it was thought unlikely that Shakespeare would have been able to cope with a Latin play; today it seems less unlikely. Whether or not Shakespeare read *Richardus Tertius,* it seems to me highly probable that he knew of its existence, and that if we want a source for the *idea* of an 'intentional trilogy', Legge's drama provides it.

Although never printed in the sixteenth century, *Richardus Tertius* was fairly well known. It survives in several manuscripts. It seems to have been written in 1579 and acted in the same year at St. John's College; it was acted again, according to the Bodleian MS., in 1582, also at St. John's. Since Greene was at St. John's from 1578, and Nashe from 1581, and since Marlowe was also in Cambridge from 1581, there is a fair chance that all three may have seen it. Indeed there is no doubt that Nashe knew of it, since he refers to it in *Have with you to Saffron Walden* (1596): '. . . his fellow *qui quae codshead,* that in the Latine Tragedie of K. *Richard* cride, *Ad urbs, ad urbs, ad urbs,* when his whole Part was no more but *Urbs, urbs, ad arma, ad arma'.*[2] The play is referred to by Sir John Harington in the Preface to his translation of Ariosto (1591; this was the essay he called 'A Preface, or rather a Briefe Apologie of Poetrie'), where it is the only example of tragedy mentioned: 'And for tragedies, to omit other famous Tragedies, that that was played at *S. Johns* in Cambridge, of *Richard the 3,* would move (I thinke) *Phalaris* the tyraunt, and terrifie all tyrannous minded men from following their foolish ambitious

---

[1] The so-called *Parnassus* trilogy post-dates the Henry VI plays. The plays were acted between 1598 and 1601.

[2] *Works,* ed. R. B. McKerrow, 1910, iii. 13.

humors . . .'[1] In Francis Meres's *Palladis Tamia* (1598), Legge is placed among 'our best for Tragedie', along with Shakespeare, Marlowe, Kyd, and Jonson.[2] The play was clearly felt to be a notable event in the new English drama, whose interest was not confined to the more academically minded. Neither Harington nor Meres bothers to mention that Legge's play was in Latin: Legge is thought of simply as one of 'our' English writers of tragedy.

The exceptional nature of Legge's work is well brought out by G. B. Churchill in the course of his very full discussion of it:

. . . *Richardus Tertius* appears to have been the first real history-play, or 'Chronicle History', written in England. Bale's *Kyng Johan* had been acted in 1539, and was the first play to introduce an English monarch upon the stage; but it has no title to be called a history, following as it does the lines of the old moralities. *Gorboduc* . . . takes its story from the chronicles, but this belongs to mythical and not actual English history. The University plays, as well in English as in Latin, appear to have been down to 1590 and later confined almost wholly to Biblical or classical material. Nowhere in this list appears a play that deals with English history, save Legge's, and a transcript of his play by Henry Lacey in 1586.[3]

The importance of Legge's play for Shakespeare has never been appreciated because it has been studied only within the context of *Richard III*; and since it cannot be shown with certainty that Shakespeare made use of it there, *Richardus Tertius* has been left in the twilight realm of possible sources and analogues. It seems feasible that Legge's conception of a trilogy of history plays dramatizing the reign of a fairly recent English king may well have prompted Shakespeare's own entry into the same field of drama. Presumably Legge himself derived the idea of a trilogy directly from Greek tragedy.

Richardus Tertius was divided into three 'Actiones', each of which was a full-length play in five acts and intended for performance on successive evenings. The material is taken from the chronicles, the diction and sentiments largely from Seneca's tragedies. But the Unities are not observed, and the copiously episodic action flows with an unclassical lack of inhibition and restraint. Each 'Actio' concludes with a spectacular visual effect: the first with the public

[1] *Elizabethan Critical Essays*, ed. Gregory Smith, ii. 210.
[2] Ibid., ii. 319.
[3] *Richard the Third up to Shakespeare*, Berlin, 1900, p. 270.

penance of Jane Shore; the second with Richard's coronation procession; and the third with a long climactic sequence showing the Battle of Bosworth, with bands of armed soldiers running over the stage, and finally, to the accompaniment of a choric hymn, the crowning of Richmond and the inauguration of the Tudor peace. One of these effects may have struck Shakespeare, whether he read the play or merely heard about it. 'The Shew of the Procession' at the end of the first Actio included 'A Tipstaffe, Shore's Wife in her petticote, haveing a taper burninge in her hand, The Verger, Singinge men, Praebendaries, The Bishope of London, and Citizens.'[1] There is nothing corresponding to this in *Richard III*, since Jane Shore does not appear, but the scene in *2 Henry VI* of Eleanor's penance makes a comparable stage picture: '*Enter the* Duchess of Gloucester *in a white sheet, and a taper burning in her hand, with* Sir John Stanley, *the* Sheriff, *and* Officers' (II. iv).

According to the Renaissance theory of imitation, the aspiring writer was advised to aim not at a close copy but at a likeness-within-difference. So Shakespeare may be imagined as imitating Legge, but making the result very unlike. Accordingly his trilogy, like Legge's, dramatizes a single disastrous reign; only the king is different—not only a different man, but different in every respect. (The contrast between Henry VI and Richard III may in any case have been rhetorical commonplace: as we saw earlier, Thomas Wilson has one in his *Art of Rhetoric*.)

Legge's trilogy is an academic work with something of the freedom of popular drama. Shakespeare's Henry VI trilogy and *Richard III*, on the other hand, are plays written for the popular theatre which are yet in some ways also academic. There seems nothing inherently implausible in supposing that Shakespeare took a hint—a momentous hint—from a senior Cambridge don.

---

[1] *Richardus Tertius*, ed. B. Field, 1844, p. 108.

7. 1 Henry VI: *Hereafter Ages*

SHAKESPEARE belonged to an age in which the idea of fame was taken with considerable seriousness. Not only were men becoming increasingly tender towards their country's past, collecting and preserving relics and records, but those who could pay for it were also anxious to hand on worthy images of their own achievements. In the course of a discussion of tomb sculpture, Eric Mercer remarks:

The concept of immortalising a calling could ... be extended to the monumental recording of an exploit, and the inscription to Sir John Pelham (d. 1557) at St. Michael's, Lewes, records his defeat of a French raid at Seaford. By the reign of Charles I this function of a tomb had become sufficiently important for Weever to open his book, *Ancient Funeral Monuments* [1632], with a definition of them as things 'erected, made, or written, for a memoriall of some remarkable action, fit to be transferred to future posterities'.

During the last years of the sixteenth century, this led to a fashion for 'scenic representation', as in the case of Sir John Farnham's tomb at Quorn. He was shown standing in soldier's dress 'before a detailed scene of the siege of a city'.[1] Shakespeare's historical plays therefore run concurrently with a new 'scenic' tendency in funerary sculpture.

Like *Henry V* and like *Antony and Cleopatra*, *1 Henry VI* is a play suffused with the idea of fame, the posthumous life that great men and their achievements enjoy in the memory of others. In the second act, after a bitter campaign, the English have recaptured Orleans and put the French to flight. Old Salisbury has died during the fighting, and Talbot now arranges a fitting memorial for him.:

> Now have I paid my vow unto his soul;
> For every drop of blood was drawn from him
> There hath at least five Frenchmen died to-night.
> And that hereafter ages may behold
> What ruin happen'd in revenge of him,

[1] *English Art* 1553–1625, Oxford, 1962, pp. 236–7.

Within their chiefest temple I'll erect
A tomb, wherein his corpse shall be interr'd;
Upon the which, that every one may read,
Shall be engrav'd the sack of Orleans,
The treacherous manner of his mournful death,
And what a terror he had been to France.

(II. ii. 7–17)

For Talbot it is vital that posterity should remember, and that it should remember circumstantially. Salisbury's monument must bear a true image of his achievements and of the way he met his end. When at the close of the fourth act, Talbot himself meets his death, Sir William Lucy comes to collect his body and insists on reciting to the French the long list of Talbot's titles. The list was apparently taken from Talbot's actual epitaph in Rouen cathedral. The interest in funerary monuments implied by both these passages, the practice of cherishing the memory of the dead so that they do not altogether die, are entirely characteristic of the first four acts of the play. Unless we bear these ideas in mind, much of *1 Henry VI* will be artistically unintelligible.

Talbot's speech comes at a pause in the fighting in and around Orleans. The previous scenes had shown the English and French locked together in a long campaign. Now, however, for a short space the soldiers can take respite—and in this same scene, while Talbot, Bedford, and Burgundy talk over the night's events, a Messenger appears with an invitation for Talbot. A new subject is broached, the Countess of Auvergne's plot against Talbot.

On the face of it, what happens is straightforward and self-justifying. The Countess sends her messenger to beg Talbot to grant her a visit: she had long wished to see such a famous hero. He agrees to go, but first whispers something inaudible to a Captain. As soon as he arrives and has assured the Countess that he is indeed Talbot, she treats him as a prisoner: he has walked into a trap. For she hates him as a cruel enemy of France. She will imprison him and see that he does no more harm to her country. At this Talbot laughs and speaks what to her seem mere paradoxes. She has in her power, he tells her, not the substance of Talbot but only his shadow; the real Talbot would be too big to be confined within her walls. He explains himself by blowing on his horn. At this signal, his soldiers appear. They are his 'substance'. The Countess understands and apologizes, and Talbot agrees to accept her now sincere offer of hospitality.

Although the surface meaning of this little episode is clear enough, one may feel puzzled as to why it was included at all. The Countess's invitation is fictitious. Shakespeare may have remembered something like it in a romance, but in its present form it was his invention. The question remains: why did he invent it? If we take the scene 'straight', there seems to be no obvious difficulty—except that there is something rather arbitrary about it, which teasingly prompts the question why it should be here. For the Countess is never seen or referred to again. The incident, so vividly written and so curiously pointed in its sudden reversal and denouement, stands all alone in the play. It must surely have been written—or so one would like to believe—with a further purpose than its immediate one of providing entertainment.[1]

This further purpose can be clarified by looking more closely at the way Shakespeare phrases the exchanges which make up the episode. The Countess's invitation is first announced by her Messenger:

> All hail, my lords! Which of this princely train
> Call ye the warlike Talbot, for his acts
> So much applauded through the realm of France?

The theatrical metaphor ('acts . . . applauded') marks a complete break in tone from what has gone before. The fierce acrimony of the battle scenes gives way to a more relaxed atmosphere, in which the warriors partake of a little refreshment and amusement. (And in any case we may feel that Talbot's 'acts' would hardly be 'applauded' by the French). The playfulness inherent in the metaphor is such as to put us, perhaps no more than subliminally, on our guard. He goes on to issue the Countess's invitation: she admires Talbot's 'renown' and wishes to

> boast she hath beheld the man
> Whose glory fills the world with loud report.

The last word is almost comically ambiguous: for Talbot's glory does undeniably fill the world with bangs as well as with admiring talk. Talbot's ally Burgundy speaks next:

---

[1] For another reading of the scene, see Sigurd Burckhardt, *Shakespearian Meanings*, Princeton, 1968, pp. 47–72.

> Is it even so? Nay, then I see our wars
> Will turn unto a peaceful comic sport,
> When ladies crave to be encount'red with.

This is the second metaphor suggestive of the theatre; while 'peaceful comic sport' implies not only a comic interlude in the full dramatic sense but also love-dalliance, as the next line makes more nearly explicit. And Bedford, too, in a similarly bantering courtly tone, declines to accompany Talbot. He must go alone: to him only was the invitation issued. But before he goes Talbot mysteriously whispers to the Captain. Something is afoot: what it is must not yet be disclosed. We next see the Countess giving instructions to her porter, and, left alone, she soliloquizes:

> The plot is laid; if all things fall out right
> I shall as famous be by this exploit
> As Scythian Tomyris by Cyrus' death . . .[1]

Her 'plot' is yet another theatrical term: not only is her conspiracy under way but we are about to see a carefully devised 'interlude' performed.

The dialogue that follows between the Countess and Talbot turns on whether or not he is in fact Talbot. When she sees him the Countess exclaims that the man before her cannot be the famous hero: she had expected 'some Hercules' or a 'second Hector', not 'this weak and writhled shrimp'. The immediate point is the same as one made in an emblem book of the period: 'Minuit praesentia fama': presence lessens fame.[2] Talbot seems less great than his fame. But on being assured that he is indeed Talbot, she announces that he is in her power:

> Long time thy shadow hath been thrall to me,
> For in my gallery thy picture hangs;
> But now the substance shall endure the like
> And I will chain these legs and arms of thine . . .

---

[1] Tomyris is now an unfamiliar figure: editors have to explain that she was a Queen of Scythia who decapitated the Persian Cyrus. But in Tudor times she was more familiar; she was occasionally referred to in poems and pageants, as in Mary Tudor's accession celebrations, when she was presented as a 'figure' of the Queen. The true explanation is that Tomyris was one of the female Nine Worthies, as J. Huizinga remarks in *The Waning of the Middle Ages* (Harmondsworth, 1955, p. 72). The mention of Tomyris here may have contributed to the theatrical or pageant-like associations of this scene.

[2] Geoffrey Whitney, *A Choice of Emblems*, ed. H. Green, 1866, p. 20: 'Praesentia minuit fama'—(literally) 'Fame grows less in presence'.

Talbot's response is to laugh. He tells her that, although he really is Talbot, she has only his 'shadow' (the word could mean 'picture') in her power, not his substance. His reply is in fact the thematic climax of the scene: it leads immediately to the 'recognition' and 'reversal' of this drama-in-little:

> *Talbot.* No, no, I am but shadow of myself.
>   You are deceiv'd, my substance is not here;
>   For what you see is but the smallest part
>   And least proportion of humanity.
>   I tell you, madam, were the whole frame here,
>   It is of such a spacious lofty pitch
>   Your roof were not sufficient to contain 't.
>
> *Countess.* This is a riddling merchant for the nonce;
>   He will be here, and yet he is not here.
>   How can these contrarieties agree?
>
> *Talbot.* That will I show you presently.
>
> *Winds his horn; drums strike up; a peal of ordnance. Enter Soldiers.*
>   How say you, madam? Are you now persuaded
>   That Talbot is but shadow of himself?
>   These are his substance, sinews, arms, and strength . . .

The Countess capitulates at once:

> Victorious Talbot! pardon my abuse.
>   I find thou art no less than fame hath bruited,
>   And more than may be gathered by thy shape.

In this key passage theatrical terms are still present, though less prominent. 'Shadow', opposed here to 'substance', in Elizabethan English was a synonym for 'actor', while 'shape' could also be used to mean 'role' or 'theatrical part', sometimes 'theatrical costume'.[1] These theatrical terms point to the same idea: throughout the episode there runs an undercurrent of thought about imagination and reality—and what is imagined includes the life enjoyed in the minds of others by the famous, fame itself being as much a matter of imagination as the idea of drama, the imaginary events imitated by actors on a stage.

The meeting between Talbot and the Countess brings out two sets of contrasts: first, between the fame of Talbot and the

---

[1] 'Shadow' translates 'umbra' which in Latin as in English could mean 'actor' as well as 'shadow'. I am grateful for this point to Mr. John Norton-Smith.

unimpressive physical appearance—the 'shape'—of the man himself, at least as it appears to her; and second, between the fame
of the historical Talbot in the minds of Shakespeare's audience and
the 'shape' it assumes, reincarnated by the actor, in the present
play. In each case the visible 'shadow' of Talbot as he stands
before the Countess and before the audience is something
separable from, although referable to, the unseen 'substance',
which to the Countess, is his army, his 'real' strength, and to us,
the audience, is the historical reality which the play as acted
serves to bring to mind. By means of this invented incident,
therefore, starting perhaps from the rhetorical commonplace
'Minuit praesentia fama', Shakespeare is alluding to the nature of
the imaginative work he is engaged in as the author of a new kind
of history play.

In *I Henry V*, his other English history which celebrated a
famous military hero, Shakespeare was to make his meaning more
straightforwardly clear and explicit. Indeed a few passages from
the Chorus of that play form the best commentary on the present
episode. One may note too that the voice of the Chorus has
something of the courteous and humorous note of Talbot himself in his dealings with the Countess:

> But pardon, gentles all,
> The flat unraised spirits that hath dar'd
> On this unworthy scaffold to bring forth
> So great an object. Can this cockpit hold
> The vasty fields of France? Or may we cram
> Within this wooden O the very casques
> That did affright the air at Agincourt?
> O, pardon! since a crooked figure may
> Attest in little place a million;
> And let us, ciphers to this great accompt,
> On your imaginary forces work.
>
> (Prol., 8–18)

The Chorus is saying that the great events of his story can be
brought upon the stage only through the exercise of imagination
and through the use of symbols. There is an immense gulf
between the scale of the actual historical events and the token
representations of them which is all that the conditions of the
drama allow. As he is to say before the fourth act, the audience
must

> sit and see,
> Minding true things by what their mock'ries be.

And again, before the fifth act, he pleads the 'excuse'

> Of time, of numbers, and due course of things,
> Which cannot in their huge and proper life
> Be here presented.

His position is in fact curiously close to Talbot's—with of course the difference that the Chorus is talking overtly about dramatic illusion, while Talbot is entirely concerned with the circumstances of his meeting with the Countess. For just as the Chorus uses the metaphor of a 'crooked figure'—an arithmetical symbol, which properly used may multiply units—so does Talbot at first appear to the Countess 'a weak and writhled shrimp', an unimpressive figure in a different sense. And yet the unheroic-looking man standing before her—also a 'crooked figure'—is merely a 'shadow' whose 'substance' is, like the historical events referred to by the Chorus, such that its 'huge and proper life' cannot be got under the Countess's roof:

> . . . were the whole frame here,
> It is of such a spacious lofty pitch
> Your roof were not sufficient to contain 't.

The Chorus appeals to the audience's co-operative imagination:

> Piece out our imperfections with your thoughts . . .

Analogously, the Countess is led to confess to Talbot that

> thou art no less than fame hath bruited,
> And more than may be gathered by thy shape.

Talbot's physical weakness and crookedness—his 'imperfections' —are therefore precisely symbolic (there is nothing in Shakespeare's sources to suggest that Talbot was physically unimpressive). In this scene he stands for the shadow-actor who must imitate what is so much greater than himself. And yet with imagination—actor's and audience's—the imitation may succeed.

The Countess episode is a kind of witty conceit on the dramatist's part. It works obliquely as a comment on the imaginative activity which the play stimulates in its audience. It also tells us something about our response to the fame of the famous dead. The Countess thinks she can capture and so conquer Talbot; she discovers that she cannot. She cannot conquer the man who has already, through fame, conquered death. For the play's imaginative mode is not in the least naturalistic. Talbot, as he appears in *1 Henry VI*, is not only a brave and loyal soldier; he is also a legendary figure. That is, he is presented to us both as he was in life and as he was to become after death—someone who has 'gone down in history', immortalized in the memories of his countrymen. When Talbot, before leaving for the Countess, *whispers* to the Captain, he is doing what, in Shakespeare's last play of fame, Cleopatra did to Charmian: she too, after her interview with Octavius in v. ii, whispers to a subordinate. Like Talbot, she is preparing to outwit the plotter. For both Talbot and Cleopatra, having (historically speaking) already achieved the empyrean of fame, are invulnerable. The Countess cannot put Talbot in a dungeon, nor can Caesar make Cleopatra walk in his triumph. In trying to do so they are ineffectually trying to avert what is already a part of history. When Burgundy says, in the lines already quoted, that

> I see our wars
> Will turn into a peaceful comic sport,
> When ladies crave to be encount'red with

he is reminding us of what has in fact happened. The French wars of the fifteenth century have indeed turned into 'a peaceful comic sport' for Elizabethan theatre audiences. Talbot has become a famous hero of the history books. We know that he did not languish in a dungeon but died fighting bravely with his son against the French. But in the present play that scene is yet to come.

We have been considering the Countess episode in isolation. But it has a context within the play's sequence of scenes which will certainly affect the way we take it. For it comes immediately after the battle scenes located at Orleans (i. ii; i. iv, v, vi; ii. i and the earlier part of ii. ii) to which it acts as a kind of epilogue. These battle scenes and the Countess episode throw light on each other: they are part of the same conception, and that conception itself is more interesting than has usually been admitted.

One of the most striking features of *1 Henry VI* is the prevalence
of action, the high frequency of staged incident. The opening
scene is static, its interest predominantly verbal: the praise of
Henry V, the lamentations for his death, the bickering between
Gloucester and Beaufort, and the messenger speeches. The four
noblemen stand in a formal group around Henry V's coffin;
apart from the entries of the messengers, there is no movement
to arrest the eye. In the second scene the action moves to Orleans,
and at once a change is felt. The scenes that comprise the Orleans
sequence are intensely animated. The dialogue is of course still
important: there is a wide range of tone, from Talbot's formally
'heroic' account of his captivity to undercutting cynical repartee.
And yet these scenes are rounded out with a surprising number
of sharply defined *actions*, some of them involving considerably
detailed stage business. At times indeed the action gives rise to
a quality approaching mime. Readers of this part of the play can
easily overlook this dimension of closely imitated military
activity. But scrutiny of the text proves that much was expected
of the actors—and, by implication, of the audience. Those on stage
as well as those watching them are to be engaged in a corporate
act of imagination.

The first Orleans scene (1. ii) briskly introduces the Dauphin
and his allies. They decide to attack the English once more.
They march away, and the first 'action' follows: '*Here alarum.
They are beaten back by the English, with great loss.*' The terse stage
direction, clearly authorial, leaves it to the actors to work out
exactly how it was done, but something in the way of a skirmish, and
possibly a protracted one, must have been planned in rehearsal.
This is after all the first battle scene of a play which boldly brings
to the stage the famous French wars, and this action must at
once establish the war atmosphere. The Dauphin and the
others re-enter, and a kind of council scene follows, in the course
of which the Bastard of Orleans introduces Joan la Pucelle.
First Charles tests her clairvoyance by substituting Reignier
for himself; but she is not deceived and promptly picks out the
Dauphin. She then describes herself in 'high terms' which astonish
him—and would remind an audience of the 'high astounding
terms' of Tamburlaine. Her physical prowess is equally surprising, as the Dauphin discovers when he tests her valour by
engaging her in single combat. Their fight, with Joan's victory,

is the next striking action; no doubt it would have offered an elaborate exhibition of swordsmanship. The French are heartened by their new ally and make one more effort to raise the siege.

The next Orleans scene (I. iv) introduces Talbot, and he is at once shown in a milieu of minutely realized activity. We are made to imagine a setting unusually particularized for an Elizabethan play of this date. The first stage direction reads: '*Enter, on the walls, the* Master-Gunner *of Orleans and his* Boy'. The Master-Gunner explains his plan:

> The Prince's espials have informed me
> How the English, in the suburbs close intrench'd,
> Wont, through a secret grate of iron bars
> In yonder tower, to overpeer the city,
> And thence discover how with most advantage
> They may vex us with shot or with assault.

The Boy is left (off stage) with 'a piece of ordnance' aimed at the English position. Then, '*Enter* Salisbury *and* Talbot *on the turrets, with* Sir William Glansdale, Sir Thomas Gargrave, *and* Others'. Talbot gives Salisbury an account of his captivity, couched in high epic terms; and while they are looking through the 'grate' at the city they are shot at by the Boy. Salisbury and Gargrave are fatally wounded. The scene is, potentially at any rate, an exciting piece of action: we are told by the Master-Gunner what is going to happen and are then made to wait for it (the dramatic formula is elementary but effective). What is of more interest perhaps is the number of details carried over from Hall's history: the Master-Gunner and his Boy, the tower and the grate, the view they have through the grate of 'the bulwark of the bridge', even the fact that 'it is supper-time in Orleans' (in Hall the Master-Gunner 'was gone doune to dinner'). These details work together to evoke a curiously vivid and convincing picture of an actual incident in a particular time and place. In Hall, however, Talbot is not present at this incident. For this his first appearance Shakespeare places him on the tower along with Salisbury and the others and makes him deliver his narrative while exposed in that dangerous spot. The narrative is thus superimposed on the gunnery incident, making a dramatic equivalent to a painted or sculptured memorial scene: the hero posed heroically in the foreground, with the violence of war displayed around him (as in the tomb of Sir John Farnham, already mentioned). Talbot is still standing over Salisbury vowing revenge when he is interrupted by a new development: '*Here an alarum, and it thunders and lightens*'. 'What stir is this?' cries Talbot, 'What tumult's in the heavens?' A messenger explains that the Dauphin's army has arrived, along with 'one Joan la Pucelle'. She, presumably, is somehow responsible for the aerial tumult, which heralds the clash between herself and the English hero.

In textual or verbal terms, on the other hand, the following scene (I. v) looks short (only thirty-nine lines) and uninteresting. The scene's real substance is revealed in the stage directions. Talbot has just made his exit to the sounds of an '*Alarum*'. Another stage direction follows immediately with a symmetrical double-action: '*Here an alarum again, and* Talbot *pursueth the* Dauphin *and driveth him. Then enter* Joan la Pucelle *driving* English-men *before her. Then enter* Talbot.' They exchange a few words of defiance, and '*Here they fight*'. A pause for breath, while Talbot excoriates her, and then '*They fight again*'. Neither wins, and while the French enter Orleans, Joan takes her leave: '*A short alarum; then enter the town with soldiers.*' Talbot is left alone, bewildered by his inability to overcome the French 'witch'. The sounds of warfare continue while he speaks: two distinct *alarums* are called for, until finally '*Exit* Talbot. *Alarum; retreat.*' The new scene (I. vi) begins at once: '*Flourish. Enter on the walls* la Pucelle, Charles, Reignier, Alençon, *and* Soldiers.' The occasion is one of triumph and jubilation: 'Rescu'd is Orleans from the English.' And Joan is acclaimed as 'France's saint'. They leave, to the ear-blasting sounds of another fanfare. A pause follows, since the next scene (II. i) takes place at night, and everything is now hushed. A Sergeant is positioning sentinels; he leaves them to their watch; and then, unseen, '*Enter* Talbot, Bedford, Burgundy, *and* Forces, *with scaling-ladders; their drums beating a dead march.*' They take up positions at different points, and then '*The English scale the walls and cry "Saint George! a Talbot!"* ' The sentries are roused, and more spectacular actions follows: '*The French leap o'er the walls in their shirts. Enter, several ways,* Bastard, Alençon, Reignier, *half ready and half unready.*' The French take stock of the situation and blame each other for the ignominious defeat until, as a final blow to their self-esteem, they are once again interrupted: '*Alarum. Enter an English* Soldier, *crying "A Talbot!*

A Talbot!" They fly, leaving their clothes behind.' The mere name of
Talbot is enough to make them run. One can imagine this final
laughter-rousing incident serving as a kind of invitation to the
audience to applaud.

The Orleans war sequence ends here. Talbot pays tribute to
the dead Salisbury, in the speech already quoted, and then the
messenger arrives from the Countess of Auvergne. That episode
rounds off the sequence by making us reflect on what we have
just been witnessing. A close look at the whole sequence, giving
full attention to each of the actions just listed, would show that
in acting-time it is much longer and more resourcefully contrived
than a cursory reading would suggest. A reader is likely, for
example, to overlook or understress the indications of 'noises
off': the *flourishes*, *alarums*, and *retreats* that signalize the various
military movements—not to speak of the thunder and lightning
that herald the approach of Joan. Moreover the three or four more
developed actions are well contrasted: the single combat between
the Dauphin and Joan, the gunnery incident, the English assault
on Orleans using ladders, and the rout of the unprepared French
who leap over the walls. And these larger incidents grow out of
a whole series of battles and skirmishes which at times seem more
or less continuous. The amount of physical action pressed into
this sequence needs insisting on.[1] Its only rival elsewhere in
Shakespeare is the sequence, similarly placed early in the play, in
Coriolanus, where we are required to keep distinct in our minds
the whereabouts of two Roman armies when they engage simultaneously with the Volscians. The Actium sequence in *Antony
and Cleopatra*, which is structurally modelled on this Orleans
sequence, is at once more spaced out and less given to the direct
presentation of action: all the fighting is relegated to an area off
stage. A comparison with *Tamburlaine*, by far the most ambitious
history play (if it can be called that) preceding *1 Henry VI*,
would show that Marlowe's battle scenes are almost entirely
theoretical: they hardly exist dramatically. When Tamburlaine and
Bajazeth leave for battle, no attempt is made to give definition
to the fighting other than a generalized 'alarum': the women on
stage exchange insults until Bajazeth appears running, pursued

---

[1] One might compare the elaborate stage actions of Robert Wilson's *The Three
Lords and Three Ladies of London* (*c.* 1589), as described and analysed by Richard
Southern in *The Staging of Plays before Shakespeare*, 1973, pp. 558–78.

by Tamburlaine. These Orleans scenes, on the contrary, are methodically shaped into well-defined actions; especially notable is the skill with which different levels of the acting space are exploited. Talbot makes his first appearance 'on the turrets'— on the 'top' of the theatre, one stage higher than the upper stage. (Later in the play, in the Rouen sequence, Joan is also to appear *'on the top'* when she signals her entry into the city: *'thrusting out a torch burning'*.) Indeed this part of the play is remarkable for the way the physical form of the theatre is made to yield imaginative potential: we are given just enough stimulus for us to make our own transformation of the tiring-house façade into specific locations of the Orleans siege. Towards the end of the sequence, however, Shakespeare goes further. We are first shown the English assault on Orleans when they scale the wall with ladders. But afterwards that same action is verbally described in such a way as to confirm our sense of its reality. So, after they have leapt over the walls in their shirts, the French try to collect themselves by talking over what has just happened:

> *Reignier.* 'Twas time, I trow, to wake and leave our beds,
> Hearing alarums at our chamber doors.

> *Alençon.* Of all exploits since first I follow'd arms
> Ne'er heard I of a warlike enterprise
> More venturous or desperate than this.

The English exploit, which we have just witnessed, is thus at once distanced in fame—as if it were already a *famous* action, remembered by the participants and written down in histories. Something similar happens in the following scene, when the English leaders bestow a comparable immortality upon the French response to the attack, but this is the other sort of fame—shame and ignominy:

> *Bedford.* 'Tis thought, Lord Talbot, when the fight began,
> Rous'd on the sudden from their drowsy beds,
> They did amongst the troops of armed men
> Leap o'er the walls for refuge in the field.

> *Burgundy.* Myself, as far as I could well discern
> For smoke and dusky vapours of the night,
> Am sure I scar'd the Dauphin and his trull,
> When arm in arm they both came swiftly running . . .

We know that what they hesitantly affirm is true: we have ourselves just witnessed those events. The order of things here—action followed by verbal report—serves to support the credibility of the record. In such a sequence we see history actually in the making.

And so we return to the Countess of Auvergne. The Countess tries to entrap the famous hero. But all she can do is seize a shadow, a ghost—an actor—who, long after the historical Talbot's death, mimics his invisible substance, presenting 'a weak and writhled shrimp' in place of the Hercules, the Hector, that—metaphorically at any rate—constituted the Talbot of reality.

The Countess episode brings to an end the long first sequence of *1 Henry VI*. Shakespeare's company may well have arranged an interval after it. For if the time taken by its many extended stage actions is borne in mind, the sequence from the opening of the play to the end of II. iii is quite a long one. The following scene introduces an entirely new set of characters (Plantagenet, Warwick, Somerset, and the rest) and an entirely new plot-interest. The plucking of the roses does not concern the present theme: Talbot and the idea of fame. Here one may simply observe of Talbot that, throughout the remaining scenes in which he appears, he inhabits a different dimension from that of the others. He is a walking legend, whose famousness gives him a special kind of *mana*, as if he were surrounded by a golden light like a saint's aureole. When the young king meets him in Paris (III. iv), he gazes at him as at some famous old monument, or as if the shade of a long-dead hero had been summoned up by a magician:

> *King.* Is this the Lord Talbot, uncle Gloucester,
> That hath so long been resident in France? . . .
> When I was young, as yet I am not old,
> I do remember how my father said
> A stouter champion never handled sword.

Henry VI was only nine months old when his father died, as he himself elsewhere reminds us; the present memory is invented so as to enhance Talbot's credentials: no less a one than Henry V—himself 'too famous to live long' (I. i. 6)—paid tribute to him.

Talbot has little more to do in the play than die into fame—a 'fame-death' comparable to the 'love-death' of legendary lovers.

His death is more than once anticipated. In the very first scene
the Messenger is misunderstood by Bedford to say that Talbot
has been killed in battle:

> *Messenger.* A base Walloon, to win the Dauphin's grace,
>   Thrust Talbot with a spear into the back;
>   Whom all France, with their chief assembled strength,
>   Durst not presume to look once in the face.
>
> *Bedford.* Is Talbot slain? Then I will slay myself . . .
>
> (I. i. 137–41)

Here, interestingly, the Messenger is made to anticipate Talbot's
actual death, for according to Hall: 'his enemies . . . cowardly
killed him, lyenge on the grounde, whome thei neuer durst
loke in the face, whyle he stode on his fete . . .' It is as if, again
like Henry V, he is 'too famous to live long': he is feared dead
before he has even once appeared in the play. Later, in the
Rouen sequence (III. ii), Bedford's death takes us closer in feeling
to Talbot's own. He dies honourably on the battlefield, sitting in
a chair, his dying moments counterpointed against the ignominious flight of the cowardly Fastolfe. Bedford—'a man half
dead', as Talbot calls him—compares himself to Uther Pendragon,
who 'in his litter sick / Came to the field, and vanquished his
foes'. A passage in Geoffrey of Monmouth explains Shakespeare's
reference: 'Then, with a laugh he [Pendragon] called out in a
merry voice: "These marauders called me the half-dead king,
for that I was lying sick of my malady in the litter, and so in
truth I was. Yet would I rather conquer them half-dead, than be
conquered by them safe and sound and have to go on living
thereafter. For better is death with honour than life with shame." '[1]
Bedford's honourable death juxtaposed with Fastolfe's dis-
honourable flight makes Geoffrey's point succinctly, as well as
preparing us for the longer-drawn-out process of Talbot's end.

This ambitious sequence (IV. ii–vii) is designed entirely with a
view to providing a suitable setting for Talbot's fame-death.
At its very beginning we are told quite clearly what we are going
to see. This is the function of the French General's words as he
speaks down to Talbot from the walls of Bordeaux:

---

[1] *History of the Kings of Britain*, tr. Sebastian Evans, rev. C. W. Dunn, 1958, Bk.
8, Ch. 23, p. 181.

> . . . no way canst thou turn thee for redress
> But death doth front thee with apparent spoil
> And pale destruction meets thee in the face . . .
> Lo, there thou standst, a breathing valiant man,
> Of an invincible unconquer'd spirit!
> This is the latest glory of thy praise
> That I, thy enemy, due thee withal;
> For ere the process of his sandy hour,
> These eyes that see thee now well coloured
> Shall see thee withered, bloody, pale, and dead.
>
> (IV. ii. 25–38)

Just as Bedford sitting in his chair was a 'half dead man', so Talbot is already marked by death. The general sees him in that moment as 'a breathing valiant man' who within an hour will be 'withered, bloody, pale, and dead'. What we see, however, in the scenes that follow is a metamorphosis not of a living man into a discoloured corpse—or not only that—but of a mortal man into a hero immortalized in fame. From now on, changes are repeatedly rung on the topics of fame and shame, honour and ignominy, until, at the end of the fourth act, when Sir William Lucy learns of Talbot's death, we are left with two wholly disparate ways of seeing Talbot. Lucy chants his roll-call of Talbot's many titles—

> But where's the great Alcides of the field,
> Valiant Lord Talbot, Earl of Shrewsbury,
> Created for his rare success in arms
> Great Earl of Washford, Waterford, and Valence,
> Lord Talbot of Goodrig and Urchinfield,
> Lord Strange of Blackmere, Lord Verdun of Alton . . .

—only to be rebuffed by Joan's contemptuous

> Here's a silly-stately style indeed!
> The Turk, that two and fifty kingdoms hath,
> Writes not so tedious a style as this.
> Him that thou magnifi'st with all these titles,
> Stinking and fly-blown lies here at your feet.

The French see nothing but a corpse, the English a glorious image in Fame's temple.

In these final scenes of Talbot's apotheosis Shakespeare uses a method quite different from anything earlier in *1 Henry VI*. Whereas in the Orleans sequence lively action was at a premium, bustle, noise, elaborately mimed movements, here the burden is carried by the verse—for of the three scenes that make up this movement, the first two are duologues spoken by the Talbots, father and son, while the third is almost a monologue, in which Talbot has become '*old* Talbot', alone and desolate and finally with his son's body in his arms. Accordingly the verse too is in a different style from anything previously heard: uniformly elevated, musical, artificial. With the exception of a few lines, most of these scenes are in heroic couplets, a form which Shakespeare never uses elsewhere in a tragic passage. But the dying of Talbot into fame is not quite a tragic subject, nor are these scenes meant to be taken as tragic. The rhymes insulate and uplift him, shutting him off from other men, while painfully—like Hercules—he ascends into a higher life. The stress falls on that new life, the life of fame.

We can allow this conception of Talbot's death to have interest, but in actual effect it must be admitted a failure. Whatever Nashe may have thought about their emotional force, these scenes now seem strained and thin, their exaltation something of an effort, their pathos somewhat unmovingly 'official'. In the comparable but immeasurably finer scene of Cleopatra's death Shakespeare grounds the exaltation in common humanity. But here the preoccupation of the Talbots with their own honour and fame becomes altogether over-insistent. At the same time the loftily pitched chiming verse moves the discourse far away from naturalism. We are not meant, perhaps, to listen too closely to *what* the Talbots are saying: as so often in opera, the music should beneficially drown the words. Still, these scenes no longer affect us, for what is finally unsatisfying about them is the excessive simple-mindedness of the postures adopted. Sir William Lucy's schoolboy jingoism ('Submission, Dauphin! 'Tis a mere French word: / We English warriors wot not what it means') and his pompous recital of Talbot's titles deserve Joan's deflationary riposte. Her reply gives relief and rights a balance, wrenching the play back into its characteristic dialogue method, in which each speaker is humanly partial.

Once Talbot is safely dead, Shakespeare is free to bring out into the open his lack of enthusiasm for him. Until the fifth act, this alternative less favourable estimate has been almost, though not quite, suppressed. When Talbot speaks of his revenge for

Salisbury's death (in the speech quoted at the beginning of this chapter)—

> For every drop of blood was drawn from him
> There hath at least five Frenchmen died to-night

—one may have one's doubts as to how admirable the man is who can make such a boast. To the French he has never been a hero at all, but a 'bloodthirsty lord' (the phrase is used by the 'virtuous lady' the Countess of Auvergne), for he has

> by tyranny
> Wasted our country, slain our citizens,
> And sent our sons and husbands captivate.

Talbot does not deny any of this; he says of himself, in phrases matching hers and so in a way corroborating them, that

> he yoketh your rebellious necks,
> Razeth your cities and subverts your towns,
> And in a moment makes them desolate.

But later, when 'bloody Talbot', as the Dauphin calls him, has died, the perspective shifts abruptly. We no longer need to accept uncritically the warrior's work of massacre and devastation. Instead all thoughts are for 'a godly peace', for 'stopping effusion of our Christian blood', French as well as English. These phrases are Gloucester's, but King Henry goes further:

> I always thought
> It was both impious and unnatural
> That such immanity and bloody strife
> Should reign among professors of one faith.

This is hardly a sentiment we can imagine falling from Talbot's lips but, while it need not be assumed that we must endorse absolutely all Henry's expressions of piety, such a remark as this, coming so soon after Talbot's death, cannot but qualify our estimate of his achievement. Henry's position on this matter is not in fact an extreme one by sixteenth-century standards. It happens to be identical with Erasmus', as it was expressed in his *Institutio Principis Christiani* as well as in such famous pacifist writings as the *Querela Pacis* and the long essay included in the *Adagia* called 'Dulce Bellum Inexpertis' ('War is sweet to those who have never experienced it'). The military hero has his glory, but according to another scale of values, both more Christian and more simply human, the great soldier may be no more than a great barbarian.[1]

Shakespeare is far too reasonable to give the full weight of his sympathy to simple fame-hungry Talbot. The play accordingly suffers from a lack of authorial conviction in many of Talbot's scenes: the writing often rings hollow. More than anything else, perhaps, it is this felt insincerity that has prevented *1 Henry VI* from surviving the century in which it was written.

[1] See R. P. Adams, *The Better Part of Valor: More, Erasmus, Colet, and Vives on Humanism, War, and Peace* 1496–1535, Seattle, 1962. Behind Erasmus' denunciations of military heroes are such things as Seneca's verdict on Alexander the Great and his father Philip: '. . . they were no lesse plagues to mankinde, than an over-flow of waters, drowning all the levell; or some burning droughth, whereby a great part of living creatures is scorched up' (quoted by Sir Walter Ralegh in *The History of the World*, ed. C. A. Patrides, 1971, p. 320).

8. 2 Henry VI: *A Commonwealth Tragedy*

EACH of the three Parts of *Henry VI* has certain themes in common with the other two. The fatal danger of strife within the state—what Lydgate called *The Serpent of Division*—is the most obvious. But to a large extent the three plays are designed as self-contained wholes. Since they were meant to be acted on separate days, they needed to make their effect as single works. The first four acts of *1 Henry VI* took a special colouring from the idea of fame : the choice of many of the incidents and the way they are dramatized were conditioned by it. The second play in the trilogy, however, is quite differently orientated. The idea of fame is now of no importance. Its action is set wholly in England, unlike *1 Henry VI*, which straddled England and France. Nor is it primarily a play of civil war, like *3 Henry VI*, although the Wars break out in the fifth act. (But the fifth act of this play, like the fifth act of *1 Henry VI*, is transitional : it looks forward to the next Part of the trilogy and so anticipates the character of the next play. Accordingly Suffolk's proxy wooing of Margaret takes place in Act Five of Part One, while the open conflict between York and Lancaster flares up in Act Five of Part Two). The main business of the first four acts of *2 Henry VI* is not military —neither the loss of the French territories nor civil war— but civic. Its prime concern is government.

That this is so can be seen from the fact that the chief character in the first three acts is Duke Humphrey of Gloucester, who is not a soldier but a counsellor to the King and a judge. For most of this time he is the King's Protector and as such a Governor— *the* Governor—of the realm. Government is Humphrey's business, and it was probably from this fact, supplied by his chronicle sources, that Shakespeare developed his over-all conception of the play. It is in the role of a governor that Holinshed sums up Gloucester's character :

But to conclude of this noble duke : he was an upright and politike governour, bending all his indevours to the advancement of the common-wealth, verie loving to the poore commons, and so beloved

of them againe; learned, wise, full of courtesie; void of pride and
ambition: (a vertue rare in personages of such high estate, but, where
it is, most commendable).[1]

For Shakespeare the key phrase seems to have been 'bending all
his indeuours to the aduancement of the common-wealth'. For as
he has written it, 2 *Henry VI* is above all else a play of the commonwealth, a tragedy in which the commonwealth's Protector
is conspired against and murdered and in which as a result the
commonwealth itself is torn to pieces.

The first scene of the play establishes at once its main terms of
reference: commonwealth, government, lords and commons.
As soon as Henry, Margaret, and Suffolk have left, Gloucester
embarks upon a bitter attack on the humiliating marriage treaty
which has entailed surrendering Anjou and Maine: 'Brave peers
of England, pillars of the state . . .' In it he ignores their divisions
and presents the English nobility in an ideal light as the conscientious government of the country, all of them working together, both on the French battlefields and at home round the
council table:

> Have you yourselves, Somerset, Buckingham,
> Brave York, Salisbury, and victorious Warwick,
> Receiv'd deep scars in France and Normandy?
> Or hath mine uncle Beaufort and myself,
> With all the learned Council of the realm,
> Studied so long, sat in the Council House
> Early and late, debating to and fro
> How France and Frenchmen might be kept in awe?

When Gloucester goes, his enemy Beaufort at once sneeringly
calls his sincerity in question. But the terms in which he does so
again alert us to the commonwealth preoccupations of the play,
this time by introducing the idea of the commons as opposed to
the lords who had been the subject of Gloucester's speech:

> Look to it, lords; let not his smoothing words
> Bewitch your hearts; be wise and circumspect.
> What though the common people favour him,
> Calling him 'Humphrey, the good Duke of Gloucester',
> Clapping their hands, and crying with loud voice
> 'Jesu maintain your royal excellence!'
> With 'God preserve the good Duke Humphrey!'

[1] *Shakespeare's Holinshed*, ed. W. G. Boswell-Stone, 1907, p. 246.

When Beaufort goes, Somerset and Buckingham murmur ambitiously together, and on their departure Salisbury and his son Warwick are left to speak up virtuously for the common good and to repudiate Beaufort's aspersions against Gloucester. Once more the commonwealth theme is sounded. Holinshed said of Warwick that he was 'one to whom the common-wealth was much bounden and euer had in great fauour of the commons of this land, by reason of the exceeding houshold which he dailie kept in all countries where euer he soiourned or laie . . .'. Shakespeare worked this passage into his opening scene, but in such a way as to reflect credit on Gloucester. So Salisbury comments on Beaufort, Somerset, and Buckingham:

> Whiles these do labour for their own preferment,
> Behoves it us to labour for the realm.
> I never saw but Humphrey Duke of Gloucester
> Did bear him like a noble gentleman.
> Oft have I seen the haughty Cardinal—
> More like a soldier than a man o' th' church,
> As stout and proud as he were lord of all—
> Swear like a ruffian and deamean himself
> Unlike the ruler of a commonwealth.
> Warwick, my son, the comfort of my age,
> Thy deeds, thy plainness, and thy house-keeping,
> Hath won the greatest favour of the commons,
> Excepting none but good Duke Humphrey . . .

Although Salisbury and Warwick are soon to ally themselves with the ambitious York and so forget their care for the commonwealth, Salisbury's words serve to impress on us an ideal of civic responsibility which no one but Gloucester lives up to. Warwick and he himself, Salisbury says, should join together 'for the public good' and 'cherish Duke Humphrey's deeds / While they do tend the profit of the land'. When Salisbury and Warwick in turn leave, only York is left on stage, the most dangerous of them all, to plan his strategy for exploiting the quarrels of the nobility until he can wrest the crown from Henry:

> And force perforce I'll make him yield the crown,
> Whose bookish rule hath pull'd fair England down.

His soliloquy ends the scene, the stress finally falling on 'bookish', a slightly surprising choice of epithet, since although Henry has been characterized by 'church-like humours' he has not so far been associated with book-learning. However, studiousness in the service of the state, an interest in books for themselves, is to emerge later in the play as one of its minor themes. We have already heard Gloucester refer to 'the learned Council of the realm', but Jack Cade and his followers, in the rebellion which has been secretly fomented by York, declare themselves against book-learning of any sort. They inflict death on 'clerks'—literate men—merely because they can read and write. But literacy, in the Tudor understanding of the term, is an essential part of government. It stands for the power of those in authority to *think* on behalf of the nation. And as such it forms part of the complex of ideas centring on government and commonwealth.

A standard Tudor work on government was Sir Thomas Elyot's *The Book named The Governor* (1531; at least 7 editions by 1580). Elyot's book has often been cited as a probable source for two Shakespearian passages of explicit theorizing about the commonwealth: the speeches by Exeter and Canterbury in i. ii of *Henry V* and the Degree speech by Ulysses in i. iii of *Troilus and Cressida*. It has never been cited in connection with *2 Henry VI*, yet it was probably much more distinctly present in Shakespeare's mind during its composition. Of particular relevance are its opening three chapters, and especially the first, which gives a general description of what was traditionally called a 'common weal' or 'commonwealth' but which Elyot insists on calling a 'public weal'. He was in fact strongly opposed to the term 'common weal': it seemed to him to have wholly misleading associations with the 'the commons' as well as with the sinister idea of holding all things 'in common'. 'Public weal' was, he thought, the proper translation of the Latin *Respublica*, for 'public' was derived from *populus*, 'in which word is contained all the inhabitants of a realm or city, of what estate or condition so ever they be'.[1] His definition is given in the second paragraph of the book; his words have a challenging, almost combative, tone as if he were pressing an argument. It has indeed been argued in a recent study that Elyot was implicitly attacking some of the (apparent) positions of More's *Utopia*, particularly its suggestions that the social hierarchy could be dispensed with and that well-born 'drones' should not be supported by the labours of the lower

[1] *The Book Named The Governor*, ed. S. E. Lehmberg, 1962, p. 2.

orders.[1] It is quite as likely, however, that the Peasant War in Germany (1524–5) with its alarming attempt to lay flat the hierarchy may have given urgency to Elyot's writing here. Shortly after Elyot's book appeared, occurred the terrible Munster Rising (1534–5), with the Messianic rule of John of Leyden—still a disturbing memory for Elizabethans, as the Munster episode in Nashe's *Unfortunate Traveller* proves. Such memories as these would almost certainly enter into an audience's reponse to *2 Henry VI*.

Elyot's definition begins as follows:

> A public weal is a body living, compact or made of sundry estates and degrees of men, which is disposed by the order of equity and governed by the rule and moderation of reason . . . Public (as Varro saith) is derived of people, which in Latin is called *Populus*; wherefore it seemeth that men have been long abused in calling *Rempublicam* a common weal. And they which do suppose it so to be called for that, that everything should be to all men in common, without discrepance of any estate or condition, be thereto moved more by sensuality than by any reason or inclination to humanity.[2]

The disposition of the 'public weal' into a hierarchy of ranks is essential to Elyot's definition, for from 'the discrepance of degrees . . . proceedeth order'. And when in turn Elyot thinks of Order, he does so in terms which have suggested to many that Shakespeare recalled them when he wrote Ulysses' Degree speech:

> Moreover take away order from all things, what should then remain? Certes nothing finally, except some man would imagine eftsoons *Chaos*, which of some is expound a confuse mixture. Also where there is any lack of order needs must be perpetual conflict, and in things subject to nature nothing of himself only may be nourished, but when he has destroyed that wherewith he doth participate by the order of his creation, he himself of necessity must then perish, whereof ensueth universal dissolution.[3]

In the final section of this chapter Elyot returns once again to the question of differing social estates. It is, he argues, right and proper that the lower labouring orders should support those above

---

[1] John M. Major, *Sir Thomas Elyot and Renaissance Humanism*, University of Nebraska, 1964, pp. 109 ff.

[2] *Governor*, p. 1.

[3] Ibid., p. 2.

them in the social scale who are more directly involved with the
responsibilities of government:

> Now to conclude my first assertion or argument: where all thing is
> common there lacketh order, and where order lacketh there all thing
> is odious and uncomely. And that have we in daily experience; for the
> pans and pots garnisheth well the kitchen, and yet should they be to
> the chamber none ornament. Also the beds, testers, and pillows
> beseemeth not the hall, no more than the carpets and cushions be-
> cometh the stable. Semblably the potter and tinker, only perfect in
> their craft, shall little do in the ministration of justice. A ploughman or
> carter shall make but a feeble answer to an ambassador. Also a weaver
> or fuller should be an unmeet captain of an army, or in any other office
> of a governor.[1]

The accepted historical sources of 2 *Henry VI*—Hall, Holinshed,
Foxe—together with the substance of Elyot's political doctrine
which he could have absorbed from a number of places (though
they almost certainly included Elyot's *Governor*), supplied Shakespeare with the subject-matter of his play; what was wholly
original was his way of converting this historical and political
matter into dramatic form. And characteristic of the early Shakespeare is the unflagging invention, the profusion of thematically
pointed episode and incident.

The play makes a markedly different impact from *1* and *3 Henry
VI* in virtue of the fact that the lower orders—'the commons'—
make several important appearances. They do not appear in the
other two plays. A related fact, more noticeable perhaps to a
reader than to someone seeing it performed, is the occurrence of
prose. There is no prose in the other two plays, whereas *2 Henry
VI* has a number of prose scenes, which are of course precisely
those which admit commoners to the stage. For in keeping with
its commonwealth subject, *2 Henry VI* follows Elyot in setting
before us the different degrees and estates of society.[2] There are
the plebeian petitioners at the beginning of i. iii, who are intercepted by Margaret and the haughty Suffolk; among them is
Peter Thump, the armourer's apprentice, who accuses his master
of saying the King was a usurper. In ii. i occurs the incident of
Saunder Simpcox and his false miracle, and in ii. iii the combat

---

[1] *Governor*, p. 5.

[2] The words *commons*, *commonweal*, and *commonwealth* occur more often in *2 Henry
VI* than in any other of Shakespeare's plays.

between Peter and his master, in which they are joined by neighbours and apprentices.

The third act of the play shows, in its first scene, Gloucester's arrest for treason and, in its second, his murder and its immediate repercussions. The commons do not appear in the first of these scenes. But at one point in the second their off-stage presence is made powerfully effective; indeed they now influence the course of the action. Soon after Gloucester is discovered dead, there is an off-stage commotion: '*Noise within. Enter* Warwick, Salisbury, *and many* Commons.' We have just been shown how the lords responded to Gloucester's death; now we hear how the commons take it. Warwick speaks:

> The commons, like an angry hive of bees
> That want their leader, scatter up and down
> And care not who they sting in his revenge.

The King asks Salisbury to stay with 'the rude multitude' while Warwick examines Gloucester's body. The simile of the bees, used here and frequently found in political treatises, occurs also in Elyot's second chapter, where bees are commended for having a single 'governor'—as they are in Canterbury's description of the bees' kingdom in i. ii of *Henry V*. Here perhaps the bee simile works as a kind of signal that 'commonwealth matters' are at issue. A little later in this same scene of Gloucester's death, Salisbury returns bearing the message given him by the commons:

> (*To the Commons within*) Sirs, stand apart, the King shall know your
> mind.
> Dread lord, the commons send you word by me
> Unless Lord Suffolk straight be done to death
> Or banished fair England's territories,
> They will by violence tear him from your palace
> And torture him with grievous ling'ring death . . .

His speech is a long one, and is formally eloquent; it has as a kind of refrain the words 'They say', so giving a semblance of indirect speech ('They say by him the good Duke Humphrey died; / They say in him they fear your Highness' death'). It is an interesting passage. Salisbury speaks as the cultured voice of the rude commons. It is the moment in the play when the precarious harmony of Humphrey's commonwealth is overturned. Though seemingly decorous, there is something slightly perverse about the speech. For, by means of the venerable Earl of Salisbury, the commons are threatening violence—we are made to feel that they can hardly be restrained from swarming into the King's chamber. When Salisbury finishes, the commons shout off stage for an answer. Suffolk's reply is characteristic: he accuses Salisbury of being an accomplice of the commons ('rude unpolish'd hinds'), but all the honour he has won, he says, is that of acting as their messenger-boy—

> the lord ambassador
> Sent from a sort of tinkers to the King.

The expression pinpoints the social and civic incongruity of the occasion and prepares for the scenes of social upheaval that are soon to occur. In its keen awareness of indecorum, of the overthrow of degree, it recalls Elyot's remark, already quoted: 'A ploughman or carter shall make but a feeble answer to an ambassador.' But despite Suffolk's sarcasm, the King acts on the commons' ultimatum and promptly banishes him.

In Act Four the commons succeed in taking over the stage. The victims of their violence include some of their aristocratic masters. And another phrase of Elyot's seems apposite: 'where there is any lack of order needs must be perpetual conflict'. In IV. i Suffolk is captured by pirates. In the long-drawn-out dialogue in which he braves his captors, a startling degree of class hatred is given vent. Suffolk addresses the Lieutenant, who is the captain of the crew, in deliberately insulting terms: 'Obscure and lowly swain', 'jaded groom', 'Base slave'. It seems that the Lieutenant had formerly been in his service, as Suffolk now reminds him:

> Hast thou not kiss'd thy hand and held my stirrup,
> Bareheaded plodded by my foot-cloth mule,
> And thought thee happy when I shook my head?

But Suffolk's contempt for his former servant is fully returned when the Lieutenant, before ordering Suffolk's head to be cut off, makes his own reply, addressing himself to 'Poole! . . . Ay, kennel, puddle, sink, whose filth and dirt / Troubles the silver spring where England drinks . . .' Suffolk's response is to go to even further extremes of pride. His loathing knows no bounds for the 'paltry, servile, abject' drudge who has him in his power:

> It is impossible that I should die
> By such a lowly vassal as thyself.

And, although finally beheaded, he never cringes or begs mercy or relinquishes his pride of rank.

The ferocity of this exchange is at once converted into the more protracted ferocity of the Jack Cade scenes, which in many ways enact Elyot's social doctrines. For a number of short scenes the commoners rule the stage. First the hapless Clerk of Chatham is taken off to be hanged 'with his pen and inkhorn about his neck'; then the Staffords are killed in an armed scuffle; finally Lord Say and his brother-in-Law are beheaded and their heads made to dance upon poles. This is the climax of the theme of the shattering of the commonwealth. Cade's 'then are we in order when we are most out of order' is simply a variation on Elyot's 'where all thing is common there lacketh order, and where order lacketh there all thing is odious and uncomely'. And when Cade leads his army of rude mechanicals into a form of battle, we recall—perhaps Shakespeare recalled—'a weaver or fuller should be an unmeet captain of an army, or in any other office of a governor'.

It has often been noticed that for these scenes of rebellion Shakespeare used details taken from accounts of the Peasants' Revolt of 1381. On that occasion the rebels attacked lawyers and all those associated with the law, so that (as Holinshed put it) 'hauing made all those awaie that vnderstood the lawes, all thinges should then be ordered according to the will and disposition of the common people'.[1] Also in 1381 the rebels compelled 'teachers of children in grammar schooles to sweare neuer to instruct any in their art . . . it was dangerous among them to be knowne for one that was lerned, and more dangerous, if any men were found with a penner and inkhorne at his side: for such seldome or neuer escaped from them with life'.[2] The most prominent of Cade's victims is Lord Say, who, as J. P. Brockbank notes, is in part conflated with the Lord Chief Justice beheaded by Wat Tyler in 1381: he is thus to some extent an embodiment of the law.[3] But he is also an embodiment of book-learning and is associated with the provision of grammar-school education to which the 1381 rebels had also been so hostile. The reason why Shakespeare

---

[1] Boswell-Stone, p. 271. [2] Ibid., p. 272.
[3] 'The Frame of Disorder: *Henry VI*', *Stratford-upon-Avon Studies, 3: Early Shakespeare*, ed. J. R. Brown and Bernard Harris, 1961, p. 88.

goes back to the reign of Richard II for these details is to bring out yet again the idea of the commonwealth in which each of the estates or degrees of society has its proper work. So Elyot argued that those with greater powers of 'understanding' and 'knowledge' should be raised to the more honourable estates where their gifts can be suitably employed on behalf of the whole community:

for as much as understanding is the most excellent gift than man can receive in his creation, whereby he doth approach most nigh unto the similitude of God, which understanding is the principal part of the soul, it is therefore congruent and according that as one excelleth another in that influence, as thereby being next to the similitude of his maker, so should the estate of his person be advanced in degree or place where understanding may profit; which is also distributed into sundry uses, faculties, and offices, necessary for the living and governance of mankind . . . And unto men of such virtue by very equity appertaineth honour, as their just reward and duty, which by other men's labours must also be maintained according to their merits. For as much as the said persons, excelling in knowledge whereby other be governed, be ministers for the only profit and commodity of them which have not equal understanding; where they which do exercise artificial science or corporal labour do not travail for their superiors only, but also for their own necessity. So the husbandman feedeth himself and the cloth maker: the cloth maker apparalleth himself and the husband; they both succour other artificers; other artificers them; they and other artificers them that be governors.[1]

In Elyot's understanding of the term the 'governors' of the realm are the product of a long and laborious process of education: his *Book named The Governor* is largely a programme for their education. And inevitably prominent in his scheme is a training in the arts of language: an ability to write and speak with maximum power and fluency. It is in virtue of the fact that they are, at least in theory, well-educated in this sense that qualifies them to govern the 'public weal'.

Such considerations colour the scenes in which Cade and his followers attack the Clerk of Chatham and Lord Say. When the rebels get Lord Say into their power the occasion is used for an attack on all literacy and book-learning, for Say is identified with both:

Thou hast most traitorously corrupted the youth of the realm in erecting a grammar school; and whereas, before, our forefathers had

[1] *Governor*, pp. 4–5.

no other books but the score and the tally, thou hast caused printing to be us'd, and, contrary to the King, his crown, and dignity, thou hast built a paper-mill. It will be proved to thy face that thou hast men about thee that usually talk of a noun and a verb, and such abominable words as no Christian ear can endure to hear . . .

Cade moreover objects not only to Say's educational efforts but also to the very fact that he enjoys a higher style of life than himself: 'Thou dost ride in a foot-cloth, dost thou not? . . . Marry, thou ought'st not to let thy horse wear a cloak, when honester men than thou go in their hose and doublets.' He objects to differences of rank in themselves. His attack is answered by Say in a long speech written by Shakespeare with a conspicuous rhetorical suavity: it betrays indeed precisely the literary education which has helped to fit Say and others like him (for the incident is entirely exemplary) for his role as a civil servant. First, unwisely in the circumstances, Say reveals that he knows Latin. Then after a reference to Caesar's Commentaries, he embarks on the substance of his appeal:

> Justice with favour have I always done;
> Pray'rs and tears have mov'd me, gifts could never.
> When have I aught exacted at your hands,
> But to maintain the King, the realm, and you?
> Large gifts have I bestow'd on learned clerks,
> Because my book prefer'd me to the King,
> And seeing ignorance is the curse of God,
> Knowledge the wing wherewith we fly to heaven,
> Unless you be possess'd with devilish spirits
> You cannot but forbear to murder me.
> This tongue hath parley'd unto foreign kings
> For your behoof.

Cade. Tut, when struck'st thou one blow in the field?
Say. Great men have reaching hands. Oft have I struck
  Those that I never saw, and struck them dead.
Geo. O monstrous coward! What, to come behind folks?
Say. These cheeks are pale for watching for your good.
Cade. Give him a box o' th' ear, and that will make 'em red again.
Say. Long sitting to determine poor men's causes
  Hath made me full of sickness and diseases . . .

In the course of his self-justification Say turns into a prototypical servant-governor of the state: an incorruptible dispenser of justice, a lover of learning and so a generous patron, a practised speaker on ambassadorial missions, a member of the 'intelligence' service, in short a man of heavy responsibility who wakes while others sleep. The speech is an idealized self-portrait of a 'governor'. Inevitably, in this play, we are reminded of Duke Humphrey himself, an upholder of just government and a patron of learning (as Duke Humphrey's library in Oxford's Bodleian still testifies 500 years later).

The attack on Say is the climax of Cade's depredations: it aims a blow against the very principles of government. Cade's followers soon melt away before the emotional appeals of Clifford. And in the fifth act the commonwealth theme yields to the civil wars which now break out. Hostility between the estates of society, however, does not exhaust the way in which Shakespeare dramatizes the break-down of the commonwealth ideal. *2 Henry VI* has a strikingly large number of trial scenes, scenes which show justice being administered. But with one exception the charge brought against the accused is in all cases the same: treason. The words 'treason' and 'traitor' ring out from the first act to the last. In I. iii the apprentice Peter accuses his master of 'high treason'. In the next scene Eleanor and her witchcraft accomplices are similarly arrested as 'traitors'. In II. ii York has a secret talk with Salisbury and Warwick and argues his claim to the throne. They acclaim him as King. Nothing could be more treasonable than their behaviour. In III. i Gloucester himself is arrested for 'high treason', and after his death the commons demand Suffolk's banishment. Suffolk's entire career within these plays has been a traitor's progress. The theme reaches a climax in the fifth act when York and Somerset precipitate the outbreak of civil war by calling each other traitor, each attempting to have the other arrested. Treason is of course an offence—rather, *the* offence—against the King and the state. The definition given by the Oxford Dictionary is simply 'an offence against the king's majesty or the safety of the commonwealth'. It helps explain why, in a commonwealth tragedy such as *2 Henry VI*, treason, whether real or imputed, should figure so prominently. During the first four acts, as well as in V. i, every incident turns on treasonable conduct, the culmination being York's open repudiation of Henry and his claim to the throne.

There is, however, one exception. This is the striking incident of Simpcox's false miracle, in which Gloucester exposes the fraud of the man who claimed he had been cured of his blindness by St. Alban. It is worth examining this excellent scene (II. i) in detail. For this incident, not in Hall or Holinshed, Shakespeare had to go to Foxe's *Acts and Monuments;* Foxe in turn had taken the account more or less verbatim from Sir Thomas More's *Dialogue of the Veneration and Worship of Images* (1529). More himself heard the story from his father. For the most part Shakespeare follows More's story faithfully. The beggar, unnamed by More, had come to St. Albans, prompted by a dream, hoping to be cured of his blindness; but no cure had resulted. Then, as soon as the King and his company arrived, his sight was restored, everyone supposing that a miracle had taken place. Duke Humphrey asked the man to come to him, and exhorted him not to let his head be turned by the adulation of the people.

. . . at last he looked well upon his eyne, and asked whether he could see nothing at al, in al his life before. And when as well his wife as himselfe affirmed fastly no, then hee looked advisedly upon his eyen againe, and seyd: I beleve you very well, for me thinketh ye cannot see well yet. Yes, syr, quod he, I thanke God and hys holy martyr, I can see now as well as any man. Yea can (quod the duke) what colour is my gowne? Then anon the begger told him. What colour (quoth he) is this mans gowne? He told him also, and so forth without any sticking, he told him the names of all the colours that could be shewed him. And when the Duke saw that, he bad him walke traytour, and made him to be set openly in the stockes: For though he could have seene sodenly by miracle the difference between divers colours, yet could he not by the sight so sodeinly tell the names of al these colours, except he had known them before, no more then the names of all the men, that he shuld sodaynly see.[1]

In *2 Henry VI* this incident is set within a larger scene involving the King, Queen, and nobles. They have just been hawking, and at once they quarrel, using the language of falconry as a cover for their attacks on each other. The miracle is announced and, as in Foxe, Simpcox (the name supplied by Shakespeare, a compound of

[1] *Narrative and Dramatic Sources,* ed. G. Bullough, iii. 128. Foxe departs from More in one detail. Instead of More's 'he bad hyme walke faytoure', Foxe has 'he bad him walke traytour'. 'Faitour' means 'impostor', 'cheat'. In this Shakespeare is closer to More: 'Then Saunder, sit there, the lying'st knave in Christendom.' Simpcox is not called a traitor. Possibly Shakespeare read More's *Dialogue* or deliberately softened the word which was being used often enough in the play already.

simpleton and coxcomb) and his wife are brought before the royal party. One detail is added: Simpcox is lame. His blindness, he claims, has been cured, but not his lameness, and so he is carried in a chair.

> *Beaufort.* What, art thou lame?
> *Simpcox.*   Ay, God Almighty help me!
> *Suffolk.* How cam'st thou so?
> *Simpcox.*   A fall off of a tree.
> *Wife.* A plum tree, master.
> *Gloucester.*   How long hast thou been
>   blind?
> *Simpcox.* O, born so, master!
> *Gloucester.*   What, and wouldst climb a
>   tree?
> *Simpcox.* But that in all my life, when I was a youth.
> *Wife.* Too true; and bought his climbing very dear.
> *Gloucester.* Mass, thou lov'dst plums well, that wouldst venture
>   so.
> *Simpcox.* Alas, good master, my wife desir'd some damsons
>   And made me climb, with danger of my life.
> *Gloucester.* A subtle knave! But yet it shall not serve.

Gloucester interrogates Simpcox, as in Foxe, and goes on to ask him the names of some of those present (Shakespeare is adapting Foxe's final phrase) before bursting out with his judgement: 'Then, Saunder, sit there, the lying'st knave in Christendom . . .' But the incident is prolonged a little further than it is in Foxe. Gloucester sends for a beadle ('have you not beadles in your town, and things called whips?') and asks for a stool to be brought. When the Beadle appears *with whips*, Gloucester turns to Simpcox: 'Well, sir, we must have you find your legs. Sirrah beadle, whip him till he leaps over that same stool.' Simpcox protests that he is not able to stand, but

> (*After the Beadle hath hit him once, he leaps over the stool and runs away;
>   and they follow and cry 'A miracle!'*)
> *King.* O God, seest Thou this, and bearest so long?
> *Queen.* It made me laugh to see the villain run.
> *Gloucester.* Follow the knave, and take this drab away.
> *Wife.* Alas, sir, we did it for pure need!
> *Gloucester.* Let them be whipp'd through every market town till
>   they come to Berwick, from whence they came.

The incident is usually taken as a straightforward example of Humphrey's justice, what Foxe called his 'prudent discretion'; and it may be that this is all Shakespeare intended. The additions he made to his source, however, suggest that he had something more in mind. Simpcox's lameness, added by Shakespeare, leads to the exchange in which he says it was to satisfy his wife's appetite that he climbed the tree, so injuring himself by a fall. The lameness leads in turn to the extension of Foxe's incident with the beadle, the whips, and the stool. Finally the punishment imposed by Gloucester is much more severe than it was in the source. In More and Foxe the beggar was merely 'set openly in the stockes'. Shakespeare's Gloucester has both Simpcox and his wife whipped 'though every market town till they come to Berwick'. Berwick of course is on the Scottish border and so a considerable distance from St. Albans. The verdict might be thought harsh. They would be whipped many times over.

It seems possible that this incident, on the face of it so simple and straightforward, has more to do with Gloucester than at first appears. Simpcox has a wife, who made him climb the dangerous tree. We have just seen Gloucester's own ambitious wife plot with witches and be arrested; immediately after the Simpcox incident and in this same scene Buckingham is to arrive with news of Eleanor's crime. Unlikely though it may seem to everyone present, Gloucester has something in common with the 'knave' whom he judges. Secondly, it may be that we are meant to find Gloucester's severity distasteful. Shakespeare was fully aware of the element of cruelty and even sadism which might enter into the administration of justice, and particularly into the imposition of punishment. (Lear makes it the subject of some of his speeches on Dover Cliff.) Humphrey's tone is surely not intended to be very sympathetic: 'have you not beadles in your town, and things called whips? . . . Well, sir, we must have you find your legs. Sirrah beadle, whip him . . . Follow the knave, and take this drab away.' In Margaret's harsh laughter we can recognize something very unpleasant. Her tone is different from Humphrey's, but has a kinship with it. Though not overtly cruel, his voice has a judicial relish which is not very engaging, while his reference to Simpcox's wife as 'this drab' is gratuitous.

We must ask what purpose Shakespeare could have had in presenting Humphrey here as open to criticism. In all his other scenes he is established as an entirely innocent man assailed on all sides by his enemies who never scruple to accuse him of every kind of administrative and judicial misdemeanour. It may be that in an irrational way their accusations are not entirely wasted: they have a way of sticking, even of suggesting that the situation may genuinely be more complex than Humphrey admits—that he may, in short, actually be culpable in some way or other. Eleanor's grave misdeeds work in the same direction: although Humphrey is innocent of them, he is guilty (so to speak) of being Eleanor's husband, and is tainted by her guilt. Moreover any severe judge is expected to be free of fault himself: if he is not, he is not worthy, we feel, to pronounce judgement on others. What all this amounts to is that there is a dimension of mysteriousness about Humphrey's innocence which, if anything, adds to the tragic nature of his fall. Later, in his scene of farewell to Eleanor (II. iv), she warns him of the coming danger, and he responds with a secure confidence in the power of his innocence that is again recognizably part of a tragic pattern. He has a touch of blindness about himself which increases the fearfulness of his situation.

But there is something else about Gloucester's behaviour in this Simpcox scene not yet mentioned. Before Simpcox appears, the nobles arrive in a group: they have been hawking. As usual they bicker together spitefully, only the King trying to preserve amity. The two most violent antagonists are Gloucester and Beaufort. Indeed Gloucester is quite as bad as any. His behaviour here is like a relapse to the undignified scuffles of *1 Henry VI*. Using asides and under cover of falconers' terms he and Beaufort come to the point of arranging a duel:

King. . . . blessed are the peacemakers on earth.
Beaufort. Let me be blessed for the peace I make
    Against this proud Protector with my sword.
Gloucester. (*Aside to Beauf.*) Faith, holy uncle, would 'twere come to that!
Beaufort. (*Aside to Glouc.*) Marry, when thou dar'st.
Gloucester. (*Aside to Beauf.*) Make up no factious numbers for the matter;
    In thine own person answer thy abuse.
Beaufort. (*Aside to Glouc.*) Ay, where thou dar'st not peep; and if
      thou dar'st,
    This evening on the east side of the grove.
King. How now, my lords!
Beaufort.   Believe me, cousin Gloucester,
    Had not your man put up the fowl so suddenly,

We had more sport. (*Aside to Glouc.*) Come with thy two-hand
    sword.
Gloucester. True, uncle.
Beaufort. (*Aside to Glouc.*) Are ye advis'd? The east side of the grove?
Gloucester. Cardinal, I am with you.
King.   Why, how now, uncle Gloucester!
Gloucester. Talking of hawking, nothing else, my lord.[1]

(II. i. 35–50)

Gloucester's behaviour here could hardly be less admirable; he is
indistinguishable from Beaufort. Quarrelling in the presence of the
King, and actually arranging a duel, he has entirely forgotten
his duty to the commonwealth. He seems carried away by anger
and pride and is hardly recognizable as the sage upholder of order
and national unity that he was in the opening scene. This dis-
creditable exchange is cut short by the Simpcox incident; it ends
in this way:

> *Gloucester.* (*Aside to Beauf.*) Now, by God's Mother, priest,
>   I'll shave your crown for this,
>   Or all my fence shall fail.
> *Beaufort.* (*Aside to Glouc.*) Medice, Teipsum;
>   Protector, see to 't well; protect yourself.
> *King.* The winds grow high; so do your stomachs, lords.
>   How irksome is this music to my heart!
>   When such strings jar, what hope of harmony?
>   I pray, my lords, let me coumpound this strife.

Beaufort's last gibe tells Gloucester 'Physician heal thyself': the
Protector will need protecting. And as we have seen, the impostor
Simpcox reflects at least a partial mirror image of Gloucester
which he, secure in his own innocence and virtue while in the act
of judging, fails to recognize. His severity is a sign of his sense of
impregnability. Yet at once, on the heels of Simpcox, comes
Buckingham with news of Eleanor's arrest, and at once Gloucester's enemies pounce. Beaufort murmurs ''Tis like, my lord,
you will not keep your hour', while Margaret warns him and in so

---

[1] This cleverly orchestrated scene seems to owe something to the scene in *The
Jew of Malta*, in which the two suitors of Abigail similarly quarrel (and later fight a
duel and kill each other), and in which a good deal of the significance of the rapid
dialogue is carried in asides and innuendos. Humphrey's 'Talking of hawking;
nothing else, my lord' recalls Barabas's 'Tush, man! we talk'd of diamonds, not of
Abigail' (II. iii. 153). The sordidness of the context in Marlowe's play is perhaps a
pointer to Shakespeare's own estimate of Gloucester's and Beaufort's behaviour.

doing brings out the implications of the incident we have just witnessed:

> Gloucester, see here the tainture of thy nest;
> And look thyself be faultless, thou wert best.

We have just seen that he is not faultless.

The King's words on the discord of his quarrelling peers echo like an elegy for the elusive commonwealth ideal: 'When such strings jar, what hope of harmony?' Shakespeare is alluding to the idea of the music of the state, expressed by Plato and by many others after him, including Elyot, who had written of music: 'how necessary it is for the better attaining the knowledge of a public weal; which, as I before have said, is made of an order of estates and degrees, and by reason thereof containeth in it a perfect harmony.[1] Or as Exeter put it, in the play given to Henry's father:

> For government, though high, and low, and lower,
> Put into parts, doth keep in one consent,
> Congreeing in a full and natural close,
> Like music.

[1] *Governor*, pp. 22–3.

9. 3 Henry VI: *Civil Swords*

THE preoccupation of *2 Henry VI* with the idea of the common-wealth contributes to the play's close-knit unity. Despite the varied material taken from the chronicles it gives the action, at least of the first four acts, a philosophical focus which goes far to explain the dense rounded shape the play in retrospect assumes. It is a play of high and low, lords and commons, verse and prose. In all this it makes a contrast with the third play of the trilogy. Far more than its predecessors, *3 Henry VI* is written on one stylistic level; much the same vocal pitch prevails throughout. And yet this gain in smoothness of texture is not entirely to the play's benefit. When in these early plays Shakespeare is writing with deep creative involvement, a certain roughness or abruptness often shows itself. Stylistically this may appear in terms of dis-junction, as if a massive collision of opposed viewpoints were taking place far beneath the perceptible verbal surface. An order-ing conception may be glimpsed, but more immediately felt is a challenging incompatibility between the parts, invigorating in its suggestion of the fullness and complexity of the dramatist's vision. We find something like this in *1 Henry VI*—in the utterly different voices given to Talbot and Joan, or in the quite different kinds of dramatic action of the Orleans battle sequence on one hand and the rose-plucking scene on the other. Or in another contemporary play, *Titus Andronicus*, we find it in the mutually opposed render-ings of Titus's high sustained passion in the third act ('When will this fearful slumber have an end?') and Aaron's brilliantly relaxed humorous low animal energy in the fourth ('Weeke weeke! / So cries a pig prepared to the spit'). There are other plays, however, in which the creative clash of viewpoints is more faintly felt. Such plays may seem to have a high degree of stylistic unity, but the absence, relatively speaking, of discord points to a lack of pro-found engagement. After Mercutio's death, *Romeo and Juliet* runs aground into dramatic shallows; among the comedies *The Two Gentlemen of Verona*, despite Launce's efforts, is altogether too much on a single level. And although *3 Henry VI* is always far more dramatically ebullient than the last two acts of *Romeo* or than the whole of *The Two Gentlemen*, the play suffers from a slight imaginative malaise, a falling-off in the abruptness and roughness that, for the early Shakespeare, is a sign of deep involvement. In certain fundamental ways *3 Henry VI* is living off inherited capital: as the last play in the trilogy it runs the risk of doing again what had already been done more freshly in Part Two. Of course there are new characters, notably the three sons of York, but the dramatist is still working within the area demarcated in Part Two; we have not radically shifted ground. And yet much of the writing of *3 Henry VI* is finely pointed; the play is filled with sharply turned exchanges, while the numerous characters are well discriminated throughout. In a comparison between *2* and *3 Henry VI*, we should probably conclude that, if there is a slight loss in force, there is no loss in artistry; if anything, the new play shows more signs of artistic ordering, of a care for the meaningful sequentiality of scenes and for the shaping of the scenes themselves.

The events of history as Shakespeare found them in the Tudor historians posed him with a dramatic problem of exceptional difficulty. These events were protracted over a long period of time; more important, they were repetitive, confused, and without a pattern of significant development. There were many battles, often of only temporary importance. The only factor which remained stable was the hostility of York and Lancaster, whose supporters stayed loyal to their chosen sides except for the two notable turncoats Warwick and Clarence. Accordingly *3 Henry VI* is to be a play of the splitting of the realm, England divided into two populaces. Here the red and white rose badges were of particular value to the dramatist, for from the Quarto stage directions it is clear that they helped audiences to distinguish visually the play's many characters. In the opening scene, the Yorkists arrive '*with white Roses in their hats*' and are soon joined by the Lancastrians with '*red Roses in their hats*'. In a later scene (v. i) another sharp visual moment is recorded when Clarence rejoins his brothers and betrays Warwick: 'Richard *and* Clarence *whispers togither, and then* Clarence *takes his red Rose out of his hat, and throwes it at* Warwike.' No doubt each of the main characters wore a rose throughout the play, so that ensemble scenes would take on the look of playing teams ranged against each other. The last wearer of a red rose is Henry VI himself, who is murdered by Richard Gloucester in the

penultimate scene. It is, as far as this play is concerned, the final
move in the game; in performance the dead king's rose could be
torn off by Richard and crushed or thrown away during his
forward-looking soliloquy. To an Elizabethan audience it would
seem obvious that the only satisfactory outcome was the blending
of the red and white roses in the Tudor dynasty. Such a viewpoint
would give its own irony to the deceptively harmonious tableau
of the final scene, with Edward's complacent pronouncements
and the complete ascendancy of white roses.

The use of the roses was one way of clarifying the stage action.
But the plethora of chronicle material, episodic and even atom-
istic, remained stubbornly recalcitrant to dramatic treatment.
Hall's narrative scarcely ever suggests a locality, a specific place,
on which a scene might be built. Instead the constant changes of
location, the interminable comings and goings of everyone all
round the country—to and from London repeatedly, but also to
the various battle sites in Yorkshire, the Midlands, and the West
Country as well as several excursions to France—all these movements required a special kind of scenario. Given such difficult
material, Shakespeare did what could be done. Some of it he
organized into a tragic or quasi-tragic pattern; for the rest he
decided positively to exploit the very element of formlessness which
must have seemed at first so resistant to artistic shaping. So that,
far from disguising its disorderliness, he made disorder his theme:
what he puts on the stage is England without a king. In having
two kings, in reality it had none. It was a real achievement to
work out a dramatic plot which would convey a sense of significance to a theatre audience. And although much good work has
been done in recent years towards elucidating the play, the structure of *3 Henry VI* is still perhaps inadequately understood. But
unless Shakespeare's design is recognized, the play is bound to
seem clogged with detail, muffled in impact, fatally lacking in the
beauty of firm imaginative definition.

The first thing to grasp is that the play falls into two parts,
with the division coming after the second act.[1] A five-act structure
is also clearly marked, but is accommodated within this two-part
division. Whether or not there was an interval intended after the

---

[1] Cf. E. W. Talbert, *Elizabethan Drama and Shakespeare's Plays*, Chapel Hill,
1963, p. 220. Professor Talbert's book contains valuable analyses of all Shakespeare's
early history plays.

second act, Shakespeare disposed his material in such a way as to make the most of this bipartite arrangement. Once this division is accepted, the whole play begins to make better artistic sense. Warwick's role, for example, adheres closely to the division. In the first two acts he is on the side of York; in the last three he supports the Lancastrians, beginning with his disaffection from Edward when at the French court (III, iii) he hears the news of Edward's marriage. But each of the two parts is organized in its own way with its own emotional range and even its own tempo; each has a different end in view. In coming to this structural arrangement Shakespeare was probably influenced by the most famous play of his time. Marlowe's *1 Tamburlaine* falls (or can be argued to fall) into two similar parts. At the end of its second act Tamburlaine is crowned King of Persia, so bringing to a conclusion the first movement of the play, while the last three acts, beginning with the appearance of Bajazeth the Great Turk and ending with his death, form a separate movement. The second Part of *Tamburlaine* divides in a similar way, with Zenocrate's death concluding the second act and Tamburlaine's death the fifth.

The first two acts of *3 Henry VI* contain the most savage fighting of the Wars. They are in fact conceived as a kind of formal brief tragedy whose object is to show the barbarousness of civil war. Clifford is the typical character of this two-act tragedy. His father had been killed by York at the first battle of St. Albans (*2 Henry VI*, v. ii); and over his corpse he had spoken words which might serve as a prologue to the present play:

> Even at this sight
> My heart is turn'd to stone; and while 'tis mine
> It shall be stony. York not our old men spares;
> No more will I their babes.

In these first two acts, most of the characters, with the exception of Henry, are, like Clifford, pledged to a fierce vengefulness. Indeed revenge specifically for a father becomes, as the New Arden editor notes, a reiterated motive for action.[1] In the opening scene not only Clifford but Northumberland and (in defiance of history) Westmoreland have had their fathers killed by the Yorkists. The situation has therefore a kind of elemental tragic potentiality: the theme is 'death of fathers', as in *Hamlet*, and like

[1] New Arden *3 Henry VI*, ed. A. S. Cairncross, 1964, p. 4.

Hamlet and like Orestes these three men cannot possibly escape 'a deed of tragic violence'. What Clifford says to the child Rutland as he stabs him to death could be the motto of the others too: 'Thy father slew my father: therefore die.' This intensity of passion, associated with Clifford and carried over from the penultimate scene of *2 Henry VI*, charges these opening scenes from the beginning, enabling Shakespeare with very little preparation to climb steeply to an exceptionally early scene of climax, the death of York (I. iv).

This two-act movement is itself, however, divided into two, each half corresponding to one act. The effect is symmetrical, not too obviously neat, but offset by differences, and so ethically suggestive. The first act comes to a climax with York's death. This is matched in the second act by the scene at Towton, traditionally the bloodiest of all the civil war battles. In this scene Henry meditates on the battle and sees the Father who has killed a Son and the Son who has killed a Father. Both scenes exhibit the horrors of civil war, but with marked differences. The one is a rawly direct presentation of atrocity—particularly if taken with Clifford's murder of Rutland, which immediately precedes it. The other distances the horrors: the tableau of the King sitting on the molehill with the Father on one side and the Son on the other does not attempt to disguise its stiffly formal nature—on the contrary, it insists on it, so impressing on us that this is a frank meditation on the unnaturalness of civil war. For a few moments we are hardly in the world of drama at all but of civic pageant. Moreover each scene involves the leader of the rival houses. The death of York at the hands of Clifford and Margaret was supplied by history, whereas the scene of Henry at Towton was invented by Shakespeare—and so supports the idea that he intended a deliberate matching of effects. And there are further resemblances. When York is captured, he is made to stand 'upon this molehill here'. When Henry meditates on the battle he says, 'Here on this molehill will I sit me down.' The point is that neither is a true king; each is a 'king of a molehill'. Lastly, the first and second acts are verbally matched in their beginnings (though this is a detail unlikely to be noticed at a performance of the play). So the first act opens with the line, spoken by Warwick of Henry:

I wonder how the King escap'd our hands.

While the second act opens with Edward saying of York:

> I wonder how our princely father scap'd . . . .

But if their openings are alike, their endings are not. The first act ends with a Lancastrian victory, the second with a Yorkist. But the symmetry is not at all mechanical. When fighting first breaks out in the first act the Lancastrians at once gain the upper hand. In the off-stage fighting between the acts they keep their ascendancy and even at Towton the Yorkists nearly give way before them. The Yorkist leaders rally only by a supreme effort of will (II. iii) and for the first time in this part of the play wrest victory from the Lancastrians. So although each of these acts ends with a victory, one for each side, the movement of action has the fluidity of history. We can discern a pattern in the events, but the pattern itself is not over-obtrusive.

The two climactic scenes at Wakefield and Towton are each highly patterned, and in each a heightened sense of occasion is aroused by the opening monologue. In the first, it is clear at once that York has given up the fight and knows he is about to die. As usual with his death scenes, Shakespeare informs his audience at the start what they are about to witness. And what they are about to see here is a quite exceptionally rabid expression of pure hate (in conception the scene is a development from the death of Suffolk at the hands of the Lieutenant). We have just seen Clifford butchering York's child, so we know what mercy his father can expect. But Clifford is a butcher, not a sadist; left to himself he would have stabbed York to death without delay. It is Margaret who decides to lengthen out the business to a ritual of torment: 'Hold, valiant Clifford; for a thousand causes / I would prolong awhile the traitor's life.' Clifford takes no notice: 'Wrath makes him deaf'.[1] She appeals to Northumberland, who wins his attention and together they bind York and place him on the molehill.

---

[1] 'Wrath makes him deaf': this vivid phrase recalls one used by Erasmus–'fervore surdus'–in his account of a barbarously cruel schoolmaster, whom he calls a 'butcher' (a word also applied to Clifford). The schoolmaster flogged a boy without cause and, although others tried to intervene, 'that tormentor, deaf with ferventness, made no end of his butchery, till the child was almost in a swoon'. See J. H. Lupton, *Life of John Colet*, D.D., 1887, pp. 260–1. The sentence quoted here was translated by Richard Sherry, who included in his *Treatise of Schemes and Tropes* (1550) the whole of Erasmus' 'Declamation of the Education of Children' in which the phrase occurs. If Shakespeare did in fact recall the phrase, he was perhaps prompted by the previous scene (I. iii), in which the child Rutland, about to be killed by the 'butcher' Clifford, appears with his schoolmaster.

The essence of the scene is Margaret's formal mocking of
York, and his equally formal reply. It is the moment, at the centre
of this two-act tragedy, when York and Lancaster confront each
other with unrestrained fury. The occasion is barbarous, yet the
dramatist's control does not waver; in fact only the sense that it is
subdued into a shape makes it bearable. For the collision of their
opposed wills is given symmetry. The length of the two speeches
is exactly calculated: Margaret's (66–108) looks longer than York's
(111–49) to a reader—but only at first glance. Her first four lines
are addressed to Clifford and Northumberland; she turns to York
only with her fifth line: 'What, was it you that would be England's
King?', and this address to York is exactly the same length
(thirty-nine lines) as his address to her. So within the symmetry
of the two acts, Shakespeare placed this symmetry of the two
speeches. The arrangement is not simply a formalistic one; it
expresses rather the ethical parity of the two sides, and the appall-
ingly wasteful bankruptcy of their policies.

Margaret's hatred for York issues in a perverted unnaturalness
of feeling. In *3 Henry VI* she is characterized primarily as a mother
—no longer as Suffolk's mistress or Henry's wife. Yet she, a
mother, attacks York where he is most vulnerable, in his love for
his four sons. So she lists them, calling them a 'mess' (a set of
four at a table):

> Where are your mess of sons to back you now?
> The wanton Edward and the lusty George?
> And where's that valiant crook-back prodigy,
> Dicky your boy, that with his grumbling voice
> Was wont to cheer his dad in mutinies?
> Or, with the rest, where is your darling Rutland?

The order is that of seniority (according to Shakespeare's own
version, which makes Rutland the youngest); but what makes her
tone peculiarly disturbing is the affected geniality and the twisted
use of family slang. She invades his home privacy in order to
desecrate it. But she is preparing for her climax, the moment when
she produces the blood-stained 'napkin' and breaks to him the
news of Rutland's death.

> Alas, poor York! but that I hate thee deadly,
> I would lament thy miserable state.
> I prithee grieve to make me merry, York.

Even at this inhuman moment, her choice of words shows that she is violating her own humanity: something in her does in fact 'lament' his state; while proclaiming her amusement she betrays a sense of misery. Yet she persists in the taunting and self-ravaging ritual, now turning it into a parody of a children's game ('Stamp, rave, and fret, that I may sing and dance'), now pressing a paper crown on his head, treating him as a king in sport, giving way to an impulse to strike off his head and then holding herself back to hear what he has to say.[1]

When York replies he speaks out of a deep emotional wound, inflicted by the sight of his child's blood. But the bulk of his speech is massive in its solemn and distanced formality. What he does, or what Shakespeare makes him do, is to follow the procedure of formal laudatory addresses—her origins and personal qualities in due order—in such a way as, almost impersonally, to annihilate her. She makes no reply, except to jeer at Northumberland for being moved. York's collapse into tears, and Northumberland's sympathy with him, give the scene its Shakespearian seal. Natural feeling, the capacity to be moved, is a symptom of strength not weakness. And in finally butchering York, Margaret and Clifford seem more losers than winners, more deeply defeated than their victim.

If York's scene is one of unmitigated atrocity, Henry's scene at Towton is in every way a complement to it, in which the noise and agony of the long-drawn-out fighting are distanced and muted while from a point of view almost outside the play we participate in a communal act of remembrance, a memorial service for the victims, both the killed and those who survived the killings. York's scene focused on a single atrocity; Henry's is generalized, including in itself all such atrocities, all the sufferings of civil war.

Like York's scene, Henry's opens with a monologue which also prepares in its own way for the scene that is to follow. This long speech is poetically the most elaborate passage in the play. It is not only highly wrought: it is the most delicate in feeling. The scene as a whole, until Margaret's entry, is an occasion for feeling, for withdrawal and contemplation—not only on Henry's part, but on the audience's.

From the very beginning, the formality of Henry's language

[1] See Appendix C.

and the marked patterning of the verse induce us to anticipate a
formal patterned scene:

> This battle fares like to the morning's war,
> When dying clouds contend with growing light,
> What time the shepherd, blowing of his nails,
> Can neither call it perfect day nor night.
> Now sways it this way, like a mighty sea,
> Forc'd by the tide to combat with the wind;
> Now sways it that way, like the selfsame sea
> Forc'd to retire by fury of the wind.
> Sometime the flood prevails, and then the wind;
> Now one the better, then another best;
> Both tugging to be victors, breast to breast,
> Yet neither conqueror nor conquered.
> So is the equal poise of this fell war.

The battle, taking place off stage, is held in a firm similitude, and
is further quietened and subdued by the pastoral reference with
its cosmic scope and its literary pastoral style ('What time . . .').
The simile in the first line ('like to the morning's war') has a
metaphor inside it, which reduces the very notion of war to the
commonest of harmless natural phenomena, the silent daily strife
between light and darkness. And since the second and fourth lines
rhyme, these four lines sound like a closed quatrain, a part of a
poem, so furthering the effect of contemplative withdrawal. The
lines on the wind and tide with their expressively suspended
syntax, epistrophe ('. . . wind', '. . . wind') and rhyme all heighten
the pitch of speech, so preparing for the exceptionally figurated
passage on the shepherd's life that opens out from it, with its
extended anaphoric scheme ('How many hours . . .', 'So many
hours . . .') and its formal exclamations, questions and answers.

The entire beautiful speech has become for us perhaps an all
too easily detachable anthology-piece, its function in the setting of
the bloody conflict at Towton obscured. For it is of course its
context that gives its delicate lyrical feeling its full power. From
his very first appearance in *1 Henry VI*, Henry has been associated
with pastoral diction. Just as the shepherd is the antithesis of the
heroic warrior, so Henry reverses the qualities of his famous
battle-winning father. But not until now has he been allowed to
indulge to the full his longing to escape the cares of kingship for
the obscure lot of the 'homely swain'—'Living low where fortune

cannot hurt me', as he is to say in a later scene (IV. vi. 20). The topic, a literary commonplace, could hardly be triter, yet never before perhaps, in either poetry or drama, had its nostalgic appeal been given such urgency. For the speech is no more than an interlude, almost an act of truancy, from the trilogy's endless verbal and physical conflicts—an escape from the civil war to 'the morning's war'.[1]

After such a speech, the carefully arranged tableau of King, Father, and Son, is inevitably something of an anti-climax. The stiff slightly old-fashioned pageant verse seems to ask a less close verbal attention of the audience than did Henry's speech; we are rather required to look and think, meditate, on this ultimate collapse of civilized society. In referring to himself as 'a king more woeful than you are', Henry might seem to be tastelessly egoistic. We must allow him to be speaking less as a person than as a voice of the regal office that subsumes the nation. Through him the kingdom's soul laments its own suffering—for the further benefit of the play's Elizabethan audience, itself so close to another civil war.

The last scene in this civil war movement (II, vi) opens with yet another monologue. Clifford is fatally wounded (the Quarto stage direction gives him '*an arrow in his neck*'). In substance and even in length his speech matches York's in I. iv. Both acknowledge defeat, and call on their enemies to finish them off. Clifford's role has run through both acts of this two-act tragedy; as we have seen, it was he who announced the theme of civil war and un-sparing revenge at the close of *2 Henry VI*. There is therefore an appropriateness in concluding this movement with his death, for although not personally as important as York or Henry, he can be seen as the typical figure of civil war, almost the protagonist of this now to be completed action. At the end of his monologue he faints, and his death when it comes a few moments later is oddly powerful. His enemies, Warwick and the sons of York, now appear, fail to see him at first, but then hear him groan as he dies. Hoping he is alive, they gather round him and 'vex him with eager words'. But being in fact dead, he is beyond their malice.

[1] It may be (as I suggested in *Scenic Form in Shakespeare*, p. 166) that this scene originated in a tradition that, at the second battle of St. Albans, Henry was left in the company of two guards under an oak tree and that during the battle he laughed and sang. The King in his insanity is as removed from the battle as the shepherd envied by Shakespeare's Henry.

They are reduced to taunting a corpse. The scene is Shakespeare's invention and shows eloquently the futility of the revenge ethic. No one had been more savage than Clifford, but even he acquires a pathos, perhaps even a dignity, in death. As York, Clifford's victim, had said to his own victim, Clifford's father: 'Thus war hath given thee peace, for thou art still.'

The two-act movement ends here, with the Yorkists about to move south to London. The sense of coming to a conclusion is strong. Henry and Margaret have fled to Scotland; Edward is about to be crowned king. As if rounding off a successfully completed business, Edward has announced: 'Now breathe we, lords. Good fortune bids us pause.' A 'pause'—an interval—in the play's performance seems in place.

The opening of Act Three coincides with a new chapter in Hall: 'The Prosperous Reigne of Kyng Edward the Fourth'. Accordingly Shakespeare's last three acts are quite differently orientated from the first two. If his first movement expressed the vengefulness of civil war, his second starts from the premiss that England has two crowned kings. Such a situation, it goes without saying, was for Elizabethan citizens unpleasant merely to contemplate, not to speak of actually putting it to the test of experience. For this second movement of the play, therefore, Shakespeare constructs a sequence whose chief quality is a giddying instability. Its characters are for the most part constant only in their struggle for power. Otherwise, violent and unprincipled, they change as their interest changes, breaking oaths, repudiating treaties, betraying friends, and re-forming into newly constituted groups. Since selfish impulse is as fickle as the outcome of battle, mere chance emerges as the dominant power. And this is in fact our impression as we watch these last three acts of *3 Henry VI*: they are governed by Fortune. If in the earlier sequence the typical figure was the butcher Clifford, here it is the turncoat Clarence, 'false, fleeting, perjur'd Clarence', who at the crucial moment betrays Warwick his friend, ally, and father-in-law. It follows that this second movement, with its long succession of reversals, is never as moving as was the first, with its two great scenes of passion and tragic contemplation. Nor is it meant to be: it is instead plotted so as to make the most of its ironical possibilities. There is a kind of witty precision in the way each step is taken, from Edward's coronation to the final Yorkist tableau, which draws from the audience a keen intellectual attention hardly compatible with the more emotional involvement of the first two acts.

The sequence is opened by the short scene (III. i) in which Henry steals over the Scottish Border into England and is arrested by two Keepers. (A member of Shakespeare's audience would probably be reminded that Mary Queen of Scots also came into England from Scotland, so creating the intolerable situation of two Queens in one Kingdom.) The scene is well placed, since even before we first see Edward as crowned king we are reminded that there is now another king on English soil. The dangerous awkwardness of Henry's presence is further brought out in his dialogue with the Keepers. He gently reminds them that they have sworn an oath of allegiance to him which they have now conveniently forgotten in swearing another to Edward. This passage on oath-swearing and oath-breaking sets the tone for the whole of this second movement; at the same time the volatility of the commons is described in Henry's own elaborate delicate manner:

> Look, as I blow this feather from my face,
> And as the air blows it to me again,
> Obeying with my wind when I do blow,
> And yielding to another when it blows,
> Commanded always by the greater gust,
> Such is the lightness of you common men.

The blown feather is an emblem of all English subjects during the disputed reign of the two kings. The entire principle of allegiance has been confused; every one is at the mercy of circumstances.

Edward's impulsive wooing of Elizabeth Woodville (III. ii) is the act that gives motive power for the whole sequence. Richard and Clarence observe him throughout, commenting sarcastically and coarsely on the openly sexual interest he takes in the fair widow. Something of their sardonic coolness is carried over to the scene at the French court which follows and which is more largely laid out (265 lines), so giving room for full dramatic development. This scene has considerable impact in performance. It comes across as powerfully robust political satire, yet the writing is studiously objective: the real eloquence of the scene inheres in its structure, in the telling order in which the events are taken so that each point is released with maximum effect. The three chief characters—Lewis, Margaret, and Warwick

—orate with blandly unblushing 'official' eloquence, scarcely bothering to cover up their true politic motives. First Margaret presents her case to Lewis. She is so dejected that she sits on the ground (or so I interpret lines 8–11) in the traditional posture of despair. When her enemy Warwick appears, offering a lucrative marriage to Lewis's sister Bona, Margaret's case seems hopeless. For Lewis takes Warwick aside and questions him about Edward's standing in England:

> *Lewis.* Now, Warwick, tell me, even upon thy conscience,
>   Is Edward your true King? . . .
> *Warwick.* Thereon I pawn my credit and mine honour.

The marriage with Bona is almost settled, when—'*Post blowing a horn within*'. A Messenger arrives with letters for Lewis, Warwick, and Margaret. They respond very differently. Margaret, we are told, 'smiles' delightedly. Warwick 'frowns'. Lewis 'stamps as he were nettled'. Edward is already married. A realignment of forces, announced in terms of high-minded indignation, follows at once. Warwick protests his innocence, and to prove it declares

> I here renounce him and return to Henry.
> My noble Queen, let former grudges pass,
> And henceforth I am thy true servitor . . .
> *Margaret.* Warwick, these words have turn'd my hate to love;
>   And I forgive and quite forget old faults . . .

In performance these words will very likely draw gasps of surprise from the audience (Margaret's use of the old proverb 'forget and forgive' is breathtaking). The exchange is almost farcically glib, and yet all too believably true to the life of power-politics.

The same care for minute ironical plotting informs the whole of Act Four, a sequence of eight short scenes, some of which contain two or three even smaller actions. Everything is in a state of precarious mobility. The kings alternately come and go, now captive, now free, until with the recapture of Henry at the end of the act things settle into place for the final struggle. This is to be the business of the fifth act: the destruction of the Lancastrian party as personified in Warwick, Margaret and Henry himself. It was unfortunate for Shakespeare that there could be no single action which focused the fall of Lancaster. The stages of its fall were diffused and discrete, so that dramatically a piecemeal effect was hardly avoidable. Warwick is betrayed by Clarence at Coventry and killed in battle at Barnet (v. i); Margaret is defeated at Tewkesbury and then sees her only hope, Prince Edward, stabbed to death (iv, v); and finally Henry too suffers death in the Tower of London at the hands of Richard (vi). Warwick's death, Margaret's courage before battle, and Henry's final moments are all given some tragic heightening, but an uncomfortable sense of compression on the dramatist's part, even perfunctoriness, makes itself felt. Thus, although Margaret suffers what York suffered—the loss of a loved child—the scene of her grief is not a true dramatic counterpart to the scene of York's death: nor indeed is it meant to be (as some critics suppose). It is altogether a slighter thing, and takes a subordinate place in this final series of Lancastrian misfortunes. Nor is Henry's death given much sense of climax. It is played on the upper stage and is unimpressively written (there are too many mythological references, which make a pedantic fussy effect), and there is too little sense of occasion. But the business of disposing of the House of Lancaster is at last completed, and the play can end. Henry has abdicated, if not from his throne, in effect from his trilogy, long before its inconclusive close.

10. Richard III: *A Tudor Climax*

I

ALTHOUGH in the obvious historical sense 'Elizabethan' literature is no more than a part of 'Tudor' literature, for the purposes of literary history the two terms are usually and justifiably distinguished. 'Elizabethan' refers to what is unique to the second half of Elizabeth's reign: a glisteningly fresh post-Pléiade world of lyrical poetry, whose high points include *The Faerie Queene*, *A Midsummer Night's Dream*, and the best songs scattered through the plays and miscellanies of the eighties and nineties. In this limited sense of the term, 'Tudor' literature is much less assured in technique. It belongs rhetorically to an altogether more primitive phase; its diction is more stereotyped just as its topics are fewer and narrower in range. If 'Elizabethan' literature celebrates Nature, the favourite 'Tudor' theme is Fortune, whose grim realm—in literature at any rate—is defined by the court, the prison and the scaffold. The most characteristic work of 'Tudor' poetry is *The Mirror for Magistrates*—but an equally apt title for it would be *The Book of Fortune*, the dice-game for which Sir Thomas More wrote his prefatory verses. In this narrow courtiers' world the ambitious scheme and climb, enjoy a few hours of power and suddenly plunge into an abyss. 'The piller pearisht is whearto I lent' begins Wyatt's sonnet, written after Thomas Cromwell's death on the scaffold. For not only do the 'great ones' fall, but their many dependants topple with them. In this world of Fortune, nothing is stable; even apparently firm pillars may suddenly give way.

In all this *Richard III* can be seen as the culmination and climax of 'Tudor' literature. More than any other of Shakespeare's early histories it is a play of Fortune, a tragedy of anxious courtiers, conspiratorial climbers and raucously lamenting losers. Above all it puts on show the ways and methods of the tyrant, his ruthlessly planned ascent to the crown, and his precarious hold on it once he has seized it. In the fourth scene of the play we are shown Clarence imprisoned in the Tower of London. He describes his terrible dream, and falls asleep. While he sleeps, his keeper speaks over him a curiously formal and impersonal comment:

> Sorrow breaks seasons and reposing hours,
> Makes the night morning and the noontide night,
> Princes have but their titles for their glories,
> An outward honour for an inward toil;
> And for unfelt imaginations
> They often feel a world of restless cares,
> So that between their titles and low name,
> There's nothing differs but the outward fame.

The speech makes a complete poem: one might call it a variant on the eight-line *strambotto* form that Wyatt practised, and its subject another variant on the Senecan dispraise of courts—one of which Wyatt himself powerfully translated:

> Stond who so list upon the slipper toppe
>   Of courtes estates, and lett me heare rejoyce;
> And use me quyet without lett or stoppe,
>   Unknown in courte, that hath such brackishe joyes . . .

Given its date, so late in the century (probably 1590–1), *Richard III* seems in surprisingly close touch with the themes and moods of earlier Tudor literature. To some extent this is explained by its subject, for in dramatizing the usurpation of Richard Gloucester Shakespeare could hardly have avoided basing his play on the early historical narrative of Sir Thomas More. But he went further than that, for in adapting More's brilliant work for the stage he drew on those other literary forms which he must have associated with the earlier Tudor court: the metrical 'tragedies' of *The Mirror for Magistrates*, in which complaining ghosts recount their misspent or victimized lives on earth; those passages from the classical moralists which were doubtless copied into many a common-place book under such headings as 'The Rule of Tyrants', 'The Evils of Court Life', and 'The Happiness of Retirement'; as well as traditional elegiac forms which by Shakespeare's time were perhaps becoming old-fashioned: *ubi sunt* laments, and emblems of the world's vanity such as appear in the volume called *A Theatre for Worldlings* (1569), to which the young Spenser contributed. Sensitive to what might be imaginatively congruent, Shakespeare drew these 'Tudor' forms together to help fill out his very ambitious historical drama. In *Richard III* he takes leave of 'Tudor' literature, for a time at least; indeed not until the end of his career will he return to it, in *Henry VIII*, and by that time so much has happened, to him and to the English language and the English drama, that those forms, though still recognizable, have become almost radically changed, viewed as they now are from the new perspective of a later cultural epoch. In *Henry VIII*, the 'Tudor' forms are Jacobeanized; in *Richard III*, they are distinctively Elizabethan, but in ways which still need clarification. Accordingly the account that follows aims to locate the play more exactly in its Elizabethan cultural setting and at the same time to define more closely a few of its more neglected features.

II

Richard III is usually regarded today as a brilliantly lurid melodrama, a work peculiarly of and for the stage. Compared with the Henry VI plays that preceded it, it has an extra dimension of theatricality, so that even the least stage-minded reader cannot ignore its status as a play, a script designed to be projected at an audience by actors. This peculiarly frank theatricality is clearly related to Shakespeare's histrionic hero. Richard has from the start a masterful habit of assuming roles, manipulating others, and devising scenes which will furnish suitable settings for his carefully studied performances. He acts like a Presenter or Master of Ceremonies, mediating between the audience and the other characters, interpreting the action for us, preparing us for the next moves in the plot and seeing to it that we savour to the full the roles we have just seen him perform. All this side of the play—its self-conscious theatricality, its deep perspectives with Richard downstage, the others further away from us—is now widely accepted and understood. As Nicholas Brooke puts it, Richard is 'more real' than the others: 'This sense of him makes everyone else mere actors in a play'; like the Vice in the moralities, 'he alone has any direct contact with the audience'.[1]

It might be asked why it was that Shakespeare chose to dramatize the history of Richard III in this way. There was nothing in

[1] Nicholas Brooke, *Shakespeare's Early Tragedies*, 1968, pp. 55, 57. See also A. P. Rossiter, *Angel with Horns*, 1961, and W. H. Clemen, *A Commentary on Shakespeare's Richard III*, 1957. Another notable essay on *Richard III* is included in Wilbur Sanders's *The Dramatist and the Received Idea*, Cambridge, 1968.

the subject that intrinsically demanded that he should have done so. We can see this by glancing at the anonymous play *The True Tragedy of Richard the Third* (printed 1594), which Shakespeare may or may not have used. *The True Tragedy* has little or nothing of the theatrical ebullience which Shakespeare has taught us to associate with this subject; one is surprised to find how undominating, by comparison, another playwright's Richard could be. This play opens, not with Richard, but with an Induction showing Truth and Poetry, whose function is simply to recall the historical situation at the time of Edward IV's last illness; and Richard does not appear until the third scene of the action proper. His characterization follows the chronicles, but he has nothing of the Vice-like humour or of the bold commandeering of audience *rapport* that Shakespeare's Richard assumes from his first appearance. Towards the end he is given some sub-Senecan rant on the miseries of the tyrant, but there is nowhere anything like the peculiarly heightened quality of *Richard III*—the repeated contrivance of effects which remind us that we are at that moment watching a play. This was Shakespeare's own contribution. Why did he do it?

A crucial factor in the immediate background of the play is Kyd's *Spanish Tragedy*.[1] The date of Kyd's play is not known for certain any more than Shakespeare's, but it probably comes somewhere between 1587 and 1590. At any rate it clearly preceded *Richard III*, and it excercised what I take to be a decisive influence on it. Indeed it is *Richard III* rather than *Titus Andronicus* or *Romeo and Juliet* that qualifies as Shakespeare's most Kydian play. Of course *Richard III* is not to be 'explained' by Kyd: it has many qualities which Kyd cannot match. And it shows the impact of other plays on Shakespeare, notably that one play of Marlowe's— *The Jew of Malta*—which was also influenced by Kyd. None the less, of all contemporary plays *The Spanish Tragedy* most deeply affected the conception of *Richard III*, and in order to appraise what Shakespeare did we need first to have a clear idea of Kyd's own achievement.

In the context of Elizabethan drama *The Spanish Tragedy* was

---

[1] This chapter was already written when I discovered that Professor M. C. Bradbrook had already noted Kyd's influence in *Shakespeare and Elizabethan Poetry*, 1951, pp. 131–2. Her discussion is not mentioned in two works concerned with Kyd's influence on Elizabethan drama: *Thomas Kyd and Early Elizabethan Tragedy* (1966) by Philip Edwards, and *Thomas Kyd. Facts and Problems* (Oxford, 1967) by Arthur Freeman. Neither gives any consideration to *Richard III*.

astonishingly original. It was not only new stylistically: it treated tragic emotion in a way new to the English theatre. It was also full of structural devices which could not fail to be of interest to other dramatists. Perhaps most suggestive was its handling of time. It discovered how to convey a sense of lived time—time experienced subjectively—which had not been done before by any sixteenth-century dramatist. To a writer with ambitions towards tragic drama such technical discoveries were invaluable.

The most obviously striking feature of *The Spanish Tragedy* was the presence on stage of Andrea's Ghost and Revenge, so that the whole of the main action is observed by them and framed by their comments. The action proper—not in the underworld but in the Spanish court—can therefore be seen as a hugely extended play within a play, which itself contains smaller inset units, including a formal dramatic entertainment performed before a stage audience in the last act. The effect at such times as the last is one of several recessional planes or concentric circles, whereby one level of action is enclosed or framed within another. Nothing quite like this had been seen on the English stage before. Another device is not so obvious, and is again probably original to Kyd in its working out. This is the conception of the hero Hieronimo, which can from a dramaturgical point of view be regarded as a structural feature. Hieronimo is at first presented to us as two things: he is a father and a judge (Knight Marshal of the Spanish court, with certain duties such as providing entertainment for state occasions). This at least is how he appears in the first act, but so far he has not really come dramatically alive. He does that only after his son's death, for only then does he begin to fulfil his essential structural function in the play. He is essentially a rememberer. For from now on, throughout the course of this long play, his dominant faculty is his memory, his obsessive, monomaniacal, Horatio-fixated memory. He cannot forget the moment when he heard his son cry out and when he went into his garden to find his body hanging there. Hieronimo's mind harks back to the arbour scene over and over again, right until the closing moments of the play when, with his playlet of 'Solyman and Perseda' finished and the royal audience still unaware of the actual deaths of Balthasar, Lorenzo, and Bel-imperia, he suddenly draws back a curtain to reveal the body of Horatio. So while the play proceeds on its course after the arbour-scene, Hieronimo, or part of him, is arrested before the picture of his hanging son; and since he is the chief character in the play he sees to it that we, the audience, are detained there with him. This then—Hieronimo's memory—is the second of the play's striking structural devices, serving to bind the action into a tight unity.

If these two features are considered together—the presence on stage of Andrea's Ghost and Revenge, and Hieronimo's obsessive memory—it will be seen that Kyd is using time in an exceptionally interesting way. In the first place, Revenge knows everything that is going to happen. He has told Andrea that he will see Balthasar killed by Bel-imperia. Everything is in some sense determined. The characters appear to have free will, but in fact they are going through motions which have been foreseen. For Revenge, therefore, it can be said that the future is in a way already present. Of Hieronimo, on the other hand, it can be said that, after Horatio's death, he refuses to relinquish the past: he detains the past in the present. So for Revenge the future is already present; for Hieronimo (after Horatio's death) the past is present. By focusing time in this way *The Spanish Tragedy* gives its audience a memorable theatrical experience. The play is not simply a linear succession of episodes: in Kyd's construct the end is implicit in the beginning, and the beginning is recalled by the end.

The whole play is framed by the extra-terrestrial presence and comments of Andrea and Revenge. Everyone in the Spanish and Portuguese action and everything that happens to them are watched and noted by the two in the upper stage (or wherever they are). Even when alone, the terrestrial characters are watched. Every trivial incident in the complicated chain of events, every apparent digression, is seen and foreseen, seen by Andrea and foreseen by Revenge. It is hardly surprising that Kyd is the first English dramatist for whom irony is a vital part of his technique. When Lorenzo, for example, lays his villainous plots and goes on to double-cross his hapless accomplices, he appears to be in a position of unqualified superiority; his power seems invulnerable. And this invulnerability is an effect of his apparent command of the stage: he seems to be the most powerful person on it. Yet in fact his command of it is shared, unknown to him, by Andrea and Revenge. They sit behind him, waiting for him to meet his fate. This stage arrangement expresses an important part of the play's meaning. The selfishly immoral schemer, who denies his natural bond with others, who rejects the law of reciprocity (the right of others to say *tu quoque*), is the one who is finally most put out to discover that he who had so coolly observed others is himself observed. Kyd's constructive method—its effects of Chinese boxes or concentric rings—brings out the extent to which everyone's vision is blinkered by egoism, seeing things from a single partial point of view. They fail to see themselves in others, others in themselves; they forget that they are themselves objects as well as subjects.[1]

Kyd is using the ancient rhetorical commonplace of the theatre of the world. For the spectators the stage is a world which they can contemplate from outside. But the world they inhabit outside the theatre is also a theatre, which is itself subject to extra-terrestrial judgement. Ralegh expressed the idea succinctly:

> What is our life? a play of passion,
> Our mirth the music of division . . .
> Heaven the judicious sharp spectator is,
> That sits and marks who still doth act amiss,
> Our graves that hide us from the searching sun,
> Are like drawn curtains when the play is done,
> Thus march we playing to our latest rest,
>   Only we die in earnest, that's no jest.

Presumably the kind of structure Kyd exploits—the recessive planes of the *theatrum mundi*—can achieve its fullest effect only in a society officially committed to a belief in God: the ultimate audience must be a heavenly one. In an agnostic society the dramatic arrangement loses its final theological sanction to become a merely piquant theatrical device.

In the last resort Kyd's play is more impressive as a theatrical construct than as a tragedy. It holds out a promise of justice, when its two worlds—the world of Spain and Portugal and the super-natural world—are brought into relation. When that comes about, justice will be executed: the good rewarded and solaced, the bad punished. Or such at least in theory Kyd's ending should persuade us to accept. That its moral confusions do not persuade us, but leave us perplexed and dissatisfied, need not concern us here. What is important is the powerfully original conception of a tragic action that Kyd bequeathed to Shakespeare—or that

---

[1] Cf. Peter B. Murray, *Thomas Kyd*, New York, 1969, pp. 28 ff.

Shakespeare, or so I now want to argue, appropriated and modified for *Richard III*.

The features of Kyd's play just described all recur in *Richard III*. If the two plays have not in the past been closely associated, it is because these features reappear in jumbled form, reconstituted in a different though discernibly related pattern. Shakespeare must have been much impressed by *The Spanish Tragedy*, but what he took over from it seems to have been largely or perhaps wholly unconscious, so completely is Kyd's influence digested; if there are any verbal echoes they are minimal. Stylistically one may see at a glance that the two plays have something in common: they share a certain hard metallic eloquence, a liking for repetitive rhetorical schemes and patterns, a high incidence of latinate formality. Of course Seneca has been invoked to explain these qualities in both cases, but it was Kyd who was the first to english Seneca in this particular manner. (Earlier English Senecans are much less sprightly and agile). But the likenesses between the two plays go far beyond the details of verbal style: they involve the fundamentals of conception and structure, as a brief comparison will bring out.

Many of Kyd's most strikingly original inventions found an echo in *Richard III*, even if distorted and so not recognizable at first glance. One of these can be mentioned briefly. Hieronimo's memory, his obsessive insistence on keeping the past alive, is essential to the experience offered by *The Spanish Tragedy;* and this has its clear counterpart in *Richard III*. The corresponding character is Margaret, whose presence in the play is quite unhistorical (she left England many years before) and whose function is almost entirely that of recalling the past and calling for judgement. Like Hieronimo, she has become an embodiment of memory.

Kyd's other main device also left its mark on *Richard III*, but its effects need rather more unravelling. Of course Shakespeare's play has nothing that literally corresponds to the presence on stage of Andrea and Revenge, with the impression it creates of an extended play within a play. But an effect somewhat like it has in fact been noticed: one critic finds Richard 'more real' than the others, everyone else seeming 'mere actors in a play'. And this, I think, is a fairly widespread impression: the play does convey a sense of recessed planes that is for its time a peculiarity of *The Spanish Tragedy*. The two plays, however, establish this impression in different ways. What Shakespeare gives us is a gradual progression from blind egoism at one extreme to, at the other extreme, a full acknowledgement of the final divine order. For he does not begin, like Kyd, by frankly presenting the supernatural world: he opens abruptly with Richard's monologue, much as Marlowe had done with Barabas in *The Jew of Malta;* but whereas Marlowe had preceded it with a prologue (spoken by Machiavelli), Shakespeare dispenses with any such preparation.

The play opens with Richard's overwhelming sense of his own self. His mind is entirely orientated to this world. He acknowledges no supernatural order—or if he mentions any such thing it is with amused incredulity:

> Simple plain Clarence, I do love thee so
> That I will shortly send thy soul to heaven,
> If heaven will take the present at our hands.

Though less overt in its contempt, this is very much in the vein of Marlowe's Machiavel-Prologue:

> I count religion but a childish toy,
> And hold there is no sin but ignorance.
> Birds of the air will tell of murders past?
> I am asham'd to hear such fooleries!

Like Machiavel, and like Barabas, Richard has no serious use for other-worldly considerations. In the course of this opening scene Clarence, then Hastings, two of Richard's future victims, pass over the stage engaging briefly in converse with him, each of them seeming merely to interrupt his continuing self-communing soliloquy. The scene is one of furious activity, but the activity is all within Richard's mind: the other characters are as pliantly obedient to his wishes as if they were no more than ideas he had thought up—they come and go as prompt upon their cue as if he were only planning some such future encounter as is in fact now taking place. And this is the point, or one of the points, being made by the scene: Richard has only to think of a scheme and it is put into act; his hypocrisy, at the service of his over-mastering will, finds no obstacle in the world of men. In the following scene Anne puts up more resistance, but she is an avowed enemy as Clarence and Hastings were not, and Richard is

out to effect a spectacular conversion in her attitude to him, which
necessarily requires more effort. Yet even so, there is never any
real suggestion that he will not finally prevail. Another soliloquy
follows her departure, so restoring the impression that the point
from which we regard the action is within Richard's mind: that
subjective angle is, or seems to be, the one which the play wants
us to adopt—as if what he sees is identical with objective reality.
It is in the third scene, however, that the play within a play effect,
with its theological implication, is more fully disclosed. The
Queen and her kinsfolk are discussing the King's illness; Buckingham and Derby join them, followed shortly after by Richard
and Hastings. Richard embarks upon yet another of his 'performances'—this time, the plain man—and is in full spate when,
unknown to any of the company, behind them, enters 'old Queen
Margaret'. So Margaret, concealed, watches Richard performing
in front of the courtiers who are his dupes. The stage arrangement
momentarily recalls the effect whereby Andrea and Revenge
watch Lorenzo and Balthasar intimidating Pedringano or, in a
later scene, brushing aside Hieronimo. In each case the confident
schemer, who is given to watching and manipulating others, is
himself now the object of another's attention and is not as
invulnerable as he supposes. Particularly close is the scene in
which Lorenzo and Balthasar eavesdrop on Bel-imperia and her
new lover Horatio:

> *Bel.* Why stands Horatio speechless all this while?
> *Hor.* The less I speak, the more I meditate.
> *Bel.* But whereon dost thou chiefly meditate?
> *Hor.* On dangers past, and pleasures to ensue.
> *Bal.* On pleasures past, and dangers to ensue.
> *Bel.* What dangers and what pleasures dost thou mean?
> *Hor.* Dangers of war, and pleasures of our love.
> *Lor.* Dangers of death, but pleasures none at all.
>
> (II. ii. 24–31)

Horatio's last two speeches are echoed and mockingly perverted
by Balthasar and Lorenzo; without the lovers' knowing it, Horatio is being isolated, though so far only in verbal terms, by his
two future murderers. In the present scene of *Richard III* nothing
quite so pointedly sinister is contrived. For Margaret soon comes
forward to reveal herself. But before she does so, she too echoes

and perverts the remarks of those she is listening to, either by sardonic replies (which remain unheard)—

Rich. 'Tis time to speak, my pains are quite forgot.
Mar. Out, devil! I do remember them too well

—or, more in Kyd's manner, by keeping the words but twisting the sense—

Qu. Eliz. . . . As little joy you may suppose in me
   That I enjoy, being the Queen thereof.
Qu. Mar. As little joy enjoys the Queen thereof;
   For I am she, and altogether joyless.

When Margaret comes forward and engages in an angry altercation with the entire company, the nature of the scene is abruptly changed. It is now an open contest, with Margaret against the rest—defeated Lancaster contesting York's victory—and although she is shown to be quite as blood-guilty as anyone else there, she also wields an authority which, in the history plays, is given only to those who have been finally defeated and are unquestionably out of the running. Her last, most elaborate, curse is reserved for Richard, but his last-moment substitution of her own name for his trips her up at the crucial point, spilling some of her venom upon herself. Since both are guilty, both are cursed. But in her clamour for what she sees as justice she has appealed to a supernatural order ('O God that seest it, do not suffer it . . . !'), and for the first time in the play Richard has met a will as immovable as his own.

In the scene of Clarence's murder (I. iv), the pattern established by the first act is completed. Richard does not appear at all; but through Clarence's dream we are apprised of the outermost circle of spiritual reality—the supernatural order of the four last things, death, judgement, heaven, and hell—which Richard has so far ignored or denied but which first Anne and then Margaret had appealed to. Our vision of reality in these first four scenes is therefore one of widening comprehensiveness. We began with the narrow, if for the time overwhelmingly forceful, egoism of Richard ('But I, that am not shap'd for sportive tricks . . . I, that am rudely stamp'd . . . I, that am curtail'd of this fair proportion, Why, I . . .'); we proceeded to a growing sense of possible resistance to him (Anne, Margaret); until now in this fourth scene it becomes clear that even Richard's enormous energy is contained by the final order of things. He is an atheist in a theist's world—unlike Marlowe's Barabas, who is an atheist in a world which may, or may not, be controlled by God.

The rest of the play repeats this pattern, but on a larger scale. For just as Act One culminates in Clarence's dream and the murderers' discussion of conscience and God's judgement, so the rest of the play leads up to the second of the great dream scenes, that on the eve of Bosworth, in which Richard himself faces the final realities of conscience and judgement.

This conception of a supernatural order that surrounds and contains the main action and from which judgement will eventually come owes something essential to Kyd; so too does a more specific feature in the structure of *Richard III*. The first act is an extended protasis or introductory movement, which concludes with Clarence's dream and death. The main action of the play also concludes with a dream shortly followed by a death. It may be that for this arrangement Shakespeare was also indebted to Kyd. Act One of *The Spanish Tragedy* ends with the dramatic entertainment, supervised by Hieronimo, for the king of Spain and the Portuguese ambassador. And the last act of the play ends with a scene in which Hieronimo is once again in charge of a courtly entertainment: this time the play of Solyman and Perseda. Both scenes involve players within the play, just as in *Richard III* the two corresponding scenes involve ghosts (strictly speaking, ghosts which appear within a dream). For the positioning of these two crucial scenes Shakespeare presumably followed Kyd. There is too a further semantic link between the two pairs of scenes: the transition from the idea of players to that of ghosts would have been easier for Shakespeare than for us since (as in *1 Henry VI*) the word 'shadow' could mean either 'player' or 'ghost'. So all four scenes have to do with 'shadows' (as far as the actors are concerned, the ghost scene before Bosworth is as much of an inset dramatic set piece as Hieronimo's playlet of Solyman and Perseda: both are presented to stage audiences).

In a number of ways, then, large and trivial, *The Spanish Tragedy* affected the conception and the shaping of *Richard III*. Perhaps the most far-reaching effect came from the two devices already described: the looking-forward of Revenge and the looking-backward of the bereaved Hieronimo. The result was a form of drama more tightly knit than anything yet seen on Elizabethan stages. The beginning of the play and the ending are closely matched: we do not, as we so often do in Elizabethan plays (including some of Shakespeare's), forget the beginning by the time we reach the end. Such a form of play required a rather different method of composition, in keeping with its more 'spatial' design. In *Richard III*, accordingly, we find a more or less continuous concern with the ending; less so in the earlier part of the play, but insistently so in the last two acts. All the lines of the action converge on Bosworth, for it is a clear assumption of the play that no member of its audience could possibly be ignorant of Richard's fate. It is this fact that the entire play is orientated towards its end, as in *The Spanish Tragedy*, that allows Shakespeare his method of matching scenes in the first act with others later in the play: the two 'wooing' scenes (Anne, Elizabeth), Anne's and Margaret's two scenes, and the two dream scenes. Indeed, as R. A. Law and J. Dover Wilson have shown, these first-act scenes were probably modelled on the later ones.[1] The wooing of Anne, which has no historical basis, was suggested by the wooing of Elizabeth for her daughter's hand, which is described by the chroniclers. Similarly, Brakenbury, who was Keeper of the Tower at the time of the murder of the Princes, was introduced unhistorically by Shakespeare into the scene of Clarence's murder. There was no circumstantial historical account of Clarence's death, so Shakespeare resorted to invention: he gave Clarence a dream so as to match Richard's own on the eve of Bosworth. Indeed he seems to have transferred to Clarence Holinshed's account of Richard's frightening dream on his last night alive: 'The fame went that he had the same night a dreadful and terrible dreame: for it seemed to him, being asleepe, that he did see diverse images like terrible divels, which pulled and haled him, not suffering him to take anie quiet or rest . . . . But I thinke this was no dreame but a punction and pricke of his sinfull conscience'. For Richard himself he invented a dream of a quite different kind.

This arrangement of matching pairs of scenes arouses a powerful awareness of before-and-after, act and consequence, sin and retribution, which is reinforced by the numerous prophecies and the quaelly numerous acknowledgements of their fulfilment. These

[1] R. A. Law, '*Richard III*: A Study in Shakespeare's Composition', *P.M.L.A.*, vol. 60, 1945, pp. 689–96; New Cambridge *Richard III*, ed. J. Dover Wilson, 1954.

and other insistent devices work cumulatively to erect a cage-like structure as impressive and also as oppressive as that of *The Spanish Tragedy*. We inhabit a dark, airless, prison-like sound-chamber. Metallic voices, resonant alike in invective and lament, strike the ear—indeed the lament and the invective seem strangely interchangeable. There is little natural warmth; our deep sympathies are not required. This is a world of tragedy as seen—or rather, as heard—by a 'Tudor' imagination.

III

Richard III is not only a play of brilliant local effects: the clashing of line against line, the matching of scene with scene, the careful working out of plot. It also projects a few unforgettable images, densely realized stage-pictures, some of which have achieved the authority of myth. These images are conceived not so much in visual or pictorial terms as in terms of dramatic poetry, or if there is a visual component it makes its appeal to the inner eye of imagination. Such are the images formed by the tyrant-figure of Richard himself; by Clarence dreaming of death in the Tower of London; and by Richard and Richmond asleep before the final battle dreaming simultaneously of ghosts. The last—Bosworth Eve—will be considered later; here I shall examine first Clarence's dream, and then the figure of the tyrant. The two mutually fructifying sides of Shakespeare's reading will again appear: the classical is made English, the English is enriched and rounded out on classical forms and prototypes. We seldom feel that Shakespeare is imitating classical writers for their own sake or in obedience to a pedagogical theory; the classical dimension is taken for granted, naturally digested, subdued to the needs of the context. It is easy to overlook some of it altogether; which is as it should be. But to overlook it would mean missing some evidence of the effort Shakespeare is making in *Richard III*. He is writing a large scale play (one of the longest he ever wrote) and the diversity of source-materials, as well as their quality, is some indication of the pressure his mind was working at in its task of bringing to birth an altogether new unity.

Clarence's dream is the chief poetic set-piece of the play. Holinshed provided little in the way of information: 'finallie the duke was cast into the Tower and therewith adjudged for a traitor,

and privilie drowned in a butt of malmesie'. Shakespeare invented
the rest. The general direction his mind took was no doubt
prompted by Kyd, whose play had opened with Andrea's Virgilian
account of the underworld. In most of its details it was pedestrian
and lacking in immediacy:

> Then was the ferryman of hell content
> To pass me over to the slimy strond
> That leads to fell Avernus' ugly waves . . .

The epithets are conventional, the rhythms something less than
urgent. But Kyd was useful in giving Shakespeare something
to measure himself against and go beyond: at only one point
does Clarence touch on the obvious stock properties of Hades-
descriptions, and then with a literariness that draws attention to
itself:

> I pass'd, methought, the melancholy flood
> With that sour ferryman which poets write of . . .

But elsewhere the details are all peculiar to Clarence's situation
(the drowning, the meetings with Warwick and Prince Edward)
and are compellingly first-hand and real.

The dream's anticipation of the drowning was dictated by the
historical account of Clarence's drowning in the butt of malmsey,
but the circumstances that lead up to it are Shakespeare's. Clarence
and Gloucester are on ship bound for the Low Countries. Their
war experiences are over, and as they walk on the hatches they
talk of the past:

> Thence we look'd toward England,
> And cited up a thousand heavy times,
> During the wars of York and Lancaster,
> That had befall'n us. As we pac'd along
> Upon the giddy footing of the hatches,
> Methought that Gloucester stumbled, and in falling
> Struck me, that thought to stay him, overboard.
> O Lord, methought what pain it was to drown . . .

For this incident Shakespeare was, like Kyd, under Virgilian inspiration, but what prompted him was a part of Virgil's Sixth Book
not usually chosen for imitation. When Aeneas visits the underworld, the first ghost he meets is that of his former helmsman,

Palinurus, who had fallen off his ship and been drowned. The exchange that follows between Aeneas and the ghost is full of a sense of pain, remorse, and regret. Palinurus feels guilt at having left his ship without pilot or tiller, and is further desolated by the fact that his body has been left unburied. The circumstances of his death are shadowed in mystery: in Book Five we have been told that Neptune requires the death of one of Aeneas' men, and that subsequently Somnus overcame Palinurus' efforts to stay awake and flung him into the sea. Somnus moreover had appeared to him in the shape of an old comrade who had been killed at Troy. Now, in the underworld, Palinurus must wander on the banks of Styx for a hundred years.

Shakespeare's use of the drowning incident is entirely free and personal: it may have been quite unconscious—certainly there is no suggestion that he is doing a piece of deliberate neo-classical imitation. Instead, by a startling imaginative collocation, the malmsey-drowned Clarence of the chronicles and the sea-drowned steersman of Virgil come together to give us Clarence's dream-narrative of drowning followed by judgement in the underworld. Few of the exact circumstances of Palinurus' fate are recalled, although both men are voyaging away from home in a period following a long war and both are pushed overboard by an apparent friend and war-comrade. Perhaps more important is the fact that Palinurus is a ghost who speaks with that plaintive reproachful voice which Virgil usually reserved for his ghosts. For something of this ghost-tone may come through to Clarence —who is in any case close kin to Andrea's Ghost, who had also described his experiences in Hades. Indeed Clarence might be said to be almost a ghost himself. When we see him he is already more like a visitant to this world than a natural inhabitant of it: he has woken up from a dream in which he dies and suffers judgement; he then falls asleep again, and wakes up a second time to find himself about to be murdered; and then he *is* murdered. His scene is a kind of narrow isthmus—a starkly 'Tudor' tragic apprehension—with a dream of death on one side and actual death on the other.

The image of a man toppling into the sea occurs elsewhere in *Richard III*. Just before his execution, so utterly unexpected by him, Hastings uses it: the man who neglects God's grace for the favour of mortal men

> Lives like a drunken sailor on a mast,
> Ready with every nod to tumble down
> Into the fatal bowels of the deep.[1]

(III. iv. 101–3)

The terror of falling from a high place or into an abyss seems a recurrent nightmare of the Tudor mind. Richard sounds the theme for the last time and with a hint of sardonic rodomontade when, on the eve of Bosworth, he sends a warning to Stanley to be ready with his army 'lest his son George fall / Into the blind cave of eternal night' (v. iii. 61–2). But the act of plunging specifically from a ship into the sea has long-standing Tudor affiliations: in Skelton's dream-satire *The Bouge of Court* the court actually is a ship, and the hero Drede, the nervous new man, finally escapes the menaces of the others by leaping overboard.

Before passing to judgement in Hades, Clarence is given a vision of the ocean bed, with its 'thousand fearful wracks', its scenes of death and decay—but also its fabulous wealth:

> Wedges of gold, great anchors, heaps of pearl,
> Inestimable stones, unvalued jewels,
> All scatt'red in the bottom of the sea;
> Some lay in dead men's skulls, and in the holes
> Where eyes did once inhabit there were crept,
> As 'twere in scorn of eyes, reflecting gems,
> That woo'd the slimy bottom of the deep
> And mock'd the dead bones that lay scatt'red by.

This is the most emblematic passage in the play, and to be understood needs to be related to traditional imagery of the storms and wrecks of fortune. In the course of his interpretation of Giorgione's painting *La Tempesta*, Edgar Wind remarks: 'In the parlance of that period the word *Fortuna* was a synonym of *Tempesta*'.[2] He goes on to give many instances, including a design by Wenceslas Hollar in which Fortune appears as Storm personified. Fortune moreover could be mastered only by resolution and patience; Wind aptly quotes Pope's *Essay on Man*: 'The rising tempest puts in act the soul'. There is no doubt that Shakespeare shared this association of storm and fortune. In *3 Henry VI* (III. iii. 38), the French King cheers Margaret in her despair: 'with

---

[1] T. W. Baldwin follows Johnson in tracing this simile to Horace's Pyrrha Ode (I. v). See *Small Latine*, ii. 499–500.

[2] *Giorgione's 'Tempesta'*, Oxford, 1969, p. 3.

patience calm the storm'. (The sentiment recurs in *Pericles*, III. i. 59: 'Patience, good sir, do not assist the storm'—not to speak of the storm scenes in *Lear*.) Clarence finds himself, in short, as Nero does in *The Mirror for Magistrates*

> Amongst the wreckes whom Fortunes tempestes tore.[1]

Shakespeare probably also owed something to the allegorical imagination of Spenser. Among the epigrams which Spenser contributed to *A Theatre for Worldlings* (1569) was one describing a costly ship laden with rich treasure. A sudden storm drives it on a rock and it sinks:

> O great misfortune, O great griefe, I say,
> Thus in one moment to see lost and drownde
> So great riches, as lyke can not be founde.

Some such emblem of the world's vanity probably lies behind Clarence's vision. But, more certainly, other details from the first three books of *The Faerie Queen* (published in 1590) also contributed. Clarence's description of the sunken treasure has been linked to the somewhat similar descriptions of treasure in the Cave of Mammon (II. vii); and there may be more Spenserian echoes than Dover Wilson noted.[2] An important idea for the meaning of Clarence's dream is suggested by Spenser's line 'Great heapes of gold that never could be spent' (II. vii. v): for the gold and jewels viewed by Clarence can serve no possible human use— they 'mock'd the dead bones that lay scatt'red by'. Indeed the whole description amounts to a mockery of worldly ambition: the wealth is 'unvalued' in being incalculable and in the fact that there is no one in the vicinity to give it value—it lies there priceless and useless. Finally, in Spenser's narrative the temptation in Mammon's cave gives way to a description of hell, since the one place is next door to the other. Clarence's dream observes a similar sequence:

---

[1] *Parts Added to The Mirror for Magistrates*, ed. Lily B. Campbell, p. 319. This is from the 1587 edition. In *Troilus and Cressida* I. iii. 47, the two terms are brought into immediate conjunction—'storms of fortune'—in a phrase perhaps formed on Seneca's 'procella Fortunae' (*Agamemnon*, 594). Cf. *Othello*, I. iii. 249. Reuben A. Brower quotes Seneca's phrase for *Titus Andronicus*, I. i. 154: 'Here grow no damned drugs, here are no storms . . .' See *Hero, and Saint: Shakespeare and the Graeco-Roman Heroic Tradition*, Oxford, 1971, p. 179.

[2] Dover Wilson, pp. 185–6. Clarence's phrase 'dreadful noise' occurs in *Faerie Queen* II. xii. 25 in a sea context, while in II. vii. 30 Spenser has 'But al the ground with sculs was scattered, / And dead mens bones . . .'

the tempting vanities of the world only serve to lead to 'the tempest to my soul' and the place of 'perpetual night' where he faces 'torment'. Like the Cave of Mammon canto it encapsulates a brief allegory of the life of man in his spiritual struggle against the blandishments of the world.

This episode has been criticized for being too obscure to be understood by an audience: 'its general application is not made immediately apparent, other than by juxtaposition with the last scene'.[1] No doubt some members of any audience would miss its application; but others would surely be alerted to the nature of what was coming by Clarence's opening speech:

> . . . That, as I am a Christian faithful man,
> I would not spend another such a night
> Though 'twere to buy a world of happy days . . .

What is coming is a passage of 'moral poetry', as Clarence's designation of himself as a 'Christian faithful man' hints, and the following two lines, with their play on 'spend' and 'buy' would surely have been related by a Biblically conscious audience to the text in St. Matthew: 'For what is a man profited, if he shall gain the whole world, and lose his own soul? or what shall a man give in exchange for his soul?' Clarence's narrative speaks for itself, but the figurative nature of his experience is underlined by the Keeper's baldly naturalistic questions ('Had you such leisure in the time of death / To gaze upon these secrets of the deep?') which, through their sceptical tone, are merely a way of calling attention to the true nature of Clarence's communication.

This image of man's choice between God and Mammon is focused into a single set-piece. The tyrant, who has entirely embraced the world, is diffused through the play, although ultimately it too coheres into a single image.

Shakespeare's historical source for the portrayal of Richard was More's *History of Richard III*, which was faithfully relayed by successive historians. It was, however, only in his third act, after Edward IV's death, when Richard was actively plotting to clear a way to the throne, that Shakespeare kept at all close to More. His first act was largely fictitious, a series of episodes invented with a view to establishing Richard's character and the situation at Edward's court. Act Two contained Edward's death and showed

---

[1] Nicholas Brooke, p. 73.

its effect on his womenfolk. Richard himself was given a subordinate role, and the whole act was relatively low-pitched. Act Three, on the other hand, restores Richard to the centre of the stage and is powerfully dramatic. At the same time it keeps close to the historical accounts of what happened, for More's narrative was itself at its most dramatic in telling exactly how Richard brought off his usurpation.

More's *History* is not in any sense an impartial study of Richard but a work of propaganda into which mythological elements are freely admitted. Richard is not just a particular man in a unique and particular situation but a usurper and tyrant and as such has much in common with other usurpers and tyrants.[1] Accordingly, after the murder of the Princes, he is said to behave as all tyrants behave (the marginal note reads, 'The out and inward troubles of tyrauntes') : 'Where he wente abrode, his eyen whirled about, his body privily fenced, his hand ever on his dager, his countenance and maner like one always ready to strike againe, he toke ill rest a nightes, lay long wakyng and musing, sore weried with care and watch, rather slumbred than slept, troubled with feareful dreames . . .'[2] This is very like the generalized account of tyrants found in sixteenth-century treatises on kingship (e.g. Erasmus's *Education of a Christian Prince*); indeed, as the Yale editor suggests, More was probably as much concerned with the political situation of his own day as with that of Richard's—Henry VIII may already have seemed a budding tyrant potentially quite as dangerous as Richard III ever was.[3]

The most compelling passage of narrative in More's *History* tells in detail how Richard manœuvred his way to the crown. First, Hastings was disposed of, in a scene which Shakespeare faithfully transposed (III. iv). But the second phase was more devious and made use of various public speakers—Dr. Shaw, Friar Penker, and Buckingham. The object was to impute bastardy both to Edward IV and to his children by Elizabeth Woodville, thus leaving Richard as the apparently rightful heir to the throne. The whole strategy was such that Richard himself was to seem the mere pawn of events, an unambitious man, decent and patriotic, unquestioningly loyal to Edward and his children, swept along

---

[1] Cf. *The History of King Richard III*, ed. Richard S. Sylvester, New Haven, 1963, p. xcviii.

[2] Ibid., p. 87.

[3] Ibid., pp. xcix-civ.

by the will of the people into accepting the crown. All the drive, all the public activity, was to be left to others. The final move in the plan came when a delegation from the City of London, led by the Mayor, was to join with Buckingham in seeking an audience with Richard and vehemently urge him to take upon him the royal title. As More narrates it, the earlier moves succeed, but only narrowly: the common people are unenthusiastic and unco-operative. Only in the final phase, when Buckingham and Richard themselves become the chief interlocutors, does everything go according to plan. Richard's reluctance to displace his nephew is masterfully overcome by Buckingham's eloquence, and he is at last acclaimed king: 'With this there was a great shout, crying kyng Richard, king Richard.'

At the end of this long, finely managed narrative movement, More gives vent to the most outspoken comment on Richard's hypocrisy that he has yet allowed himself—for the delegation from the City have not been taken in by the play-acting of Richard and his henchmen, and when they disperse afterwards they say what they really think:

But muche they talked and marueiled of the maner of this dealing, that the matter was on both partes made so straunge, as though neither had euer communed with other thereof before, when that themself well wist there was no man so dul that heard them, but he perceiued well inough, that all the matter was made betwene them. Howbeit somme excused that agayne, and sayde all must be done in good order though. And menne must sommetime for the manner sake not bee a knowen what they knowe. For at the consecration of a bishop, euery man woteth well by the paying for his bulles, that he purposeth to be one, and thoughe he paye for nothing elles. And yet must he bee twise asked whyther he wil be bishop or no, and he muste twyse say naye, and at the third tyme take it as compelled ther vnto by his owne wyll.

More's final comparison is explicitly with actors on a stage:

And in a stage play all the people know right wel, that he that playeth the sowdayne is percase a sowter. Yet if one should can so lyttle good, to shewe out of seasonne what acquaintance he hath with him, and calle him by his owne name whyle he standeth in his magestie, one of his tormentors might hap to breake his head, and worthy for marring of the play. And so they said that these matters bee Kynges games, as it were stage playes, and for the more part plaied upon scafoldes. In which pore men be but the lokers on. And thei that wise be, wil medle no farther. For they that sometyme step vp and playe with them, when they cannot play their partes, they disorder the play and do themself no good.[1]

The theatrical comparison did not go unnoticed by Shakespeare. But More's immediate point is the typicality of Richard's behaviour and his methods of acquiring power. As Richard Sylvester has made clear in his excellent edition, More applied to Richard a number of details from Tacitus and Suetonius which they ascribed to Tiberius, the first great tyrant of the Roman empire.[2] According to them, Tiberius was a terrifyingly cold hypocrite. When, after the death of Augustus, he was approached by the senators and offered the imperial throne, he persistently refused—all the time meaning to have it. Suetonius put it as follows:

Tiberius did not hesitate to exercise imperial power immediately by calling on the Praetorians to provide him with a bodyguard; which was to be emperor in fact and appearance. Yet a long time elapsed before he assumed the title of Emperor. When his friends urged him to accept it he went through the farce of scolding them for the suggestion, saying that they did not realise what a monstrous beast the monarchy was; and kept the Senate guessing by his carefully evasive answers and hesitations; even when they threw themselves at his feet imploring him to change his mind .... Finally, with a great show of reluctance, and complaints that they were forcing him to become a miserable and overworked slave, Tiberius accepted the title of Emperor; but hinted that he might later resign it.[3]

Suetonius' phrase for this elaborate piece of duplicity was 'impudentissimus mimus' ('a most shameless farce'). The phrase may have suggested More's comment, just quoted, about 'Kynges games, as it were stage playes', which rounds off his account of the usurpation. Tiberius, like Richard, is an actor in a black farce. More's comment is important since it ultimately affected the whole of Shakespeare's conception of Richard Gloucester.

Shakespeare opens his dramatization of the usurpation strategy by pointedly calling our attention to the hypocritical performance that is to follow:

Rich. Come, cousin, canst thou quake and change thy colour,
  Murder thy breath in middle of a word,

---

[1] *The History of King Richard III*, ed. Richard S. Sylvester, New Haven, 1963, pp. 80–1.   [2] Ibid., pp. lxxxii–xcviii.
[3] Suetonius, *The Twelve Caesars*, tr. Robert Graves, Harmondsworth, 1957, p. 123.

And then again begin, and stop again,
As if thou were distraught and mad with terror?
Buck. Tut, I can counterfeit the deep tragedian;
Speak and look back, and pry on every side,
Tremble and start at wagging of a straw,
Intending deep suspicion . . .

(III. iv. 1–8)

These speeches are Shakespeare's equivalent to More's comment about 'Kynges games'. Indeed what Shakespeare seems to have done is to move More's comment from the end of the episode to the beginning. This is in accord with what is practicable in a play: it is far more effective for the audience to be apprised of what they are about to see than to be given the comment after the scene is finished. It was perhaps from this episode that Shakespeare's whole conception of the histrionic, role-playing Richard took its rise. If this is true, then this tense sequence (III. v–vii), so like a play within a play in that its chief speakers perform before a stage audience, was the original nucleus of *Richard III*, the scenes in Act One with Richard's various role-assumptions coming later in order of composition.

Although I argued earlier that Kyd's influence was decisive for *Richard III*, there was nothing in *The Spanish Tragedy* to prompt Shakespeare's conception of Richard as a specifically actorish villain. Kyd's Lorenzo is a flatly conceived character, without flamboyance or histrionic gusto. Marlowe's Barabas is closer to Richard in having something of these qualities, but is still not quite what Richard is, one who deliberately assumes different roles in such a way as to remind us pointedly of the arts of the theatre. In this important respect, More—and behind him, Suetonius (perhaps more than Tacitus)—must be seen as giving Shakespeare his inspiration.

The scene in which Richard refuses the offer of the crown and even rebukes Buckingham and the rest for troubling him with it is one of the most brilliant of the play. It imposes itself as one of the play's great moments, with Richard in the balcony between two bishops ('Two props of virtue for a Christian prince') and, below, Buckingham pleading on behalf of the City deputation. Nowadays perhaps we tend to take the scene in too frankly comic a spirit. Recent acting tradition (stamped by Olivier's impress) has made us see it primarily as outrageously funny, the hilarious climax to Richard's comic performance. That the scene lends itself to touches of broad farce is undeniable, but performances which heighten the clowning at the expense of grim political realities are missing something essential. Like More, Shakespeare is displaying the characteristic arts of the tyrant, among whose vices hypocrisy had a traditional place. We are watching not just how Richard behaved but how many tyrants have behaved and still behave.[1] In his *Education of a Christian Prince*, a key book for the period and a compendium of sixteenth-century ideals, Erasmus makes a stock contrast between the good king and the tyrant, and remarks: 'According to Plato [*Republic*, 1. 347], no one is fit to rule who has not assumed the rule unwillingly and only after persuasion.'[2] The thought is one which might occur to any reader of Suetonius' *Tiberius* and More's *Richard III* as to any audience of Shakespeare's play, but only as an ideal desired in its absence. For Richard, posturing as a 'Christian prince', this is the climax of his Tiberian hypocrisies, as for the audience it is the theatrical climax of the first movement of the play.

More never acknowledges his debt to the Roman historians, and it may be asked whether the parallel between Richard and Tiberius would have been noticed either by Shakespeare or his audience. A firm answer is impossible, but it should not be assumed that Tiberius' feigned indifference to empire would have been little known to Elizabethan readers. In the 1587 edition of *The Mirror for Magistrates* (the edition closest in date to *Richard III*) a series of 'tragedies' was included spoken by Roman emperors. Among them was Tiberius, who says of himself:

> So when I had obtayned my desire,
> Who then but *Caesar*: I did rule alone:
> By nature proude, presuming to aspire,
> Desembling that which afterwarde was knowne.
> For when the fathers minde to me was showne,
> Of their electing mine Emperiall place,
> I seemde to stay, refusing it a space.[3]

---

[1] Twentieth-century audiences can compare Brecht's play about Hitler's seizure of power, *The Resistible Rise of Arturo Ui*.

[2] *The Education of a Christian Prince*, tr. Lester K. Born, New York, 1936, p. 160. More makes the same point, though reversing the terms: 'But anyone who deliberately tries to get himself elected to a public office is permanantley disqualified from holding one' (*Utopia*, tr. Paul Turner, Harmondsworth, 1965, p. 106).

[3] *Parts Added to The Mirror for Magistrates*, p. 305.

Later than *Richard III*, the anonymous play *Tiberius* (its full title
runs *The Statelie Tragedie of Claudius Tiberius Nero, Romes greatest
Tyrant*, printed 1607) opens with a scene dramatizing this same
episode.[1] References to the Roman emperors are frequent in
sixteenth-century literature, and the more strikingly tyrannical
incidents as recorded by Tacitus and Suetonius are cited again and
again.

Whether or not Shakespeare recognized that More's Richard III
had some things in common with Tiberius, in later years he seems
to have resorted to Suetonius's Life of Claudius for his own
Claudius, in *Hamlet*, as well as for Macbeth.[2] A memory of Suetonius's Claudius also perhaps coloured his portrayal of Richard
III—though there is no need to suppose he had read Suetonius at
this time: there were many intermediaries available to him. One
such derivative of Suetonius would be the 1587 *Mirror for Magistrates* just mentioned, which included a 'tragedy' spoken by
Claudius. It begins by referring to his notorious stupidity (real or
merely alleged):

> My mother by her proverbs me a foole defynde,
> Which often sayd when any foolishly had done:
> In faith you are as wise as *Claudius* my sonne.

But what particularly linked Claudius and Richard was their
personal deformity—both were lame:

> It pleased her not onely so to name me sot,
> But also me a monster oft she namde,
> Unperfect all, begun by nature, but begot
> Not absolute, not well, nor fully framde.
> Sith thus my mother often me defamde,
> What meant the men of *Rome*, which so elected me,
> A foole, a monster foule, their governour to be?[3]

Richard too, of course, is 'unperfect all, begun by nature, but
begot / Not absolute':

> I—that am curtail'd of this fair proportion,
> Cheated of feature by dissembling nature,
> Deform'd, unfinish'd, sent before my time
> Into this breathing world scarce half made up . . .

---

[1] *The Tragedy of Tiberius*, ed. W. W. Greg (Malone Society Reprint), 1914.
[2] Cf. pp. 27–8 above.
[3] *Parts Added to The Mirror for Magistrates*, p. 315.

And like Claudius, he is reviled for it by his own mother. There is nothing corresponding to this last resemblance in More or in the historians who followed him.

One reason why the play's portrait of Richard seems so full and rounded is that Shakespeare shows particular skill in what the rhetoricians called 'invention'. Once the writer had selected his topic—in this case, the Tyrant—his next task was to gather as much material as possible on that topic. Shakespeare shows his resourcefulness in 'inventing' material in this sense through the number of details relevant to his theme which he has worked into the play. No doubt like other writers of his time he collected his material from his own reading and arranged it in easily usable form in his own notebooks.[1] More's *History* supplied most for the figure of Richard, but other suggestions were gathered from a wide variety of places.

When he devised the unhistorical scene of the wooing of Anne, Shakespeare recalled a scene in Seneca's *Hercules Furens* and used it as a point of departure.[2] This was where the tyrant Lycus woos Megaera, believing her husband Hercules to be dead. This debt to Seneca is not in itself very important; what is interesting is the ability to light on potentially rich material which fitted, or could be made to fit, with extraordinary naturalness in a new context. In this case, Lycus was one of Seneca's tyrants, so that what he did on this occasion—pressing his unwanted attentions on a woman—would be felt to have a prototypical value: any subsequent aspiring tyrant, like Richard, might do the same. So too, when he later becomes the murderer of the Princes in the Tower, Richard briefly recalls a very different tyrant, the New Testament Herod, the prototypical slaughterer of innocents.

Richard's first scene as crowned king (IV. ii) shows him at once taking up the quintessential posture of the Renaissance tyrant: unable to enjoy his power, he can only make frenzied plans to stabilize his state which by definition is unsteady. He at once broaches to Buckingham his plan of dealing with his young nephew Edward V. But Buckingham is slow to take the point:

Rich. But Edward lives.
Buck. True, noble Prince. *Rich.* O bitter consequence:
    That Edward still should live—true noble Prince!

---

[1] For the use of literary notebooks, see p. 21 above.
[2] This was first noted by T. Vatke, *Shakespeare Jahrbuch*, vol. iv, 1869, p. 67.

This sinister double-entendre, involving two ways of punctuating, is perhaps a recollection on Shakespeare's part of Marlowe's recent *Edward II*, in which Young Mortimer, now very much a stock tyrant, sends the ambiguous message '*Edwardum occidere nolite timere, bonum est*'. No doubt such equivocation was felt to be a typical tyrant's trick. Later in the scene Buckingham returns, having had time to consider Richard's suggestion. The dialogue that follows is a brilliant one, with Buckingham pressing his claim for some properties due to him and Richard parrying him and coming to a point with the 'What's a clock?' exchange ('I am not in the giving vein today'). It is another case of Shakespeare's inventiveness, for this is an adaptation of a certain kind of anecdote told of famous men in antiquity. Erasmus's *Apophthegmata* was a much used collection of such anecdotes, which often took the form of a witty or unexpected riposte. Among these, jokes involving the thwarting of impertinent suitors amount almost to a sub-species in themselves.[1] Richard's snub is admittedly not in the strict sense tyrannical, though certainly arbitrary and ill natured. But he is now a king, and the incident displays him as an absolute ruler, one of whose typical duties was to hear suitors.

A last example of Shakespeare's inventiveness: in IV. iv, when Richard approaches marching with his 'train', his mother the Duchess of York and Queen Elizabeth confront him, hoping to overwhelm him with 'exclaims'. They are not allowed to get very far, for he orders his drums and trumpets to drown them, thus acting as Lepidus did, who 'commanded all the trumpets to sound together to stop the soldiers' ears, that they should not hearken to Antonius' (Plutarch, *Life of Marcus Antonius*).[2] Such behaviour would signify extreme discourtesy, inhumanity, and (to use the word Richard himself uses here) 'impatience'; behaviour quite the reverse of that expected of the good king whose virtues would ideally include 'affability'—being easy to approach, having a ready ear for worthy suitors. Again, what is interesting is the way Shakespeare turns a detail in Plutarch into a striking and expressive stage action that seems to arise naturally out of its context.

---

[1] Several are told of Augustus. See *The Apophthegmes of Erasmus Translated into English by Nicholas Udall*, ed. R. Roberts, 1877, pp. 283, 285. Udall's translation first appeared in 1542.

[2] See *Richard III*, ed. E. A. J. Honigmann, Harmondsworth, 1968, p. 232.

IV

The last two acts of *Richard III* form a continuous movement which takes us from Richard's off-stage coronation to his on-stage death. The longest scene in this part of the play is Richard's wooing of Elizabeth for her daughter's hand (IV. iv). It has had few or no defenders. It disappoints because Richard's performance is expected to be as brilliant as his wooing of Anne, and it is nothing of the sort. The entire scene has seemed too long and woodenly written, as if Shakespeare's energies were flagging (although in fact it may well have come early in the order of composition). It is possible, however, that the real drift of the scene has been missed. And if this long scene has been misunderstood, Shakespeare's whole strategy in this final movement—including the scene of the ghosts on the eve of battle—may need a fresh appraisal.

In choosing to dramatize the usurpation of Richard III, Shakespeare was treating what was for Elizabethans one of the best known episodes of English history. It could be summed up in the one word 'Bosworth'. To Tudor audiences the real significance of Richard III was his destined role as antagonist to Richmond/Henry VII. In fighting Richmond to the death at Bosworth he was, or so he might seem to be a hundred years later, opposing the establishment of the Tudor dynasty, trying to avert the coming reigns of Henry VII, his son, and his three grandchildren. We shall not, I think, understand the final movement of *Richard III* if we fail to see that Shakespeare exploits his audience's knowledge that they were Tudor Englishmen. For within the play's world events are moving inexorably and ironically towards that final show-down; indeed only if we suppose Shakespeare to be exploiting that knowledge can we make sense of his choice of incidents and the sequence in which he chose to cast them.

Richmond is never named in the play until the first scene of the second movement (IV. i). In I. iii, Queen Elizabeth had referred once to the 'Countess Richmond', the Earl of Derby's wife, and mother to the Earl of Richmond by a previous marriage. (For those who knew the details of the story, and they must have been fairly common knowledge, Derby (or Stanley) was a key figure, whose very presence on stage must have carried a reminder of the final outcome. He kept in touch with his stepson Richmond throughout Richard's reign and, though in a difficult position, successfully worked out a plan by which he betrayed Richard at Bosworth; his own son, kept as hostage by Richard, narrowly escaped execution on the morning of the battle. All this was a well-known part of the story—one might say, legend—of Bosworth Field.) But from iv. i on, Richmond's name recurs repeatedly, becoming something of a leitmotiv throughout the fourth act until he himself makes his first appearance in v. ii. In this second movement all the sight-lines converge on Richmond's coming victory—this is clearly what the many references to him alert us to. So in iv. i Dorset, prompted by his mother the Queen and seconded by Stanley, decides to join Richmond in France; in iv. ii Richard hears of this defection and muses on Henry VI's prophecy that Richmond would one day be king; in iv. iii he hears that Morton too has fled to Richmond and, more important, that Richmond hopes to marry 'young Elizabeth', daughter of Edward IV and Elizabeth Woodville. He now determines to get rid of his wife Anne and forestall Richmond by having 'young Elizabeth' himself. This is the object of his long colloquy with Queen Elizabeth in iv. iv.

But first a slight oddity must be noticed. Before Richard appears the stage is occupied by his mother the Duchess of York and the Queen. The two women decide to overwhelm him with their curses, when he enters *marching with drums and trumpets*, on his way to deal with Buckingham's revolt. Now at the end of iv. iii his speed was insisted on, since 'dull delay' was dangerous: 'Then fiery expedition be my wing.' He is now intercepted by the two women and is made to hear his mother's curse before she goes, leaving him alone with Elizabeth. The oddity here is that the sense of urgency and haste which had been aroused before Richard's previous exit seems forgotten while he lingers with Elizabeth; and yet when she leaves, after a dialogue lasting over 200 lines, the urgency is promptly resumed as one by one the messengers arrive. Shakespeare's practice here with regard to time is quite uncharacteristic: he could easily have made Richard refer to his business with Buckingham and decide that his marriage plans took priority. But as it is, in a rather perplexing way, the military business is 'frozen'—with Richard's *train* apparently still on stage—as if time stood still while he works on Elizabeth, or as if during this wooing scene we entered a strange temporal loop, so that it is in fact out of time, not part of the otherwise convincingly realistic narrative sequence.

Richard's wooing of Elizabeth for her daughter's hand is usually taken as a repeat performance, but feebler and more long-drawn-out, of his wooing of Anne. And, though there are one or two dissentients, it is usually understood that Elizabeth finally consents to Richard's proposal.[1] In Hall's historical account the Queen does in fact allow herself to be flattered into receiving overtures from Richard, and moves out of sanctuary with her daughters into his power, though it is not clear whether she knows of his designs on her daughter; but later, when 'young Elizabeth' hears of them, she is affronted—Richard was her uncle, and marriage would have been within the forbidden degrees. Although the scene has its faults—it probably is too long—it is a mistake to see Richard repeating his triumph over another intellectually feeble woman. Shakespeare had a quite different end in view.

The dialogue is more elusive in tone than it may first appear. There is from the start a studied ambiguity—and the ambiguity is Shakespeare's, not Richard's. Richard opens the subject as follows:

> You have a daughter call'd Elizabeth,
> Virtuous and fair, royal and gracious.

One notices a peculiar neutrality of tone; it has the ring of a formal utterance. It might have been spoken by anyone, good or bad. We could certainly not infer from it that a 'villain' was the speaker. We could, on the contrary, imagine it spoken by someone as virtuous in the play's world as Richmond. Richard is speaking with, for him, a strange objectivity; his speeches are usually coloured with personality and rich in histrionic or parodic tone-effects, but this one is different. The Queen responds with alarm, fearing that since Elizabeth is her daughter she too, like the Princes, must die. Richard replies in the same graciously formal tone: 'Wrong not her birth, she is a royal princess.' But Elizabeth still mistakes his purpose and bitterly reminds him of her mur-

---

[1] E. A. J. Honigmann (pp. 27–8) believes that Elizabeth does not consent; Wolfgang Clemen (pp. 190–4) is more orthodox in thinking she does; while Dover Wilson (p. 234) takes up a more complicated position: Shakespeare, he thinks, leads the audience to believe that she yields to Richard but 'undeceives them almost immediately after, i.e. in 4. 5'.

dered sons. And he makes yet another effort to switch the subject
to his present good intentions:

> *K. Rich.* . . . . I intend more good to you and yours
> Than ever you or yours by me were harm'd!
> *Q. Eliz.* What good is cover'd with the face of heaven,
> To be discover'd, that can do me good?
> *K. Rich.* Th' advancement of your children, gentle lady.
> *Q. Eliz.* Up to some scaffold, there to lose their heads?
> *K. Rich.* Unto the dignity and height of Fortune,
> The high imperial type of this earth's glory.
> *Q. Eliz.* Flatter my sorrow with report of it;
> Tell me what state, what dignity, what honour,
> Canst thou demise to any child of mine?

The bearing of this is not obvious at once. But one notices that
the terms in which the dialogue is couched are such as to induce
us to contemplate the future—the real future—of the Queen's
daughter, 'young Elizabeth', upon whom Richard now has his
eye fixed. And this too is the effect of the slightly unctuous, almost
'official', neutrality of tone with which he opened ('You have a
daughter call'd Elizabeth . . .'). We remember in fact that 'young
Elizabeth' was to become the first Tudor queen, wife of Henry
VII and mother of Henry VIII. Officially speaking, she was
exactly what Richard here calls her: 'Virtuous and fair, royal and
gracious'. And so on throughout the dialogue: when Richard
promises to advance Elizabeth's children 'Unto the dignity and
height of Fortune', we can't help knowing that that is what—
inadvertently—he actually did. And that this—the historical irony
of this extraordinary situation—is what Shakespeare had in mind
is proved by his use of the unusual word 'demise' in the rhetorical position of climax in the speech of Elizabeth's last quoted.
This is a legal word, used only here by Shakespeare. Its general
meaning is 'convey', 'transmit'; but a further, more specialized
meaning also seems present, although the earliest example cited
by the *O.E.D.* belongs to 1670: 'To convey or transfer (a title or
dignity); *esp.* said of the transmission of sovereignty, as by the
abdication or death of the sovereign.' Shakespeare must intend
his audience to pick up, once again, the allusion to Bosworth, the
fact that Richard was soon to 'demise' his 'state', 'dignity', and
'honour' to his successor. A little later the dialogue receives
similar added point through the ambiguity of reference: but first,

Elizabeth prepares for it by deliberately mistaking Richard's meaning. When he says 'from my soul I love thy daughter', she quibblingly takes 'from' to mean 'at variance with', 'away from' his soul. Richard corrects her, but in doing so introduces the notion of 'confounding' meaning, so making Shakespeare's purpose more explicit, and more conscious, for the audience.

> *K. Rich.* Be not so hasty to confound my meaning.
>   I mean that with my soul I love thy daughter
>   And do intend to make her Queen of England.
> *Q. Eliz.* Well, then, who dost thou mean shall be her king?
> *K. Rich.* Even he that makes her queen. Who else should be?
> *Q. Eliz.* What, thou?
> *K. Rich.*   Even so. How think you of it?

Here Shakespeare has made his point more clearly. Elizabeth might actually be in the author's secret, privately enjoying the equivocation, so relaxed and colloquial her words sound: 'Well, then, who dost thou mean shall be her king?' Her next remark ('What, thou?') recalls a moment in an earlier scene, when she hears for the first time that Richard has seized the royal power: Brakenbury has just refused to admit her to the Tower to visit her sons:

> *Brak.* The King hath strictly charg'd the contrary.
> *Q. Eliz.* The King! Who's that?
> *Brak.*   I mean the Lord Protector.
> *Q. Eliz.* The Lord protect him from that kingly title!

The two situations, as far as Elizabeth is concerned, have a kind of antithetical symmetry: in the first she was unaware that her son had been deposed; in the second she is (necessarily, of course) unaware that her daughter is to be made queen.

Historical irony of this kind informs the whole of this second 'out of time' wooing scene. The topics of conversation turn pointedly on what is going to happen in the immediate future— we are constantly made to apply our historical knowledge of the outcome to the present situation. In Richard's long speech (for example) of would-be overwhelmingly forceful persuasion (291–336), he dwells on the pleasure Elizabeth will enjoy as the mother of another queen:

> The King, that calls your beauteous daughter wife,
> Familiarly shall call thy Dorset brother;
> Again shall you be mother to a king. . .

—but the effect is once more to remind us that the situation envisaged, though certainly to be brought about, will see a different 'King' on the throne. Entirely in keeping with this conception is Richard's final choice of something by which to swear: 'The time to come' (IV. iv. 387). That is what the whole scene is about.

Taken in this light, the apparent wavering of Elizabeth is seen to be deliberately plotted by Shakespeare. Richard never makes any headway in his long attempt on her: all he does on his own behalf is utter a solemn curse upon himself shortly before the end of the scene, which at this point in the play we take 'straight'— this is no histrionically amusing blasphemy but is premonitory, like so much else in this dialogue, of the ultimate despair expressed in the ghost scene of v. iii. Elizabeth, on the other hand, never loses her intensely bitter sense of maternal loss. In this Shakespeare firmly departs from the chroniclers, who say (as Hall does) that she 'putting in oblivion the murther of her innocente children . . . blynded by avaricious affeccion and seduced by flatterynge wordes, first delivered into kyng Richards handes her v. daughters as Lambes once agayne committed to the custody of the ravenous wolfe . . .'[1] Shakespeare has nothing about delivering her daughters into Richard's hands. Hall goes on to comment sharply on the culpable frailty of Elizabeth ('Surely the inconstancie of this woman were muche to be marveled at . . .'), but this is not Shakespeare's position. He gives this contemptuous expression of surprise to Richard ('Relenting fool, and shallow, changing woman!'), but made more use of it earlier, after the subjugation of Anne, where it was more deserved. (For just as he transferred the chroniclers' conception of Richard's dream to Clarence's, so he transfers their contempt for Elizabeth to Anne.) Elizabeth's final words in this scene, like so much else in it, are ambiguous: they temporarily placate Richard, but convey a different meaning to the audience:

> Shall I be tempted of the devil thus? . . .
> Shall I forget myself to be myself? . . .
> Yet thou didst kill my children. . . .
> Shall I go win my daughter to thy will? . . .
> I go. Write to me very shortly,
> And you shall understand from me her mind.

[1] *Narrative and Dramatic Sources*, ed. G. Bullough, iii. 287.

What we hear at the beginning of the next scene is that 'The Queen hath heartily consented / He should espouse Elizabeth her daughter'—where 'He' refers to Richmond. We certainly have an impression of Elizabeth's weakness—she is no Margaret. And the questions just quoted make her instability apparent to the end. But even here, in their midst, comes the flat statement 'Yet thou didst kill my children'. There is no 'putting in oblivion'; that, as she said earlier, is a string she will harp on till death.

This wooing scene, like everything else in this second movement, is orientated towards Bosworth. In dramatic terms what 'Bosworth' means is not so much the battle itself—of that we are given only a brief token show—as the *eve* of battle, the occasion richest in imaginative potential and significance: the long sequence of evening, night, and early morning during which Richard and Richmond sleep and dream and in dream are visited by ghosts. In stage terms the procession of ghosts *is* the battle of Bosworth. When the ghosts have gone, Richard is defeated, as his long soliloquy shows. But the irruption of ghosts into the stage action is by no means sudden and unheralded: at two earlier points, in iv. iv and v. i, the audience are alerted to what is to come through references to spirits who are felt to be watching the action and waiting for the final judgement. So the ghosts of the newly murdered Princes (they are called 'souls') are twice appealed to, first by their mother Elizabeth (iv. iv. 13) and then, more emphatically, by the Duchess of York in her final curse on Richard, when she looks ahead to the day of battle:

> My prayers on the adverse party fight;
> And there the little souls of Edward's children
> Whisper the spirits of thine enemies
> And promise them success and victory.
>
> (iv. iv. 190–3)

Finally, and most weightily of all, when Buckingham is led to execution (v. i) he apostrophizes the invisible souls of the dead who are watching him in his last hour:

> Hastings, and Edward's children, Grey, and Rivers,
> Holy King Henry, and thy fair son Edward,
> Vaughan, and all that have miscarried,
> By underhand corrupted foul injustice,

> If that your moody discontented souls
> Do through the clouds behold this present hour,
> Even for revenge mock my destruction!

He then goes on immediately to say: 'This is All-Souls' day, fellow, is it not?' And twice more in this short scene he refers to All Souls' day, his 'body's doomsday'. But in the last reference he converts the term into a metaphor: he is dying not on any feast-day but specifically on that day which had a special bearing on the state of his soul:

> This, this All-Souls' day to my fearful soul
> Is the determin'd respite of my wrongs;
> That high All-Seer which I dallied with
> Hath turn'd my feigned prayer on my head
> And given in earnest what I begg'd in jest.

Although this is an appropriately weighty speech to mark Buckingham's last moments (he is the last of Richard's victims), Shakespeare is still preparing for the culmination of this second movement in Bosworth eve. On that night, a very special night in the national calendar (comparable in the way Shakespeare stages it with the eve of Agincourt, another secular festival), ghosts are to walk in procession—or as Richard puts it when he wakes from his dream:

> Methought the souls of all that I had murder'd
> Came to my tent . . .

So from Buckingham's death on All Souls' day we pass almost at once to the night when 'the souls of all' Richard's victims return to curse him.

This ghost scene is often disparaged by critics who approach it more as a passage in a literary text than as part of a dramatic performance; but it is surely a remarkable invention. That Shakespeare invented it must be stressed. The historical sources gave Richard 'a dreadful & a terrible dreame' (in Hall's words) in which he was tormented by devils; Shakespeare transferred this to Clarence, and while he kept the fact of Richard's dream he gave the dream itself an entirely new content. Otherwise there is no known source for this visitation of ghosts on the eve of battle, one of the great images of the play.

In the first place, Shakespeare must have taken a hint from the

fact, provided by history, that Buckingham was executed on All
Souls' day (2 November 1483). In the chronicles, this event was
separated by a considerable space from the battle of Bosworth
(22 August 1485): only Shakespeare brings the two events so
close together. To Elizabethans, All Souls' day was a relic of pre-
Reformation England. The three days of All Saints' eve (31
October), All Saints and All Souls' eve (1 November), and All
Souls (2 November) had traditionally been a time of remembrance
of the faithful dead. Early in Elizabeth's reign, bell-ringing during
these three days was prohibited as a papist superstition.[1] But though
the observance of All Souls was suppressed, some of the traditional
associations lingered for a considerable time. What Shakespeare
was free to do was to make figurative use of the festival in a play:
being suppressed, it perhaps became all the more readily available
for imaginative adaptation. This, then, is the reason why Buckingham so pointedly draws our attention to All Souls: it prepares us
for the procession of souls that is to appear on Bosworth eve.[2]
The actual date of Bosworth is quite immaterial as far as Shakespeare's use of All Souls is concerned. What matters is that a
close link between the two occasions is established in terms of the
stage performance, so that the fifth act becomes in effect a kind of
All Souls sequence.

   All Souls was a festival of the dead. The faithful living com-
memorated the faithful dead and, through prayer and almsgiving,
tried to alleviate their sufferings in purgatory. But it was also
popularly believed to be a time when the dead might return
to the living; indeed folklorists have collected a mass of evidence
to show that throughout western Europe All Souls has been
associated with the appearance of ghosts. On All Souls' eve the
dead might return home, or else the procession of the dead (the
cours des morts) might be witnessed. 'Throughout the Middle Ages
it was popular belief that the souls in purgatory could appear on

---

[1] J. Brand, *Popular Antiquities of Great Britain*, ed. W. Carew Hazlitt, 1870, i.
218–19.

[2] In his edition of the play E. A. J. Honigmann comments: 'I think it possible
that the Buckingham scenes were slightly changed before the play was finished:
prophecy and fulfilment dovetail so meticulously elsewhere that it is odd that
Buckingham has not foretold his death on All Souls' day, as he asserts several times
in v. i' (p. 19). The comment is perceptive, but it is unnecessary to postulate any
change of plan. The three references to All Souls are used to point forward rather
than back. To have introduced the reference earlier (e.g. in II. i) would only have
muffled the effect.

this day . . . to persons who had wronged them during their life.'[1] This last belief is the one with the most obvious bearing on *Richard III*: the ghosts of Richard's victims return to plague him. In the procession of the eleven ghosts the play even offers its own version of the *cours des morts*.

All Souls probably displaced an older pagan festival which was also held in November and which also involved the return of the dead; and like Guy Fawkes' day, which came to displace Hallowmas and All Souls in post-Elizabethan England, these early November festivals were celebrated with bonfires. A folklorist has written of Guy Fawkes' day in terms which are relevant to the significance of All Souls: 'It superseded the older festival of Hallowmas, taking over the bonfires, the bell-ringing, and the general liberty which characterized the older festival.' She goes on to suggest that these fire festivals 'mark the end of the old year or the end of a particular season. . . . The bonfire is a destruction of the bad luck and rubbish of the past, so that it shall never return to vex the future.'[2] This theme of the ending of a phase of experience —of a season or a year—and the ritual destruction of the dead past is another belief which clarifies the imaginative conception of *Richard III*. The play is also concerned with the casting-off of an old order, fatigued and guilt-ridden, to make way for a new. England under Richard is like the Patriarchs in limbo waiting for deliverance (this feeling of not quite hopeless waiting is particularly acute in the scene in iv. iv of the exhausted women). It is an end-of-the-year, end-of-the-cycle play, in the course of which England is to negotiate its critical dynastic change.

The associations clustering around All Souls throw light on the conception of Bosworth eve, but without explaining it entirely. That conception is a strange and powerful one; indeed it has an imaginative grandeur which familiarity with the play may cause us to overlook. The occasion, the eve of a great battle, is to mark the inauguration of a new dynasty. The scene is the two military camps, with the chief antagonists plunged in sleep, while around them in the dead of night move supernatural visitants. No source for this nocturnal camp scene is known. There is, however, one famous event which offers some striking likenesses to it. This is the occasion of the dream of Constantine which, seen in its full

---

[1] *New Catholic Encyclopedia*, Washington, D.C., 1967, i. 319.
[2] Charlotte S. Burne, 'Guy Fawkes' Day', *Folklore*, vol. 23, 1912, pp. 409–26.

setting in the history of Christianity, was a turning-point of
unparalleled momentousness. The Roman empire had been invaded by the infidel Maxentius. The details of the story vary in
different versions; but the one most relevant is as follows (from
Caxton's translation of *The Golden Legend*):

And whan constantyn had assembled his hoost he went and sette
them ageynst that other partye, but assoone as he began to passe the
ryver he was moche aferde, bycause he shold on the morne have
batayle, and in the nyght as he slepte in his bedde an aungel awoke
hym, and shewed to hym the sygne of the crosse in heven . . . 'In this
sygne thou shalt overcome the bataylle'.[1]

Next day Constantine carried a cross into battle, routed the enemy,
and himself embraced Christianity.

The story of Constantine's dream became attached to the
Legend of the True Cross (as told, for example, in *The Golden
Legend*), and in the Middle Ages became a popular subject in art,
the best known and the best instance being the frescoes at Arezzo
by Piero della Francesca. Indeed someone coming from *Richard III*
to these paintings could hardly fail to be reminded of it by Piero's
treatment of the Dream of Constantine. The sleeping king is
shown in his tent, with other tents visible in the background;
poised above the tent is an angel holding a cross and pointing to
Constantine's face. The subject was well known in England, in
part because St. Helena, mother of Constantine and discoverer of
the True Cross, was traditionally held to be English-born.[2]
Shakespeare's own birthplace proves this as well as any: Stratford-
upon-Avon had its Gild of the Holy Cross, whose chapel had
wall-paintings showing the Legend of the True Cross. (They have
since disappeared, but were visible until the early nineteenth century: according to the sketches of Thomas Fisher, there was a
small inset in one of the paintings showing Constantine's vision.)[3]

The Constantine of this tradition was of course a medieval and
Catholic one. But after the Reformation he continued to occupy the
minds of at least some Englishmen, though now in a different role.

---

[1] *The Golden Legend* (The Invention of the Cross), tr. Caxton, ed. F. H. Ellis, 1892,
vol. 2, p. 483.

[2] The Legend of the True Cross, including Constantine's Dream, is depicted on
a fine twelfth-century cross at Kelloe, outside Durham. The cross is well reproduced
in Fritz Saxl's *English Sculptors of the Twelfth Century*, 1954.

[3] *Ancient allegorical, historical and legendary paintings . . . at Stratford-upon-Avon*, ed.
J. G. Nichols, 1838.

The first dedication to Queen Elizabeth of John Foxe's enormously influential *Acts and Monuments* (the 'Book of Martyrs') opens with the name 'Constantine' and develops an elaborate comparison between Constantine and Elizabeth—for Foxe, both were supreme benefactors to the Church. According to Foxe, Elizabeth was in fact a second Constantine, not inferior to him and perhaps even greater. In her pioneer work on this subject, Dr. Frances Yates has explained the arguments behind this comparison.[1] The English under Elizabeth were returning to the older 'purer' Christian tradition. Elizabeth, says Dr. Yates, 'represents the return to the Constantinian, imperial Christianity, free from papal shackles, the kind of religion which Foxe regards as alone pure'. The comparison with Constantine was an important thread in Elizabethan 'imperial' propaganda.[2]

For the Bosworth sequence, then, two motifs came together: All Souls gave the ghosts, returning to wound the conscience of the man who had wronged them, while Constantine's dream gave the occasion of the eve of battle and the salutations which the ghosts bestow on Richmond.

In this second movement of *Richard III* we have clearly moved into the area of dynastic drama. This is the assumption that determines the shaping of the second wooing scene as well as the Bosworth sequence. Our viewpoint in these final scenes has changed decisively to a post-Bosworth position: Richard is now surrounded not only by a divinely controlled universe but by a historically determined one. He is ruined on both counts. He remains to the end more engaging theatrical company than anyone else on stage, but he now shares the weakness which had earlier been a mark of his victims. When the ghosts have gone, he is drained of authority. He is becoming a ghost like them, an *umbra*

[1] Frances A. Yates, 'Queen Elizabeth as Astraea', *Journal of the Warburg and Courtauld Institutes*, vol. 10, 1947, pp. 27–82, especially pp. 37–43.

[2] For a comparison between Elizabeth and Constantine fairly close in date to *Richard III*, see J. Nichols, *Progresses of Queen Elizabeth*, 1823, ii. 461–80. In an oration at New Windsor in August 1586, the Mayor, Edward Hake, alludes to the Babington Plot and commends the 'mercy' of Elizabeth. He goes on to say how Constantine, 'as milde as hee was', dealt with Licinnius 'his co-partner in the empire and his brother-in-lawe', who had behaved tyrannically. After much forbearance, Constantine had him put to death. The allusion to Mary Stuart under the figure of Licinnius is obvious. (I owe the reference to Hake's oration to Roy Strong's article cited on p. 34 above.) There was also an Elizabethan play, not extant, called *Constantine*, recorded in Henslowe's Diary (Chambers, *Elizabethan Stage*, ii. 122), which presumably had some topical bearing.

from the past summoned for a time by the dramatist's theatrical magic. But while Richard recedes—fighting desperately—into the murk of history, the play itself moves forward to the sunlit position of the privileged Elizabethan audience. For although (unlike Legge in *Richardus Tertius* and the author of *The True Tragedy*) Shakespeare does not name Queen Elizabeth in the play's concluding speech, there can be little doubt that she is shadowed in the person of Richmond her grandfather (and in any case shares her name with his Queen). Richmond is the play's Constantine, while for her people Elizabeth was the second Constantine, Empress and Head of the Church. So at its first performances, and whenever it was performed within her reign, *Richard III* brought the events of the previous century right up to the present moment as it was experienced by the audience. Post-Elizabethan audiences can hardly be expected to share the *rapport* suggested by this pageant-style epilogue. But at the time it was written, only a few years after Mary's execution, feelings of relief and gratitude were perhaps not merely literary. It seems suitable that the play should end in an atmosphere reminiscent of civic ceremony and celebration. Shakespeare offers more than a theatrical entertainment: he creates an occasion for national thanksgiving and communal prayer:

> Now civil wounds are stopp'd, peace lives again—
> That she may long live here, God say amen!

11. King John: *The Self and the World*

I

OF all Shakespeare's early plays *King John* makes the least decisive impact. Its lack of popularity on the stage as well as with the reader is accordingly not in the least surprising. If we come to it from *Richard III*, it can hardly fail to seem a strangely faltering, uncertain work. The king who gives his name to the play makes a puzzling contrast to his predecessor. Like him, he is in an obvious sense a bad man, yet as a character is pale and feeble where Richard was highly coloured and thrillingly energetic. And, with one exception, none of the other characters are such as to arouse any great warmth of interest in and for themselves. Nor does the plot of *King John* unfold with the sureness of purpose which can be felt in all the other early history plays. Much of the interest of the Henry VI plays is of a purely narrative kind: the historical events claim attention in themselves, and the grandeur of the national theme ensures for the trilogy a weight and dignity which the ostensible action of *King John* cannot match. It might be thought unfair to compare a single play with a trilogy. But the over-all design of *King John* cannot be set against the intensively patterned elaboration of *Richard III* or the very special simplicity of *Richard II* either. For even after repeated readings of the play, however impressive one may find certain scenes and moments, it must be admitted to be exceptionally episodic, occasionally a little disjointed, and uneven in execution. Even within single episodes the action often has an oddly indecisive quality, a tendency to start and stop, seeming not to get anywhere or at least not in a straightforward way, sometimes indeed going into reverse as if wanting to cancel itself out. This quality we shall return to, but for the moment an example will serve. In *Richard III*, when the two murderers arrive in the Tower to dispose of Clarence, he pleads eloquently for his life. But although one of the villains quails, the other does not, and Clarence is duly put to death. When in a comparable scene Arthur pleads with Hubert not to put out his eyes, his pleadings are successful, and we are left with the perhaps slightly callous feeling that the scene was not really necessary, since the situation at the end remains much what it was at the beginning. But at this point in the play the sequence of scenes has its own strangely serpentine development which, in its shifts and turns, is very characteristic of *King John*. When Hubert reports that Arthur is dead, John welcomes the news. But the anger of the lords and the resentment of the commons frighten John into putting the blame on to Hubert. Hubert is forced to tell him that Arthur is in fact still alive. Arthur meanwhile has tried to escape from his prison, falls from the tower, and is killed. His body is at once discovered by the nobles, who regard it as proof of John's guilt. Hubert appears, believing Arthur safe in prison, and is horrified to find him dead. In the circumstances the nobles refuse to accept his plea of innocence. Nothing like this deviously ironical construction can be found in the other histories and yet, though more than usually elaborate, it is in keeping with other parts of the play which also seem designed to produce an effect of frustration—as if the course of events is bafflingly beyond human control and as if human motivation and purpose are helpless before the huge complexity of history, the unmanageable sum of actions performed in the world.

If the plot of *King John* is exceptionally episodic, the play seems also without a dominant verbal style, a consistent imaginative mode—and this has undoubtedly told against it in terms of stage performance. There is again nothing to match the homogeneity of diction which marks *Richard III* and *Richard II*, the impression made by both plays that they are each subsumed within a single comprehensive rhetorical system. If *King John* has stylistic unity, it has proved to be highly elusive. But here too the apparent lack of unity is related to the seemingly rambling sequence. Some characters drop out of the action early on or halfway; others arrive late, but with a kind of unprepared abruptness. Of those who speak in Act One, only John and the Bastard persist through the play until the end. The most dogged antagonist of the English is the Dauphin Lewis, but the other characters make only briefer appearances. We see Constance and King Philip only in the second and third acts, Pandulph in the third and fifth, while Salisbury and Pembroke move into prominence in the fourth and fifth. One character who has a central role in Act Four is Hubert, and the fact that he emerges so suddenly has given rise to a critical as well as a textual problem—for it has seemed to some critics that a role so important must have been better prepared for. The Hubert problem serves to illustrate something peculiar about the play: there is nothing comparable in the other histories.[1]

These defects and weaknesses can hardly all be illusory—waiting to be explained away by a well-informed historically-orientated criticism. It seems true that the play's over-all design is indeed unsatisfying and that certain parts remain slightly botched even when all allowances have been made. The termination of the Anglo-French conflict in III. i reads as if it might have been truncated, so inexpertly is the battle dramatized; and the first half of IV. ii, the scene at court, seems an altogether feebler repetition of the brilliant court scene at a comparable point in *Richard III*. These weaker parts of the play are not likely ever to be definitively salvaged. And yet *King John* is still misunderstood and absurdly underrated. Criticism has failed to clarify its real character, its tone, its vision. Indeed, of all Shakespeare's early plays this is the one that has receded furthest from us, so that a special effort is needed to recover it. We need to try to see it afresh, facing its oddities in the hope that, rightly understood in the context of the play as a whole, they will assume an expressive value. But it needs especially to be accepted that in this play Shakespeare was doing something quite different from what he had done in the Henry VI trilogy and in *Richard III*.[2]

II

There is an early Tudor morality play, extant only in fragmentary form, called *Mundus et Infans* (*The World and the Child*).[3] Its rudimentary action shows the hero, a moral innocent, encountering the bewildering world of experience. I am not suggesting that Shakespeare knew this play; but the title has a representative,

---

[1] See Appendix D.

[2] I have reserved judgement on the question whether the anonymous play *The Troublesome Raigne of King John* (printed 1591) is a source for *King John* or whether *King John* is a source for it. The problem is difficult, and I hope to write on it elsewhere. In this chapter I have treated the play as a finished work for which Shakespeare alone is to be held responsible.

[3] *Dodsley's Old English Plays*, rev. W. C. Hazlitt, 1874–6, vol. i. The play, or at any rate the title, has impressed at least one modern poet: see W. H. Auden's 'Mundus et Infans', *Collected Shorter Poems, 1930–1944*, 1950.

quasi-proverbial force which seems peculiarly applicable to the action of *King John*. This play too dramatizes the encounter between the inexperienced self and the world. The acquisition of moral experience is its chief concern. It is of course the Bastard Faulconbridge who embodies this theme most fully. He is the play's chief instance of the innocent eye and ear, and it is his initiation into high politics—the great world—which forms a major plot line. But, important though he is, he is not the only character to keep before us the idea of the rough encounter of the self with the world. In two scenes, while he is absent from the stage, the theme is continued through the play's two other representatives of youth: the Dauphin Lewis and Arthur. In III. iv the Dauphin is instructed in worldly policy by the astute, and presumably elderly, churchman Pandulph: 'How green you are and fresh in this old world!' Pandulph himself has no illusions about the motives of others: he has seen everything before and understands that politics is a form of mechanics, a power-struggle whose nature a practised observer can easily analyse. He coolly, and correctly, predicts that John must try to dispose of Arthur by violence, and he urges Lewis to take his chance by invading England. He never for a moment suggests that it might be worth trying to save Arthur's life. What matters is the way the situation can be turned to the French advantage. In the following scene (IV. i) Pandulph's prophecy comes to pass—or nearly does. For Hubert fully intends to carry out the task assigned him. True, he draws back from it, softened by Arthur's pleading. But until that moment their scene together is the extreme instance—it forms the play's chief tableau—of innocence confronting power, the child-like self meeting the world and almost succumbing to it. Still, the Bastard remains the chief embodiment of this theme. Indeed, in the shape of his role there may even be a memory of the morality play hero's typical progress from infancy to old age and death. The lawsuit of the first act over the Faulconbridge estate directs attention to the Bastard's begetting and birth. He seems at the time a young man ready to take his chance and follow his fortunes (and in Shakespeare's source for this scene in Hall, the Bastard of Orleans was also a mere youth). In the later stages of the play, Acts Four and Five, he no longer seems particularly young, but by acquiring moral experience has reached maturity. Finally, after John's death, the Bastard speaks in a voice which

surprisingly—to a reader of *King Lear*, at least—seems to anticipate the last words of Kent in wishing to follow his master in
death. It is almost as if he too has reached the end of life. This
entire life-pattern from birth to death, though no more than a
faint suggestion, supports the impression that the Bastard is the
chief exemplar of moral experience.

If on one side *King John* has its young innocents, its 'green'
youths, undergoing initiation in the ways of 'this old world',
on the other it adumbrates the typical features of that world
itself. Indeed the very word 'world' sounds repeatedly in *King
John*. Of course it often occurs in many other of Shakespeare's
plays too; what matters is less its mere frequency than the weight
of emphasis it receives, the extent to which it is reinforced by
the play's other thematic concerns. There is little need to argue
that *King John* is about 'the world' in a very special sense. If we are
looking for a key to the play's distinctive tone and style, its vision,
even its structure, we can hardly do better than hold on to this
word. If *Richard III* recalls in a rather specific way 'Tudor'
literature, with its typical settings in court and prison and its
preoccupation with Fortune, then *King John* has a similar affinity
with the mid-Tudor morality play, for the sense of 'the world'
communicated by those plays and by this is closely related. The
world of *King John*, like the world of those moralities, is the world
of 'the world': worldliness is one of its chief preoccupations.
For its situations are so shaped as to call attention over and over
again to questions of right and wrong, loyalty and expediency,
private integrity and public politics. 'The world' in this light is
the way other people commonly behave, and the scene of their
usually unedifying pursuits is contemplated in a mood partly
resigned, partly cynical, certainly fatigued and without illusion:

> There's nothing in this world can make me joy.
> Life is as tedious as a twice-told tale
> Vexing the dull ear of a drowsy man;
> And bitter shame hath spoil'd the sweet world's taste,
> That it yields nought but shame and bitterness.
>
> (III. iv. 107–11)

The speaker is the Dauphin Lewis, in a mood of dejection after
his defeat in battle, the loss of Arthur to the English, and the
resulting frenzy of Constance. But the weighty impersonality of

his words focuses a feeling diffused more obscurely throughout the play. *King John* contemplates worldliness at length, and a mood compounded of world-weariness and disgust is the result. This speech of the Dauphin's comes at the end of the long sequence set in France (Acts Two and Three). These scenes amount to a formal demonstration of how the great world with its self-interested great powers behaves. And Lewis's lines express a response not only to the immediate situation (defeat in battle) but, as far as the audience is concerned, to this entire sequence. The speech's true function as a choric comment on the preceding French sequence has been overlooked; it has seemed just another instance of Shakespeare's rather pointlessly extravagant rhetoric, seeming not quite to fit into its immediate context. It may, however, be taken as a hint that we are meant to *generalize* from what we see on the stage.

In keeping with the play's interest in the way of the world, the way other people typically behave, its characters often resort to proverbial expressions of dismay at the world's depravity: 'Mad world! mad kings! mad composition!', '. . . bad world the while!', 'Here's a good world!' In what is probably the play's finest moment the Bastard is like a child lost in the wood of the world's shocking callousness:

> I am amaz'd, methinks, and lose my way
> Among the thorns and dangers of this world . . .

Only in the last act, with Melun's dying repentance and John's feverish death, is a tenderer, more hopefully refreshing note admitted, as when the young Prince—now the new king— speaks over his father's dead body:

> What surety of the world, what hope, what stay,
> When this was now a king, and now is clay?

The hope consists in fact precisely in a traditionally pious attitude of *contemptus mundi*, in which the evil infection of 'the world' is mastered by an other-worldliness which dismisses it as illusion. The only solid foundation is the 'truth' recognized by Melun in the last moments of his life:

> Have I not hideous death within my view . . .?
> What in the world should make me now deceive,
> Since I must lose the use of all deceit?

Why should I then be false, since it is true
That I must die here, and live hence by truth?

(v. iv. 22–9)

The world of *King John* is a place of deceit and deceiving, in which the deceivers are themselves deceived. This at least is how it comes to look by the end of the play. In the early acts, however, the transcendental dimension is, if not missing, not much in evidence, and the worldly seem to be having things entirely their own way. The play gives little cause for optimism, is rather realistically dark, showing as it does so many cases of men impelled by the chilliest of motives, crude self-interest.

John himself is the meanest, most meagre-spirited, of all Shakespeare's kings. He has no personality, no personal voice, hardly any recognizable inner consistency at all. He is almost entirely conditioned by the immediate situation, taking his colour from it rather than asserting himself and creating the situation. Occasionally he can supply a monarchical trumpet-voice, but the effect is one of efficiency, not magnanimity, for he has no abundance of spirit, not even the bad gusto of Richard III. He is a king and no king, enjoying 'strong possession' without 'right'. Accordingly all his scenes show him in equivocal postures, trying to keep up appearances but wobbling uncomfortably. The opening of the play, at which he gives audience to Chatillon, is a tableau of guilty power: John puts on a brave front but is privately pricked by conscience. Soon the Bastard makes his appearance and at once takes the centre of the stage, pushing the king to the periphery of interest. The long Angiers scene reduces John to being one of a pair of kings, whose bellowed public utterances are essentially indistinguishable. John is never, in this scene, given the chance to act as the hero of his play: his role is no more stressed than King Philip's; and the same is true of the following scene in which they are joined by Pandulph. In this first movement, which is predominantly satirical, John is always one of a group, never a heroically isolated protagonist. (It is, no doubt, largely because the play lacks an easily recognizable hero that it is so little popular in the theatre; attempts by actors to make John the star role inevitably fail.) In his one scene in Act Four, John's own nobles upbraid him for having undergone a humiliating second coronation—quite unnecessarily, according to them, since it once more brings in doubt the legality of his reign. And as if to confirm this impression of illegitimacy, the rest of the scene shows him blown to and fro by the conflicting winds of circumstance: deprived of such supports as his mother, he is helpless ('My discontented peers! What! mother dead!'). Like Acts One and Four, Act Five opens with another tableau damaging to John's regal dignity (it is not clear whether or not the action is mimed). This is the voluntary surrender of his crown to Pandulph, which formally acknowledges that in receiving it back from him John holds it from the Pope. (The scene had appeared as a woodcut in Foxe's *Acts and Monuments*.) All these actions and postures are such as to remove him from the reach of audience sympathy. In the last scenes of the play he totters aimlessly about, shamefaced and sick, unable to defend his country against invasion, and for the most part away from the action. The last words he utters are a description of himself, and a true one: 'a module of confounded royalty'. He is not only a ruined king, he is also a mere imitation or image of a king.

It seems clear that Shakespeare deliberately withholds vitality from John. If he is weak and colourless as a character, he is so because mediocrity is his hallmark. But this is a dangerous procedure for a dramatist to adopt; and it must be admitted that Shakespeare does not technically solve the difficulties. Whereas we can accept Henry VI as a weak man, though with many virtues, and a poor king, his weakness and lack of success are interesting in their own right; he is always psychologically convincing. In the character of John, on the other hand, Shakespeare failed to light upon a universally recognizable pyschological type. The result is not only a mediocre man but an uninteresting character.

Whether technically successful or not, John's shallowness, his lack of personality and mind, are to be seen as expressions of his dreary commitment to the world's stultifying values. He is a hollow man, like the other worldlings of the play, King Philip, Austria, Pandulph. Only the innocent, only those who have rejected the world have any inward life; and only to them does Shakespeare lend his gift of piercing eloquence.

Constance and Arthur are the natural victims of the great ones. Historically Constance was at this time not a widow, nor was Arthur a child: these are adjustments made by Shakespeare for his own purposes. The nature of these purposes may be brought out by recalling a cliché of the political thought of his time.

It was a primary duty of kings and governors to see that justice was done and injustice prevented. In other words, they should protect widows and orphans. The ultimate source for this formula was Biblical. Among God's laws in Exodus is included the injunction: 'Ye shall not afflict any widow, or fatherless child' (22 : 22). Psalm 68 has the verse: 'A father of the fatherless, and a judge of the widows, is God in his holy habitation', while the following verse occurs in James: 'Pure religion and undefiled before God and the Father is this, To visit the fatherless and widows in their affliction, and to keep himself unspotted from the world.' (1 : 27). Such expressions would of course have been wholly familiar in Shakespeare's time, as would the following from the Litany: 'That it may please thee to defende and prouide for the fatherles children and wyddowes, and all that be desolate and oppressed . . .'[1] Allusions to such texts as these are common in Tudor literature. In his third sermon preached before King Edward VI in 1549, Latimer remarked: 'The greatest man in a realm cannot so hurt a judge as a poor widow; such a shrewd turn she can do him. And with what armour, I pray you . . . *Lacrymae miserorum descendunt ad maxillas*, "The tears of the poor fall down upon their cheeks," *et ascendunt ad coelum*, "and go up to heaven," and cry for vengeance before God, the judge of widows, the father of widows and orphans.'[2] And in the House of Holiness in *The Faerie Queene* the seventh beadsman has the following duty:

> The seventh now after death and buriall done,
> Had charge the tender Orphans of the dead
> And widowes ayd, least they should be undone:
> In face of judgement he their right would plead.
> Ne ought the powre of mighty men did dread
> In their defence, nor would for gold or fee
> Be wonne their rightfull causes downe to tread . . .
>
> (I. x. xliii)

It is important for Shakespeare's purpose to see that Constance and Arthur are not just individual characters (though they are that) but the embodiments of the 'widows and fatherless children' referred to in accounts of the duties of rulers. It is wholly in

---

[1] *The First and Second Prayer-Books of King Edward VI*, Everyman edn., n.d., p. 233.

[2] Latimer, *Sermons*, Everyman edn., 1906, p. 125.

keeping with the Bastard's instinct for justice that, although he is
on the opposing side, he is a natural ally of Constance and eventually abets her. The behaviour of both kings, on the other hand,
perfectly illustrates how they, as rulers, should not use their power.
Theirs is the 'powre of mighty men' mentioned by Spenser; and
when Constance majestically appeals to God for aid, she is invoking Latimer's 'judge of widows, the father of widows and orphans':

> Arm, arm, you heavens, against these perjur'd kings!
> A widow cries: Be husband to me, heavens!
> Let not the hours of this ungodly day
> Wear out the day in peace; but, ere sunset,
> Set armed discord 'twixt these perjur'd kings!
> Hear me, O, hear me!
>
> (III. i. 107–11)

Her references to 'kings' in the plural has a derisive belittling
force; she distances the worldly scene in a way that makes us
look down on it as if from a great height. And her wish is granted:
before the day is out England and France are at war again. In this
first movement of the play it is not Pandulph, the churchman,
who provides the suggestion of transcendence but the widow
Constance. She directs our gaze above the low ceiling of the play's
worldly setting to the all-witnessing heavens. (In the second
movement her role is matched by the devout-spirited Melun.)
The Angiers sequence is in fact quite as much a set piece of political and moral allegory as a dramatization of historical incidents.
Its historical component is small, while its moral purpose is trans-
parent—and is given further stress by the Bastard's epilogue on
Commodity.

'Commodity' is another term that has received too little attention. The stress given it by the Bastard makes it a key word in
King John, yet its derivation in the commonplaces of Tudor political writing has not been properly traced. It occurs repeatedly
in such contexts, and is almost regularly placed in opposition to
the idea of 'commonwealth', usually in such phrases as 'private
commodity', 'singular commodity', 'his own commodity'. The
'Commonwealth' writers of Edward VI's reign were especially
fond of the term. In his Sermon of the Plough (1548) Latimer
pointedly used it: 'The bodily ploughing is taken in and inclosed
through singular commodity. For what man will let go, or

diminish his private commodity for a commonwealth? and who will sustain any damage for the respect of public commodity?'[1] Similarly Latimer's friend and fellow martyr John Bradford wrote in prison: 'O this is a sin, dear Father, that I always have been a private man more than a commonweal man; always I seek for mine own commodity, contemning that which maketh to the commodity of others.'[2] In 1551 Ralph Robinson published his translation of More's *Utopia* in which, near the end of the second book, the famous sentence occurs: 'Therefore when I consider and way in my mind all these common wealthes, which now a dayes any where do florish, so God help me, I can perceave nothing but a certein conspiracy of rich men procuringe their owne commodities under the name and title of the commonwealth.'[3]

Shakespeare, however, does not merely take over what had by his time become a worn political term and leave it there. He reinvigorates it, extending its sense. He drops the usual qualifying epithet, 'private', 'singular', etc., and makes the Bastard invent a personification:

> That smooth-faced gentleman, tickling commodity,
> Commodity, the bias of the world . . .

The peculiarly lively linguistic activity of the Bastard's speech is very much in the style of the mid-Tudor morality plays. One such play is the anonymous *Respublica* (possibly by Nicholas Udall), acted before Queen Mary in the first year of her reign, 1553. Despite its Catholic viewpoint it shows the influence of the Protestant 'Commonwealth' writers of Edward's reign ('Respublica' is of course the Latin equivalent for 'Commonwealth'). One of its leading Vice characters is Avarice, who introduces himself in the usual monologue fashion. If we bear in mind the substance of the Angiers scene in *King John*, with its powerful politicians hypocritically pursuing their own 'commodity', what he says sounds curiously relevant:

> My veray trewe unchristen Name ys Avarice
> which I may not have openlye knowen in no wise,

---

[1] Latimer, *Sermons*, Everyman edn., 1906, p. 61.

[2] Quoted by A. G. Dickens, *The English Reformation*, 1970 rep., p. 310.

[3] *Utopia*, ed. J. Rawson Lumby, 1952 rep., p. 162. Other examples are in Latimer, op. cit., pp. 85, 87, and Elyot, *Governor*, II. i, in the verses translated from Claudian on the duties of a governor.

For though to moste men I am found Commodius
yet to those that use me my name is Odius
For who is so foolishe that the evell he hath wrought
for his owen behouff he wolde to light sholde be brought? ...
Therefore to worke my feate I will my name disguise
And call my Name polycie in stede of Covetise.[1]

For the Angiers scene is about nothing else than men who disguise
their covetousness as 'policy'. 'Smacks it not something of the
policy?' jeers the Bastard at one point, and what he suggests
satirically, for the benefit of the audience, is taken quite seriously
by the kings on stage. The word 'commodity' does in fact occur
several times in *Respublica* in the stock usage of the time. Another
scene shows its vicious characters squabbling over the prizes they
are to receive. They are by definition motivated by private commodity, and at one point the language and imagery come interestingly close to a key passage of *King John*:

> *Avarice*. I wolde have a bone here rather then a grote
>   to make thes Snarling curres gnawe owte eache others throte.
>   here be eager whelpes loe: to yt Boye / box him balle.
>   poore I, maie picke strawes / these hungri dogges will snatche all.
> *Oppression*. Eche man snache for hym selfe by gosse I wilbe spedde.
> *Avarice*. Lacke who lacke shall / Oppression wilbe corne fedde.
>   Is not dame Respublica sure of goode handlinge
>   whan theis whelpes, ere they have ytt / fall thus to skambling?[2]

The state of England after Arthur's death is also described in
terms of dogs quarrelling over a bone:

> ... England now is left
> To tug and scamble, and to part by th' teeth
> The unow'd interest of proud-swelling state.
> Now for the bare-pick'd bone of majesty
> Doth dogged war bristle his angry crest
> And snarleth in the gentle eyes of peace.
>
> (IV. iii. 145–50)

Not only is the image similar: one has 'Snarling' and 'skambling',
the other 'snarleth' and 'scamble'—though this may well be due
to a common homiletic tradition.

---

[1] *Respublica*, ed. W. W. Greg, 1952, ii. 71–80. The play seems to have existed only
in manuscript until it was printed in the nineteenth century. Whether it was known
in Shakespeare's time is not clear.

[2] Ibid., ii. 311–18.

In this account of the play's apprehension of 'the world' one feature, already mentioned, remains to be explored. It often seems to happen that the purposeful activity of its characters, their deliberate schemes, come to nothing or develop in ways which could not have been foreseen, with an effect intensely frustrating to those who initiated them. In the Angiers sequence the two kings march their armies to and fro, trying to gain entry to the town or settle the matter in battle. Yet even after battle, the balance of power remains what it was: exactly poised. What settles the matter, and then only temporarily, is the proposal by the Citizen that a marriage should be arranged. But as soon as that has been gone through, and the cause of Constance and Arthur quietly ditched, the arrival of Pandulph shatters the concord so that things are essentially back where they were. The French are once again enemies of the English, and once again they must resort to battle. In such sequences as this, activity itself seems to be mocked: the great ones, who posture on the stage of the world, and who think themselves free and self-determining agents, are incapable of achieving anything. John then plans to rid himself of Arthur but, as we have seen, this involves him in an unpredictable sequence of stop-and-go in which Arthur is alive when he is said to be dead and dead when he is said to be alive. Finding the situation as impossible in their way as John does in his, Salisbury, Pembroke, and the rest embark on their paradoxical course of loyal perfidy and perfidious loyalty, only to find out eventually, through Melun, that Lewis is to pay them back in kind with his own version of hating love and loving hate:

> He means to recompense the pains you take
> By cutting off your heads. Thus hath he sworn . . .
> Even on that altar where we swore to you
> Dear amity and everlasting love.

It was the experienced worldling Pandulph who suggested to Lewis that he should invade England. Later, however, when John has capitulated to the Pope, Pandulph asks Lewis to call it off. The political scene, we see, is constantly shifting: enemies become friends, friends enemies, as the pressures of self-interest veer and divide and re-form. All activity seems merely provisional: new circumstances may cancel it out. Lewis persists in his invasion but, with victory within his grasp, has everything snatched away largely because Melun changes his mind at the point of death, forsaking his loyalty to Lewis in favour of his duty to God. The fighting that takes place in the last act has a frustratingly unreal quality that is wholly in accord with the rest of the play. Both sides lose part of their 'power' in the sea: Lewis on the Goodwin Sands, the Bastard in the Wash. And in each case, oddly, the loss is reported twice. It seems to show that, as they fight, the opponents become drained of force—as if activity itself were unreal. Only when men confess their weakness and dependency do they paradoxically speak with strength: notably in the dying moments of Melun.

King John has many thematic affinities with *Hamlet;* and it is in the speech of the Player King that we find the clearest statement of this theme of the unsatisfactoriness of action:

> Purpose is but the slave to memory,
> Of violent birth, but poor validity . . .
> This world is not for aye; not 'tis not strange
> That even our loves should with our fortunes change; . . .
> But, orderly to end where I begun,
> Our wills and fates do so contrary run
> That our devices still are overthrown;
> Our thoughts are ours, their ends none of our own.
>
> (III. ii. 183–208)

This philosophical view of human behaviour and, by implication, of human history informs not only *Hamlet* but *King John.*

III

Mundus et Infans: the World and the childlike self: we have surveyed the world implied by *King John,* but there is also the self who is initiated into experience. *King John* would be nothing without the Bastard Faulconbridge. With him, however, it comes within hailing distance of *Hamlet.* He is the sensitive moral agent who registers the human temperature of the places through which he moves. Through his responses the true meaning of the play is mediated to us.

From its opening moments the play makes it clear that John should not by 'right' have become King of England: his majesty is 'borrowed'. And since his reign does not rest on law, it must in the nature of things stand awry. In this situation the Bastard serves as an 'illegitimate' commentator on an illegitimate reign. He is himself a figure of Conscience, Honesty, and Faithful Service—some such name might have been given him in a morality play. But from a social point of view his position is always anomalous. For though accepted as a loyal servant of the king, he always carries with him something of the equivocal mark of his birth: he is both inside and outside society, just as he is inside and outside the play, an unhistorical invention of the author's who from the start has a special relationship with the audience. He is in short a loyal illegitimate, wrong-born but right-minded, the natural son though not the heir of the former king. But he is also natural in a more positively human sense. Being the issue of Cœur-de-Lion's 'commanding love', he is himself imperiously natural in feeling, uninhibited, spontaneous, humorous, straightforwardly against art and guile and worldly compromise. He provides us with the human scale by which we assess the activities of others as well as, in the later scenes, giving in himself an example of how to act, how we ourselves should act if we were in his situation.

In *Richard III*, which was probably Shakespeare's previous history play, Richard Gloucester, like the Bastard, established a strongly humorous audience-*rapport* from the moment he stepped on to the stage. But in *King John* the device has been changed in one vital respect. Unlike Richard, the Bastard is a good man, his emotional nature not perverted but unforcedly natural. Almost the whole of the first act is given to displaying the naturalness of his demeanour. The scene is ostensibly about a lawsuit, to determine who is to succeed to the Faulconbridge estate. But what comes across is something that overflows the bounds of the occasion: the energy and life-abundance of Philip, contrasted not only with his spindly anaemic half-brother but with everyone else on the stage. The entire scene exists in effect as a frame for him, giving him full opportunity merely to show himself, to convince us that he wields the unanswerable authority of one who is fully alive. A theatre audience will respond to this authority more readily than a single reader. But even the text, read privately, will convey something of the excitement aroused by the Bastard as soon as he appears.

Unlike the remaining four acts of the play, this first act contains a large number of rhyming couplets and even complete rhyming stanzas. They are not all spoken by the Bastard, though most of them are, but stylistically they grow out of his exuberantly demotic idiom. He brings to the court the assumptions of the country: he is a 'good blunt fellow', with 'country manners', who unaffectedly uses strong-flavoured English. His speech in fact has at times a vigorous dancing lilt which rises easily into stanzaic forms:

> *Elinor.* The very spirit of Plantagenet!
> I am thy grandam, Richard: call me so.
> *Bastard.* Madam, by chance, but not by truth; what though?
> Something about, a little from the right,
> In at the window, or else o'er the hatch;
> Who dares not stir by day must walk by night;
> And have is have, however men do catch;
> Near or far off, well won is still well shot;
> And I am I, howe'er I was begot.

sixain

Taking Elinor's remark, he builds on it a couplet followed by a sixain stanza. (At the end of the scene he concludes with a couplet followed this time by a reversed sixain.) The speech just quoted has a dense folk-quality: proverbial, elliptical, gestive, it communicates on a primitive level through powerful abrupt suggestions rather than the finished syntactical forms proper to public utterance:

> Something about, a little from the right,
> In at the window, or else o'er the hatch . . .

We understand him, though we need to pitch our hearing to an unfamiliarly archaic strain. For what we hear has the slightly mysterious force of an incantation, not sinister but reassuring, because seeming to speak out of the ancient habits of settled country people—another expression of the speaker's naturalness. This is linguistically the most fully charged passage in this crucial first scene, whose entire function is to make us accept the Bastard as a human presence, a credibly lion-hearted individual. Later in the play his humanity will show itself differently: through a quick response to others, through sympathy and conscience. Here it works through humour—since a good-humoured laughter, which is the audience's tribute to such warmth and energy of mind, is, especially in the early stages of a play, the most powerful and rapid of creative solvents, an activity that effortlessly draws from the audience its own vitalizing contribution.

As always in this first scene, the Bastard seems to work his spell by appealing to a deep layer of audience-memory. He is not only the son of a folk-hero, Cœur-de-Lion, but he himself stands with one foot in history, the other in myth. He comes to us out of the past half 'real', half imaginary, like the hero of a popular medieval romance. Later in the scene he refers to 'Colbrand the giant, that same mighty man'—Colbrand, the hero's antagonist in *Guy of Warwick*. Such romance associations are not accidental. The Bastard *is* a folk-hero. Through him Shakespeare makes his audience reach back into its past for an idea of someone larger than life yet life-size, heroic yet human, above them yet on their level. The play's royal bastard is exactly such a one. Of course in the hurry of the play's progress we are not allowed to think it out consciously; the process works entirely through suggestion. Significantly perhaps, we are not even clear of his name. His Christian name is Philip, though that is used only once, and after he has been dubbed 'Sir Richard Plantagenet' by the King. Only once is he called 'Sir Richard', by Salisbury in IV. iii. But later (V. iv) Salisbury calls him 'that misbegotten devil, Faulconbridge', and it is as the Bastard Faulconbridge that we usually think of him.

When at the settlement of the lawsuit the King and the rest leave, the Bastard soliloquizes:

> A foot of honour better than I was;
> But many a many foot of land the worse.
> Well, now I can make any Joan a lady.
> 'Good den, Sir Richard!'—'God-a-mercy, fellow!' . . .
> (182 ff.)

One may wonder what purpose this long speech serves, since so little later in the play bears out his view of himself here as a social climber and observer. It sounds like a prologue to a social comedy which never materializes. However, this brilliantly intonated monologue—directly played to the audience, not in the least introspective—is not really a false start but a self-justifying set-piece, whose air of exciting incipience, of great expectations—as if fresh vistas were opening up before his and our eyes—is in fact the whole point. The speech is among other things an invitation to accept a new companion. Exactly what he says hardly seems to matter: it is the quality of the company that counts, the

improvisatory comedic gift that finds promising matter in whatever happens to catch its eye:

> And when my knightly stomach is suffic'd,
> Why then I suck my teeth and catechize
> My picked man of countries: 'My dear sir',
> Thus leaning on my elbow I begin
> 'I shall beseech you'— . . .

And yet this is only part of the reason why the speech is here: it is
more than an aria of invitation, a chance for the Bastard to display
the riches of his personality and secure his private understanding
with the audience. It also sounds for the first time the theme of
worldliness which we have already explored. Shakespeare's way
of linking the Bastard, who has just been knighted and is therefore
on the way up, to that theme is to have him expatiate on the way
of the world in a specifically social sense:

> But this is worshipful society,
> And fits the mounting spirit like myself . . .

An interest in the ways of getting on in 'society' is certainly a
form worldliness can take, and at this point in the play it is perhaps
the only one which comes within the Bastard's experience. Even
so his promise to deliver 'Sweet, sweet, sweet poison for the age's
tooth' has its relevance to what is to come, and alerts us to the
pomposities of Austria that are soon to reverberate at the beginning of the next scene. On the other hand, when he says of
worldly hypocrisies, that

> . . . though I will not practise to deceive
> Yet, to avoid deceit, I mean to learn;
> For it shall strew the footsteps of my rising

the promise is never taken up: we never see him 'rising' by a series
of steps to a high social position, as these lines might fairly lead
us to expect. In fact we hear no more about it. Once he is knighted,
he becomes what he remains for the rest of the play, a respected
royal servant, a 'brave soldier', who in the last act speaks for the
King and finally for England itself. This monologue, then, has
several functions (it also, for example, allows for an impression of
a lapse of time, so that Lady Faulconbridge can enter and challenge
her son). In essence it is a kind of displaced prologue, spoken not at
the beginning of the scene (like Richard Gloucester's) but near its

end, in the first available space, and hinting at the play's chief
preoccupation though not entirely disclosing it.

The Bastard occasionally says things which may puzzle or
confuse a reader, but will hardly ever be misunderstood by an
audience: in the *brio* and bustle of a performance they will know
intuitively what he means. At the end of his Commodity speech,
he turns on himself and, on the face of it, proclaims his own
cynical acquiescence in the self-seeking compromises he has just
witnessed:

> And why rail I on this commodity?
> But for because he hath not woo'd me yet;
> Not that I have the power to clutch my hand
> When his fair angels would salute my palm,
> But for my hand, as unattempted yet,
> Like a poor beggar raileth on the rich.
> Well, whiles I am a beggar, I will rail
> And being rich, my virtue then shall be
> To say there is no sin but beggary.
> Since kings break faith upon commodity,
> Gain, be my lord, for I will worship thee.

To say that he does not mean what he says here may sound uncon-
vincingly evasive to readers of the play (as it has to some critics),
though an audience will rightly take these lines as a joke which
rounds off not only the speech but the scene. This is because in
performance it is unambiguously clear from his first appearance
what the Bastard's moral standing is—a sympathetic man who
eventually becomes a good one, whose many jocular remarks
never violate the simple outlines of his character. His very first
words in Act One—in reply to John's question 'What men are
you?'—announce what that character is:

> Your faithful subject I, a gentleman . . .

But his goodness is humorously conceived, in keeping with his
socially undignified birth, so that a constant theme of his humour
is 'common conditions'—what human beings inescapably share.
His self-awareness makes him quick to see himself in others,
others in himself. Justice, with its assumption of reciprocity,
matters to him. In the course of the Angiers scene he has acted as
a critic and commentator: he has exposed one after another the
pretensions of the two Kings, Austria, the Citizen of Angiers,

and the Dauphin. And now, in these concluding lines of his speech, he exposes the pretensions of himself. He is really no different from the others, he says. He too follows the lure of private commodity, self-interest. In a performance, however, an audience will know that he *is* different: it will judge him by his words and actions, by the aura of his personality. Throughout this first movement of the play his posture has a Socratic or Erasmian paradoxicality: just as a wise man will freely admit to being a fool or a man of learning know how little he knows, so will a man of integrity confess in how many ways he has yielded to compromise. So here the uncorrupt 'faithful subject' Faulconbridge proclaims

> Gain, be my lord, for I will worship thee.

An audience will respond with a complex amusement, quite clear about its moral bearings. And of course we hear no more about the Bastard's pursuit of 'gain'. (The fact that later in the play he goes off to 'shake the bags / Of hoarding abbots', III. iii, is a side-issue: there is no suggestion that he becomes personally rich by it; it is a task undertaken on the King's orders.)

Such a use of irony directed against himself is one way in which the Bastard is established as someone alive on his own terms, a free agent, with a mind of his own. He can choose to say one thing, knowing that we will not take him at his word. Unlike anyone else in the play he has the freedom to surprise us. Shakespeare's method of characterization here is such as to suggest he is a fully developed self, not a fixed surface persona like the other characters. E. A. J. Honigmann interestingly notes of the Bastard's first words: 'From here to the end of Act I the pronoun I is used fifty-eight times, fifty-one times by Faulconbridge.' His explanation, however, may be questioned: it indicates, he says, 'his self-reliance, and his narrow limits'.[1] On the contrary, his egoism is not at all like Richard III's. What it communicates is not narrowness and an impetuous will but psychic reality and a generous self-being. Since he is so profoundly realized, he helps us form a right response, for much of the time acting as a spectator-surrogate, embodying not only our everyday compromising private selves but also an enlarged ideal self adequate to the public demands that will be made upon it.

[1] New Arden *King John*, p. 6.

IV

The first movement of *King John* ended with the dark scene of Constance's grief and Pandulph's wearily cynical dialogue with the Dauphin. The scene that opens the second movement (IV. i) is even darker. Arthur in prison pleads with Hubert to spare his eyes. Hubert at last relents but the fact that the horror is averted scarcely alleviates the scene's grimness. In a way it heightens it, making it more believably real. There is little or nothing in it of a melodramatic nature, nothing that makes it more of the stage than of real life. Arthur's flood of eloquence, conventionalized though it is, is acceptable in virtue of its childlike simplicity: it evokes realities even if the means are stylized. And the realities are small-scale and domestic, quite out of keeping with the atrocity Hubert is pledged to commit:

> When your head did but ache
> I knit my handkerchief about your brows—
> The best I had, a princess wrought it me—
> And I did never ask it you again . . .

But the relief given when Hubert relents is followed by a fresh sense of the play's bleakly mundane colouring. For Arthur is still to die despite Hubert's decision. He knows that his uncle's enmity will never be satisfied except with his death. When it comes, Arthur's death and its consequences are to take up the rest of the play. I want finally to look more closely at this second, more tragically conceived, movement, and especially at the fifth act which, too often read in the shadow of *The Troublesome Raigne*, has received less than its critical due.

With the scene between Arthur and Hubert we return to the play's beginning. Act One had opened with France, through Chatillon, claiming the throne of England on Arthur's behalf. In Act Two Arthur himself had appeared, and his claim had been reiterated, although in the course of the Angiers business 'Commodity, the bias of the world' had deflected the French king from his purpose. Now, in IV. ii and until John's death, the question of the competing claims to the English throne is resumed. The play takes a second breath, and this time is not to be distracted from its course. The question of allegiance is primary and is enacted in two ways: in the persons of the nobles, who desert

John for the Dauphin, and in the Bastard, who stays with
the King.

Arthur's death is surrounded with confusion. Only with the
final colloquy in this fourth act, when the Bastard faces Hubert
over Arthur's body, is the confusion dispelled. After all the confused words of these scenes, the shrill reproaches, the hysteria,
John's scrambling to find a way of keeping going, and the nobles'
high-minded choice of treachery, the sequence draws to a head
with the Bastard's moment of vision. With Arthur now dead, and
dead in circumstances which incriminate the King, all he can
foresee is imminent disaster. But his words are given such power
that they seem not so much a statement of near-despair as one of
heroically affirmative courage. For the first time the true darkness
is acknowledged; there is no doubleness or evasion, nor any
thought of self-interest. The situation is not any particular man's
but the nation's.

> I am amaz'd, methinks, and lose my way
> Among the thorns and dangers of this world.
> How easy dost thou take all England up!
> From forth this morsel of dead royalty
> The life, the right, and truth of all this realm
> Is fled to heaven; and England now is left
> To tug and scamble, and to part by th' teeth
> The unowed interest of proud-swelling state.
> Now for the bare-pick'd bone of majesty
> Doth dogged war bristle his angry crest
> And snarleth in the gentle eyes of peace;
> Now powers from home and discontents at home
> Meet in one line; and vast confusion waits,
> As doth a raven on a sick-fall'n beast,
> The imminent decay of wrested pomp.
> Now happy he whose cloak and cincture can
> Hold out this tempest. Bear away that child,
> And follow me with speed. I'll to the King;
> A thousand businesses are brief in hand,
> And heaven itself doth frown upon the land.

The visionary power of the speech comes from its scope, its
nationally inclusive sweep, and the figurative density of its language. England is fought over by snarling dogs, with chaos and
tempest impending. But the vast lowering scene is viewed by a
self, an 'I', in a particular place and time. And the presentness of

the moment is insisted on: 'I am amaz'd' he begins, and the rest of the speech fills out his sense of the imminence of the disaster: 'England now is left', 'Now for the bare-pick'd bone of majesty', 'Now powers from home'. The present moment is big with event: the enemy forces are already in movement and converging on their allies within England. Yet the last of the *now*-clauses focuses on an individual, although an indefinite one:

> Now happy he whose cloak and cincture can
> Hold out this tempest.

He is saying, anyone will be lucky to win through; but at the same time, as if merely by focusing on a single person, he recalls his own personal responsibility. Particular action is possible. His words revert to the first person, not used since the beginning of the speech: 'I'll to the King'. He will remain what he has always been: a 'faithful subject'.

Just as the fourth act culminates in this speech of the Bastard's so does the fifth eventually rise to the fully affirmative major chord sounded in the last speech of the play, also spoken by the Bastard.[1] But the shape of this last act is an intricate one, the way to that final moment devious and winding. This concluding phase of the action has often been found poorly dramatized, cramped in design and perfunctory in execution. There is admittedly something constrained about it, as if what might have been a fuller development was reduced for reasons of space. But it makes perfectly good dramatic sense, and its best moments are strangely impressive, seizing the imagination with an unexpected power.

The fourth act had ended with the expectation of disaster: '. . . heaven itself doth frown upon the land.' The fifth act is even more overtly religious in expression and develops further the theme of divine judgement. It has seven scenes, with its middle scene (Melun's dying confession), as the turning-point of the play's complex denouement.

The first scene opens with John receiving his crown again from Pandulph and being reminded that it is Ascension Day, the day mentioned by Peter of Pomfret:

> Is this Ascension-day? Did not the prophet
> Say that before Ascension-day at noon
> My crown I should give off?

---

[1] The Bastard concludes four of the five acts: the exception is the third.

The repetition of Ascension Day here is oddly like the repeated
mention of All Souls at the exactly corresponding point (v. i) of
Richard III. If All Souls associations helped to shape the Bosworth
sequence, it is just possible that Shakespeare intended something
similar here with regard to Ascension Day. Immediately after
John's speech, the Bastard enters announcing the French invasion.
These two events—John's submission to the Pope and the invasion—are widely separated in Holinshed; it is Shakespeare who
has brought them together and stressed the feast day. Ascension
Day, or Holy Thursday, occurred in Rogation week (when 'roga-
tions' or general supplications were made on behalf of the parish).[1]
Two ideas were associated with it : protecting the boundaries, and
supplicating God for his blessing. Both these ideas are present in
the fifth act, in which (for the only time in Shakespeare's history
plays) England is invaded by a foreign power. Whether or not
an Elizabethan audience would have recognized an Ascension Day
connection in this sequence, a more general theme of human
dependence on God is more certainly established. Everyone in the
fifth act, the Bastard included, seems dwarfed by events, at the
mercy of unforeseeable consequences; indeed, though the Bastard
makes an effort, no one is in control, and the last-minute unexpectedly fortunate outcome seems providentially managed. In the
process, men are shocked into acknowledging their weakness and
lack of self-sufficiency.

This religious perspective is given full expression in v. iv. The
French count, Melun, fatally wounded, is brought to the English
lords and tells them that if Lewis wins the day he plans to put them
to death as traitors. Melun's confession has the effect of driving
Salisbury, Pembroke, and the rest back to the English side, so
allowing England to show a united front at the close of the play.
What Melun says is therefore of great importance, though he
himself speaks only in this scene (he has been twice mentioned in
previous scenes, IV. iii and v. ii, so as to prepare for this his sole

---

[1] Ascension Day was devoted to the idea of boundaries, in this corresponding to
the ancient Roman festival of Terminalia, the feast of Terminus, god of boundaries
and limits. Ovid's account of the Terminalia (*Fasti*, II. 639–84) shows that it was
easy to think of boundaries in a national as well as in a small-scale rural context. In
England, however, Ascension Day observances were usually a matter of parochial
limits : the minister, accompanied by churchwardens and parishioners, went round
the boundaries praying God to withhold his righteous anger and invoking his
protection. See J. Brand, *Popular Antiquities of Great Britain*, 1870 rep., i. 110–11.

contribution), and it is as important to the thematic organization
of the play as it is to its action. For as we have already seen, his
dying words, spoken with a passionate religious sincerity, rise to
a plane where there is no longer any room for duplicity and
deceit:

> *Salisbury.* May this be possible? May this be true?
> *Melun.* Have I not hideous death within my view,
>   Retaining but a quantity of life,
>   Which bleeds away even as a form in wax
>   Resolveth from his figure 'gainst the fire?
>   What in the world should make me now deceive,
>   Since I must lose the use of all deceit?
>   Why should I then be false, since it is true
>   That I must die here, and live hence by truth?

The starkly simple truthfulness of Melun, almost out of the world,
could not be more strongly opposed to the ruthless doubleness of
the Dauphin or, in a different way, to the confused equivocations
of the English nobles. He goes on to commend himself to 'one
Hubert', for whom he expresses love—and who had earlier been
reviled as a 'dunghill' by these same nobles. By vouching for
Hubert's character, he makes it clear to them that John was not
responsible for Arthur's death, so making it possible for them
to return to him. (This is the sole reason for Melun's reference
to Hubert.) Finally he directs his mind to his own imminent
end:

>   I pray you, bear me hence
> From forth the noise and rumour of the field,
> Where I may think the remnant of my thoughts
> In peace, and part this body and my soul
> With contemplation and devout desires.

Only his soul, not his body, is his own. This is the fullest moment
of other-worldliness in the play. And although it makes its effect
at once, it continues to work its influence from now until the end:
everything that comes is modified by the memory of Melun's
devout death. His 'good end' particularly affects the way we
view the death of John, which is certainly not a 'good' one. He is
to die agitated, distracted, self-preoccupied, a 'module of confounded royalty'.

But immediately before the final scene, Shakespeare invents

a night meeting for the Bastard and Hubert (v. vi). The two men meet in the dark and exchange rapid, nervous questions:

> *Hubert.* Who's there? Speak, ho! speak quickly, or I shoot.
> *Bastard.* A friend. What art thou?
> *Hubert.* Of the part of England.
> *Bastard.* Whither dost thou go?
> *Hubert.* What's that to thee? Why may not I demand
> Of thine affairs as well as thou of mine? . . .

Their nervous irritability anticipates the opening moments of *Hamlet.* And as in that scene the self-identification of the speakers is a main point. They duly declare themselves, and Hubert goes on to announce the King's sickness, his possible poisoning. The scene is a slightly puzzling one. Though unnecessary in terms of plot, it is oddly suggestive. The occasion is one of bewilderment and dejection: hence the night setting. The news brought by Hubert is not divulged until the mid-point (the scene has 44 lines: at precisely line 23 Hubert announces 'The King, I fear, is poison'd by a monk')—so that the Bastard is kept in irritated suspense. And when at last he brings himself to it, Hubert adds some other items:

> The lords are all come back,
> And brought Prince Henry in their company;
> At whose request the King hath pardon'd them . . .

Though we may guess that Prince Henry is introduced here only in order to succeed to his father's throne, the Bastard is not in a position to know it; and it is at this point in this stangely disjointed yet evidently purposeful scene that he utters his gravest, most serious words so far. Perhaps he kneels before speaking, for they form a prayer:

> Withhold thine indignation, mighty heaven,
> And tempt us not to bear above our power!

(His words allude to St. Paul: 'God . . . shall not suffer you to be tempted above your strength: but shall with the temptation make a way that ye may be able to beare it.'[1]). For the Bastard this is his darkest moment. There seems nothing to stop the Dauphin from seizing the English throne. He then discloses more:

> I'll tell thee, Hubert, half my power this night,
> Passing these flats, are taken by the tide . . .

---

[1] 1 Cor. 10: 13, Bishops' Bible, quoted by Honigmann.

He has nothing to fight the French with. That is why, in mere helplessness, he prays. He then hurries away, hoping to see the King before he dies.

Some critics think this a moment of personal temptation for the Bastard—that he himself is tempted to seize the throne.[1] There seems nothing to support such a reading, which would run counter to everything we know of his character. In any case such a major turn in the plot would need to be much more verbally explicit for an audience to pick it up. The scene's real effect is made in immediate theatrical terms: it shows two loyal Englishmen suffering a horrible moment of dark confusion and near-despair, not knowing that the Dauphin's 'supply' has foundered on quicksands. The Bastard's prayer makes a stylistically weighty climax (a 'supplication' one might call it, remembering the Ascension Day practice), which relates back to Melun's confession and, looking forward, to the King's death that now follows.

The first half of the last scene provides a setting for that death. The Prince's elegiac lines prepare for it and at the same time establish his own promise of maturity: though young, he speaks with the authority of traditional morality and so is worthy to become king. But with the rushed arrival of the Bastard, the tempo changes:

> The Dauphin is preparing hitherward,
> And God he knows how we shall answer him . . .

—and for a second time he announces his lost forces, this time to the King, who dies without response. In a mood of heroic despair he goes on to promise revenge and to rally the defences:

> . . . To push destruction and perpetual shame
> Out of the door of our fainting land.

But this desperate moment is also the moment of his enlightenment. Salisbury replies: 'It seems you know not, then, so much as we'—for everything is really over. The Dauphin has acknowledged his defeat, and peace talks are already under way. The Bastard's frenzy was unnecessary. Now that Salisbury and the rest have come back, everything is under control, and the Bastard

---

[1] This is William H. Matchett's reading: 'The Bastard is in the situation that faced John upon the death of Richard, and the question is, will he, like John, usurp the throne?' (Signet edn., p. xxxvii.)

can at once kneel to the new young King. Unlike his father, Henry inherits lineally, by 'right', and not by 'strong possession'. The Bastard goes on:

> . . . To whom, with all submission, on my knee
> I do bequeath my faithful services
> And true subjection everlastingly.

This last reference to himself matches his first, when in answer to John's question he had called himself 'Your faithful subject, I . . .' The young King is moved to tears by the pledged loyalty of his subjects and, in lines that catch from him his emotional tone, the Bastard speaks the play's epilogue:

> This England never did nor never shall,
> Lie at the proud foot of a conqueror,
> But when it first did help to wound itself . . .

In their full context these lines are not quite as jingoistic as they are often supposed. They speak out of a mood of intense relief at having been so narrowly delivered from disaster. But the play assumes the corruptibility of the English throughout. England is only part of the world, and the world is necessarily corrupt. And not only corrupt but transient:

> What surety of the world, what hope, what stay,
> When this was now a king, and now is clay?

The mood is not simply one of patriotic elation but is mixed with a recognition of tragedy. We are left with a sense of human insufficiency along with a sense of possible human greatness. Events outrun men's purposes, as the Bastard is there to show in this last scene, while Salisbury and the other nobles seem definitively humbled by their near-fatal betrayal of the King's cause, as if something of Melun's dying perception of human littleness had remained with them.

V

Some qualities of *King John*, which were no doubt obvious to its first audiences, will always escape us. Certain episodes seem to shadow incidents in Tudor history which were readily at the call of Shakespeare's contemporaries. John's dealings with Hubert over Arthur's death have long reminded readers of Elizabeth's dealings with Secretary Davison over Mary Stuart's execution. Undoubtedly we should be cautious in developing the implied comparison, if it is there: it is much more likely to be flattering to Elizabeth than critical of her—anything else would in any case not have passed the Lord Chamberlain. John was suborning a servant to commit a murder—and the murder of one who should by right have been king; while Elizabeth, in at last consenting to the execution of Mary, was acting with the full support of her Council, and was besides genuinely reluctant to grant her consent. The implied lesson of the play must also have been favourable to Elizabeth and her government. For if such a faithful subject as the Bastard chose to stay with the King, knowing his claim to be questionable and himself a possible murderer, then the faithful subjects who in theory composed the play's audience would have had even more incentive to serve a Queen with a perfectly good claim to the throne and who was besides not in any sense a criminal.

Whatever we may think of the John–Hubert/Elizabeth–Davison analogy, there is probably more in the play of a topically allusive nature than will ever be certainly clarified. The military toing and froing of the English and French Kings before Angiers may very well have recalled Henry VIII's attempts to capture Calais. And the peculiarly futile and fatuous nature of those expeditions again recalls the atmosphere of Henry's French wars. Lacey Baldwin Smith's comment seems appropriate: 'There is a nonsense quality about the sixteenth-century international scene reminiscent of an armed band of children playing at war, mimicking the secrecy, espionage and *Realpolitik* of adult diplomacy, but possessed of a dangerously short attention-span, incapable of dissociating problems from personalities, and living in a world where everything seems possible.'[1] Moreover the absence of personality in Shakespeare's John, his odd facelessness, may in part be due to Shakespeare's caution in handling topical material. (His Henry VIII also has this blankness which is, or may be, a sign that the writer is

---

[1] *Henry VIII: The Mask of Royalty*, 1971, p. 155. For an account of Henry VIII by a contemporary of Shakespeare's, which, though later than his play, recalls his King John, cf. Ralegh's *History of the World*: '*But besides the sorrows which hee heaped vpon the Fatherlesse, and widdowes at home: and besides the vaine enterprises abroade, wherein it is thought that hee consumed more Treasure, than all our victorious kings did in their seuerall Conquests: what causelesse and cruell warres did he make vpon his owne Nephew . . .*' (ed. C. A. Patrides, 1971, p. 57).

performing in some official and therefore prudently deferential capacity.) In general the reign of King John, as presented in the play, shows the abject plight of England during the Dark Ages, when the Pope made the King do what he wanted. This is a view of English history largely taken over from Foxe's *Acts and Monuments*. It throws into relief Elizabeth's contrary role as England's Constantine, one who asserted her 'imperial' authority against the 'meddling priests' of Rome. John is merely 'God's wrathful agent', a scourge used by God only to be cast away. His weakness is never condoned; indeed the play's insistence that his claim to the throne was weak helps to make his degeneracy acceptable.

Through the character of the Bastard we seem to overhear some of the ways Tudor Englishmen privately thought about the public events of their time. Like subjects in other periods, they were inevitably mixed and confused in their feelings, essentially loyal to the monarch and government—since above all they wanted peace and stability—but without many illusions about the nature of state politics and fully capable of making an independent judgement on it. We can capture something of the Bastard's representative quality by quoting the titles of two sixteenth-century publications, one a pamphlet written just a few years before *King John* (it was prompted by the Babington Plot), the other a poem of Henry VIII's time. The pamphlet is George Whetstone's *The Censure of a loyal Subject* (1587), the poem *Vox populi vox dei*. The strength of Shakespeare's conception comes from the fact that the Bastard Faulconbridge is not only a 'loyal subject' but *vox populi*. When he speaks, he speaks not for one only but for many, the unknown multitude who make up the people of England.

12. *Conclusion*

DRYDEN was wrong: Shakespeare was not 'naturally learned', nor could he dispense with 'the spectacles of books' in order to read nature. He had been taught expertly in an age outstanding for its educational achievements. By being taught how to use for his own ends the intellectual resources of his time, he became the greatest of dramatists. The tradition that he was an untaught genius belongs to romance, not history. The other tradition, to which John Aubrey referred in 1681, must be nearer the truth: 'Though as Ben Johnson says of him that he had but little Latin and less Greek, he understood Latin pretty well, for he had been in his younger years a schoolmaster in the country.' (Aubrey's source was William Beeston, whose father Christopher had been a contemporary of Shakespeare's and had acted in the same company.) Whether or not this tradition is reliable, it seems to point to something real in the plays. They are the work of someone who had received much more than a bare minimum of formal education, who was indeed well qualified to have taught others what he himself had so intelligently absorbed.

Shakespeare's first great critic, Dr. Johnson, wrote of him that he was 'above all writers, at least above all modern writers, the poet of nature'. Shakespeare's humanity, however, was itself the achievement of training, of mental application, not simply—or not alone—an inexplicable heaven-sent gift. In another famous passage, in his Life of Cowley, Johnson described what he saw as the faults of the 'metaphysical' poets, among which he included their failure in 'representing or moving the affections':

As they were wholly employed on something unexpected and surprising, they had no regard to that uniformity of sentiment which enables us to conceive the pains and the pleasures of other minds: they never enquired what, on any occasion, they should have said or done; but wrote rather as beholders than partakers of human nature . . .

Johnson might have made his attack on Cowley and his school with Shakespeare in mind as a contrast to them: if they failed in their human responsibility to their subjects, he was always aware

of it. He brought even to his earliest plays a cultivated sense of
decorum which was to become increasingly refined and subtle.
He always 'enquired what, on any occasion,' ought to be said or
done, since his perpetual concern was with human nature as it was
already known. His Constance in *King John* is not just a particular
widow and mother (though she is that) but all widows and
mothers:

> . . . I am sick and capable of fears,
> Oppress'd with wrongs, and therefore full of fears;
> A widow, husbandless, subject to fears;
> A woman, naturally born to fears . . .

So too with that large company of always adequately discriminated
characters who populate the Henry VI plays. They are all conceived according to a certain idea of natural feeling, so that any
audience can recognize at once, from its own experience, the
emotions enacted on the stage. The capacity to create such characters shows a formidable 'knowledge of the passions' (as Johnson
calls it in a note on *King John*). However, this knowledge was not
acquired simply and solely from first-hand encounters with people.
It was the fruit of long practice in rhetoric. For us, unfortunately,
the very word 'rhetoric' is a deadening one, and much more needs
to be done towards recovering its older positive content. We need
to be able to associate it not with a dull verbal pedantry but with
the empirical study of human nature. Rhetoric used philological
means for ends that were ultimately ethical, psychological, and
even anthropological. It was the way of entry to the philosophical
study of man.

Of all these early plays *Titus Andronicus* is the one that has
least survived its time. It is too much a schoolmaster's attempt at
tragedy (though, if we allow for its early date, it must still seem
an extraordinary effort). But even in *Titus*, it is remarkable how
often we are referred to a quality of normality—of 'uniformity'—
in human nature. The acts of cruelty and malice committed by its
characters are constantly measured against a standard of natural
conduct and natural feeling. Consequently, for all its grotesquely
horrible incidents, the play has a universal applicability: it is not
just a horror story intended to shock but a tragedy intended to
move. When Tamora pleads for her son's life, she speaks as any
mother would speak. Later in the play, Titus' sufferings have

a similar generic transparency: he has become an embodiment of grief—anyone's grief, a grief any audience can recognize. Later still, even Aaron—indeed Aaron as much as anyone—proves himself a member of the human family: the delight he takes in his baby son, whose safety he puts before his own, is one of the most Shakespearian, because 'natural', things in the play. In all this, *Titus Andronicus* declares itself a product of school rhetoric. Indeed only through his training in the grammar of the passions could Shakespeare have conceived his Hecuba-like hero and so written what we can see in retrospect as an immature *King Lear*.

By the side of such contemporaries as Chapman and Jonson, Shakespeare seems distinctly old-fashioned, a conservative Elizabethan temperament. His outlook belongs to an older world, which in turn reflects an earlier phase of Tudor humanism. Unlike them, he could never adopt an intransigently exclusive modernism. He was without their arrogance, their conviction of belonging to a superior minority. He belonged not to a clique but to the public, and never relinquished his responsibility to a large popular audience. Nor, as a writer, did he belong to a sect. It is not wholly surprising that in our own day he should have been claimed by Catholics as one of themselves—nor is it, I think, out of the question that he was a Catholic, though in most ways he could equally well have been a conforming Protestant. What is important is that his work is free of sectarian bias. He preferred to conciliate than to divide and antagonize.

Shakespeare's conservatism, or rather conservationism, appears in many different areas of his work. The tenacity with which he held on to older forms is only one side of his gift of memory in the largest sense. If the arguments advanced earlier in this book are right, he was the only dramatist of his time to put to deeply significant use the originally Catholic mystery plays of his youth, just as later he was to revive such outmoded forms as the romantic saint's play. Not that he was merely backward-looking: he had an unparalleled capacity for absorbing new influences and for rapid and purposeful development. But his progress forward never entailed cutting himself off from the still living past. On the contrary it becomes more and more clear that he made use of the past—often the apparently worn-out, the primitive, the merely *passé*—more resourcefully than any of his contemporaries. The fine scene of the plucking of the roses in *1 Henry VI* contains perhaps a memory of the Fall of Man plays in the mysteries (both are aetiological myths set in a garden), but its adroit use of rhetoric is entirely new and up-to-date. So in different ways *Richard III* and *King John* compel their audiences to revisit the Catholic past while remaining conscious of their Elizabethan position in history. Neither Marlowe nor the younger writers had this gift of appealing to their audience's oldest memories; for Shakespeare, on the other hand, the appeal to memory was essential to his work as the poet of 'nature'.

The Christian and the classical, the academic and the popular, are perpetually blended in Shakespeare. But it should not be forgotten that these qualities were often already blended in the Christian humanist culture that Shakespeare inherited. The studies that make up this book have gone back repeatedly to the great disseminators of classical wisdom and experience: Erasmus and his English associates and followers. None of them wrote in vain as far as Shakespeare was concerned. They all helped to nourish his work, adding to its comprehensiveness, its timeless, but also popular, centrality. But the historical picture is still far from clear. More needs to be discovered about the years that separate Erasmus and Shakespeare. Despite all the work already done, we still need an adequate literary history of the sixteenth century, bold in outline and not overloaded with detail—a map of the region that will bring out the shape of the terrain and help explorers to master it. But the period needs to be seen as a whole from the beginning of the century to Shakespeare's retirement. It is no solution to detach the drama from the rest, as literary historians have so often done. Splitting the period down the middle merely impedes understanding; it cuts off Shakespeare from his most significant predecessors. Only when we have grasped the entire period will his work become historically intelligible. Only then will our idea of Shakespeare approach more closely to the reality.

APPENDIX A

Shakespeare and Seneca

IN recent years the debate about Shakespeare's interest in Seneca's tragedies has been revived. When Cunliffe and Lucas wrote their books (1893, 1914), the question seemed comparatively simple. They combed the plays of Shakespeare and his contemporaries for resemblances to Seneca in situation, character, and especially phrasing, and when that was done their task was finished. It was clear, it seemed, that Elizabethans had a good knowledge of the ten plays; and it was mainly from Seneca, it seemed, that Shakespeare learned what little he knew about classical tragedy and about how to write in a classical manner.

With increased knowledge of Elizabethan reading habits, the situation began to look more complex. Seneca's eminence subsided as it became clearer that there were other routes to the discovery of tragic expression. And with a new study of Ovid's tragical narratives, Seneca's standing as a tragic influence became more questionable than ever. Howard Baker's *Induction to Tragedy* (1939) sought to displace Seneca altogether in favour of Ovid. More recently, in an excellent short essay (*Shakespeare Survey* 20, 1967), G. K. Hunter furthered the campaign against Seneca, arguing that the widespread use of anthologies, etc., makes it unnecessary to suppose Elizabethans to have had any extensive knowledge of Senecan plays. They could have picked up their Senecan phrases and *sententiae* from this kind of collection without needing to have read a single play right through. 'We are left', says Professor Hunter, 'with a few well-worn anthology passages and a few isolated tricks like stychomythia (and even that occurs outside tragedy) as relics of the once extensive empire of Seneca's undisputed influence.'

In *The Tragedy of State* (1971), J. W. Lever registered a protest against such attempts to minimize Seneca's importance to Elizabethan dramatists. He argues that for them 'Seneca was a potent, omnipresent influence': 'No amount of research into the survival of medieval stage traditions can wipe out this vast presence, which shaped the imagination of Renaissance Europe' (p. 8). For Seneca was read not just for his diction and his tragical paraphernalia, but for his substance. It was with a contemporary voice that he spoke to them about such matters as 'the power of rationality, the Stoic affirmation of a kingdom of the mind, unshaken by tyranny, unmoved by horrors' (p. 9).

Lever's position seems to me sympathetic and persuasive. It seems to me likely that Shakespeare (to confine the discussion to him) would have had a knowledge not merely of phrases from anthologies or of discrete passages but of at least some entire plays. How closely he knew them we can hardly tell, of course, and there is no question of any extensive structural indebtedness. But he knew enough of the salient characteristics of Seneca's style to imitate them, and not necessarily just the more famous moments and sayings. It seems likely in fact that not only Shakespeare but many of his contemporaries had a subtler and more inward appreciation of the minutiae of Seneca's style than most classical scholars have nowadays (when Seneca is little studied)—not to speak of Shakespearian scholars who probably (like myself) tend to make use of translations. Seneca has been oddly little examined during the present century. While most of those interested in the Elizabethan drama know roughly what he is like, few, I imagine, can go beyond this. The result is, I suspect, that many passages in Shakespeare which would have seemed Senecan to the Elizabethans are not recognized as such by us.

One of the more useful essays on Seneca in English has apparently been overlooked—not surprisingly, in view of its ostensible subject. This is 'Seneca's Influence upon *Gorboduc*' by H. Schmidt (*M.L.N.*, vol. 2, 1887). What is valuable about the author's approach is the way he draws attention to some prominent items of Seneca's diction. When Elizabethan writers wanted to imitate Seneca, they did not only translate his more notable *sententiae*, they also made a liberal use of some of his favourite words. These included 'hand' (*manus* or *dextra*), 'heart' (*animus*), and 'breast' (*pectus*), the last two often with 'hard' (*durus*). In *Gorboduc*, for example, all four words occur in successive lines:

> Will ever wight beleve that such hard heart
> Could rest within the cruell mothers brest,
> With her owne hand to slay her onely sonne?
>
> (IV. ii. 181–3)

When once noticed, these words are seen to recur throughout *Gorboduc*. But they are favoured by Shakespeare too, especially in his histories and tragedies. E. A. J. Honigmann noted that 'hand' becomes something of a recurring motif in *King John*: the word occurs well over sixty times. The Kings hold hands to mark their treaty and are then urged by Pandulph to disjoin them. In the John–Hubert episode of IV. ii and iii, 'hand' is reiterated with an emphasis impossible to miss, as in the following:

> *Bastard.* It is a damned and a bloody work;
> The graceless action of a heavy hand,
> If that it be the work of any hand.
> *Salisbury.* If that it be the work of any hand!

Another early play in which 'hand' recurs exceptionally frequently is *Titus Andronicus*, where hands of course play a gruesomely prominent part in the stage business. We should probably think of such passages which use these favourite words as in some sense Senecan, though ordinarily we should hardly connect them with Seneca. 'Heart' too is a favourite Shakespearian word, and, while it would be absurd to ascribe its frequency entirely to Senecan influence, the word is notably frequent in the early histories. Lines like Anne's

> Curs'd be the hand that made these fatal holes!
> Cursed the heart that had the heart to do it!
> Cursed the blood that let this blood from hence!
> *(Richard III*, I. ii. 14–16)

were probably felt as being in a classical tragic manner, even if the listener were unable to specify Seneca. Such words are so common in English that their use in tragic contexts has been overlooked, no explanation for their frequency seeming to be required. Yet, given the fact of Elizabethan interest in Seneca and Seneca's own fondness for the corresponding Latin words, the Senecan explanation seems worth considering. Much of his real influence, like that of other Latin authors, is likely to stay invisible unless clues of this sort are picked up. *King John*, for example, was probably felt to be far more Senecan than we think of it as being. The preponderance in it of 'body images'—especially 'blood', 'hand', 'eye'—was noted by Caroline Spurgeon and further examined by Honigmann, but not ascribed to Senecan influence.

King John shows Senecan influence in other ways. The tragic figure of Constance is a case in point. In most ways Constance recalls Andromache, a widow with a beloved son at the mercy of unscrupulous politicians; and in each case the boy (Arthur, Astyanax) leaps to his death from a high tower. For all this the relevant play is Seneca's *Troades*. But at one point Constance recalls a very different heroine of Seneca's. When she hears of her betrayal by the French king and the marriage between Lewis and Blanch, she is overwhelmed with rage and shock. Shakespeare provides her with a full tragic tirade, one of the play's great set-pieces:

> Gone to be married! Gone to swear a peace!
> False blood to false blood join'd! Gone to be friends! . . .

The occasion for this speech recalls one near the beginning of *Medea*. Betrayed by her husband Jason, who is now to marry Creon's daughter, Medea hears the sounds of the marriage celebrations:

> Occidimus, aures pepulit hymenaeus meas.
> vix ipsa tantum, vix adhuc credo malum.

(116–17)

('We are undone! Upon my ears has sounded the marriage hymn. So great a calamity scarce I myself, scarce even yet can comprehend', tr. F. J. Miller). And she too launches into a tirade, comparable in length to Constance's. The resemblance is only momentary—both women find it at first impossible to believe such treachery—but enough to show that Shakespeare probably knew *Medea* as a play and not simply as a few bits and pieces in an anthology.

Senecan influence, then, is not always easy to recognize. It may be a matter of single words reiterated, or of a momentary grouping of characters or of the posture of a single character which, for those who knew Seneca, might recall him. When in *Lear* Goneril and Albany exchange a few terse words about Goneril's future course of action, they echo what was once a well-known exchange in *Octavia* (in Shakespeare's time thought to be Senecan):

Albany. Well, you may fear too far.
Goneril.   Safer than trust too far.
   Let me still take away the harms I fear,
   Not fear still to be taken.

(I. iv. 329–31)

In *Octavia* the philosopher Seneca tries to moderate Nero's tyrannical cruelty;

Nero. Steel is the emperor's guard.
Seneca.   Trust is a better.
Nero. A Caesar should be feared.
Seneca.   Rather be loved . . .

For a moment the mild Albany speaks like a latter-day Seneca, while Goneril is already a budding tyrant, making her own will the law. Whenever tyrants are in question in Shakespeare, there is likely to be a Senecan feel somewhere in the diction (most obviously in *Richard III, Hamlet, and Macbeth*). At other times there may be merely a slight colouring, no more prolonged or stressed than the more rapidly hinted leitmotivs in Wagner. *The Winter's Tale* is not a play one would normally associate with Seneca. Yet once he has yielded to his jealousy Leontes acts like a tyrant, or a would-be tyrant, and never more so than in the

scene with Paulina (II. iii) in which she brings him his new-born baby
and is roughly repulsed:

> *Leontes.*   On your allegiance,
>   Out of the chamber with her! Were I a tyrant,
>   Where were her life? She durst not call me so,
>   If she did know me one. Away with her!
> *Paulina.* I pray you, do not push me; I'll be gone.
>   Look to your babe, my lord; 'tis yours. Jove send her
>   A better guiding spirit! What needs these hands?
>   You that are thus so tender o'er his follies
>   Will never do him good, not one of you.
>   So, so. Farewell; we are gone.   (*Exit.*)

The scene is an excellent one, rich in its tragi-comic mixing of tones,
poignantly amusing; and in performance the way Paulina is got off the
stage, pushed bodily towards the door, makes a curiously sharp effect.
Just as Leontes is not a true tyrant, despite his 'tyrannous passion', so
the violence offered the plain-speaking Paulina is not true tyrannical
violence—hardly more than the apologetic nudging of essentially
polite courtiers. The vivid stage effect, however, was remembered
perhaps from a play of Seneca's—*Agamemnon*—which Shakespeare
had possibly consulted for *Macbeth*. At the end of the play Clytemnestra
and Aegisthus are in power, with Agamemnon dead, and they are
disposing of the captives. Among these is Cassandra, who had been
used by Agamemnon as his concubine. Clytemnestra points to her:
'But she shall pay her penalty with death, that captive bride . . . .
Drag her away, that she may follow the husband whom she
stole from me.' But Cassandra is not unwilling to go: 'Nay, drag
me not, I will precede your going . . . . Take me away; I hold not
back . . .':

> *Clytem.* trahite, ut sequatur coniugem ereptum mihi.
> *Cass.* Ne trahite, vestros ipsa praecedam gradus.

(1003–4)

The incident forms a tableau of tyranny: whereas good kings were
always ready (in theory at least) to lend an ear, tyrants forced unwel-
come counsellors out of their presence. In each scene violence is
offered to an outspoken woman, who in each case announces that she is
ready to go: 'Don't drag me', says Cassandra, 'I'm going'. So too
Paulina: 'I pray you, do not push me; I'll be gone.'

Much Ado About Nothing is a comedy even less likely, on the face of
it, to have Senecan connections. But its most famous, and jarring,
moment is one that threatens to tear apart the comedy's already

strained fabric. We are suddenly, and with grotesque incongruity, faced with a possible tragic solution to the situation:

Bendick. Come, bid me do anything for you.
Beatrice. Kill Claudio.

What is Shakespeare doing here? It sounds as if he is echoing a moment in *Medea*:

Jason, Quid facere possim, loquere.
Medea.   Pro me? vel scelus

('What can I do? Tell me.' 'For me? A crime—'.) For a moment Beatrice is like another Medea, furious for revenge, Benedick another Jason, weakly yielding to her savage demands. The incongrous extremity of Beatrice's reply is of course a precisely calculated effect—an unprepared shock. It is the supreme instance of the perilous instability of human response which the play takes as its chief concern, the human 'giddiness' of which Benedick finally speaks. The sudden irruption into the polite world of Messina of the spirit of Seneca's barbarous heroine exactly encapsulates that concern and makes it memorable.

We need to allow that Shakespeare's use of Seneca (as of other authors) may be more oblique and audacious than is often supposed—more a matter of glancingly rapid effects than of a laborious working out of correspondences. However, neither of the examples I have given from *The Winter's Tale* and *Much Ado* is in the form of a *sententia*. Neither of them looks as if it would have been included in an anthology of the kind mentioned by Professor Hunter. Both seem to me to imply a more extensive knowledge of Seneca's plays than he is prepared to admit.

APPENDIX B

Shakespeare and Lucan

SHAKESPEARE'S acquaintance with Lucan's epic poem *De Bello Civili* shows itself in several areas of his work. An Elizabethan play dealing with the Wars of the Roses would be expected to include a few decorous Lucanian touches; accordingly in v. ii, of *2 Henry VI*, when fighting begins in earnest, Warwick's lines

> Now, when the angry trumpet sounds alarum
> And dead men's cries do fill the empty air
>
> (3–4)

seem a freely impressionistic conflation of two of Lucan's characteristic effects: 'Tam stridulus aer / Elisus lituis conceptaque classica cornu' (VII. 475–6: 'Then a strident blast broke from the trumpets, and the war-note was sounded by the horn', tr. J. G. Duff, Loeb edn.); and later in this long narrative of the central battle: 'Nox ingens scelerum est; caedes oriuntur, et instar / Inmensae voci gemitus . . .' (571–2: 'a mighty darkness of crime and slaughter arises, and a groaning like one great cry'). In this same scene, when he has killed old Clifford, York says over his body:

> Thus war hath given thee peace, for thou art still.

Shakespeare is perhaps remembering a phrase from Marlowe's version (still unprinted) of Lucan's first book:

> War only gives us peace. O Rome, continue
> The course of mischief, and stretch out the date
> Of slaughter; only civil broils make peace.
>
> (669–71; ed. S. Orgel, 1971)

The war–peace antithesis is Marlowe's not Lucan's, though it is in Lucan's manner. When later in the scene Clifford swears vengeance over his dead father he does so in a style that again recalls Lucan's own harsh antitheses:

> York not our old men spares;
> No more will I their babes . . .

Earlier in *2 Henry VI* (IV. i. 117) Lucan had been quoted (slightly inaccurately) in Latin; these later stylistic touches, slight though they are, suggest that Shakespeare knew enough of the flavour of Lucan's poetry to wish to imitate it.

There may be more to Lucan's influence, though of a different kind. The dramatist's concern with fame, which is so prominent in *1 Henry VI*, may also owe something to Lucan. Throughout his epic Lucan is particularly conscious of the eyes of posterity watching the actions of his characters; and he has many striking phrases describing the world to come of unborn generations. So, before the fatal battle of Pharsalia begins, he pauses to reflect on posterity:

> Haec et apud seras gentes populosque nepotum,
> Sive sua tantum venient in saecula fama,
> Sive aliquid magnis nostri quoque cura laboris
> Nominibus prodesse potest, cum bella legentur,
> Spesque metusque simul perituraque vota movebunt,
> Attonitique omnes veluti venientia fata,
> Non transmissa, legent et adhuc tibi, Magne, favebunt.
>
> (VII. 207–13)

('Even in later ages and among posterity, these events, whether their own fame alone immortalizes them or I too, by my pains and study, can do some service to famous men, will excite hope and fear together and useless prayers, when the story of battle is read; and all men will be spell-bound as they read the tragedy, as if it were still to come and not past; and all will still take sides with Magnus.') In *The Misfortunes of Arthur* this passage is adapted as follows:

> When Fame shall blaze these acts in latter yeares,
> And time to come so many ages hence
> Shall eft report our toyles and *Brytish* paynes:
> Or when perhaps our Childrens Children reade,
> Our woefull warres displaid with skilfull penne:
> They 'l thinke they heere some sounds of future facts,
> And not the ruines olde of pompe long past.
> Twill mooue their mindes to ruth, and frame a fresh
> New hopes, and feares, and vowes, and many a wish,
> And *Arthurs* cause shall still be fauour'd most.
>
> (IV. iii. 26–35, ed. Cunliffe)

The historical poet's power to agitate and move unborn generations, making them feel that what was long since past was still to come, is an idea that would have had a particular interest to a writer of historical plays, especially one so alert to the potentialities of the form as Shakespeare. At another of the great moments of his epic— the death of Pompey—Lucan reverts to the notion of posterity watching the present. When his assassins close in around him, Pompey closes his eyes, stands motionless, while 'these thoughts passed through his mind':

> 'Saecula Romanos numquam tacitura labores
> Attendunt, aevumque sequens speculatur ab omni
> Orbe ratem Phariamque fidem; nunc consule famae...'
>
> (VIII. 622–4)

(' "Future ages, that will never forget the tragedy of Rome, are watching now, and from every quarter of the world time coming gazes at this boat and the treachery of Egypt; think now of fame..." '). This splendid conception did not bear fruit in the Henry VI trilogy; it had to wait until Shakespeare's next civil war play, *Julius Caesar*, where in the assassination scene it was to leap out with thrilling effect:

> How many ages hence
> Shall this our lofty scene be acted over
> In states unborn and accents yet unknown!

Pompey and Caesar were Lucan's two great antagonists; and it is by an associative link that Shakespeare takes over from Pompey's death, as imagined by Lucan, to Caesar's death the awareness that 'future ages' and 'from every quarter of the world time coming' are already in attendance. (There is too a further displacement: the thought of posterity is not Caesar's but Cassius'; while the phrase 'How many ages hence' seems recalled from Hughes's 'so many ages hence', which translated a phrase from a different passage of Lucan's epic.)

Lucan's idea of a future audience watching and appraising the hero's present actions could hardly fail to interest a writer of historical plays. It may have affected Shakespeare's conception of Talbot, who lives and moves in a dimension of fame, as if conscious of what he calls (in a Lucanian phrase) 'hereafter ages'. More certainly it helped to shape the scene of Caesar's death, and probably of much in *Henry V* and *Antony and Cleopatra*, plays of famous victories and defeats. In all these plays the theatre audience itself becomes the fame-bestowing posterity invoked by the heroes; whenever they are performed, the hero's fame is in a very real sense extended. There are no doubt many sources for sixteenth-century ideas of fame, but Lucan's epic was one of them and is one of the most neglected.

One more play is relevant here. *Hamlet* is not about civil war, nor is it much concerned with the idea of fame. However, the speech on the fall of Troy which Hamlet asks the Player to recite, and which he himself quotes, is written in a very strange and yet distinctive style:

> The rugged Pyrrhus, he whose sable arms,
> Black as his purpose, did the night resemble
> When he lay couched in the ominous horse,
> Hath now this dread and black complexion smear'd
> With heraldry more dismal; head to foot
> Now is he total gules, horridly trick'd
> With blood of fathers, mothers, daughters, sons,
> Bak'd and impasted with the parching streets . . .

Critics have occasionally tried to identify what Shakespeare is doing in this speech. Is it meant to recall Marlowe, is it a burlesque of Chapman, or what? In *Shakespeare and the Classics* (1952), J. A. K. Thomson says at one point: 'I have come to believe that the influence of Lucan on Elizabethan style is seriously underestimated.' He instances Marlowe's dramatic blank verse, and suggests that 'much in Elizabethan poetry that is credited to Seneca should be credited to Lucan' (pp. 230–1). But his subject is Shakespeare, and turning to *Hamlet* he remarks: 'The Pyrrhus speech in *Hamlet* has every quality of Lucan.' He quotes the speech, and comments: 'That seems to me pure Lucan, and not Lucan at his best. However the Player also gives us Lucan at his best:

> But, as we often see, against some storm,
> A silence in the heavens, the rack stand still,
> The bold winds speechless, and the orb below
> As hush as death, anon the dreadful thunder
> Doth rend the region . . .'

The suggestion that Lucan is behind this style is illuminating and, I think, worth considering. But, as before, we need to go beyond saying that Shakespeare was merely 'influenced' by Lucan: he was doing something much more purposeful and deliberate. He was imitating him, and imitation implies at least some close knowledge of the model. We may still wonder, however, why particularly the subject of Priam's death should have been cast into an imitation of Lucan's style. Lucan's epic is about the war between Caesar and Pompey, not the fall of Troy. A possible explanation may be found in sixteenth-century accounts of Lucan's works. In Francis Meres's *Palladis Tamia* (1598), for example, a reference is made to Lucan—not for his epic poem but for two 'excellent' tragedies, neither of which has survived: 'one called *Medea*, the other *De incendio Troiae cum Priami calamitate* . . .' (The last named work was more probably a fragment of heroic poetry.) The reference may help to support Professor Thomson's theory. What Shakespeare is doing perhaps is letting us hear what Lucan's lost tragedy sounded like. (*Hamlet* does in any case incorporate a number of details from the lives of Claudius and Nero; perhaps a Lucan pastiche is related to them: see W. Montgomerie, 'More an Antique Roman than a Dane', *Hibbert Journal*, vol. 59, 1960). For at least one classical scholar, the result is 'pure Lucan'. It is probably the best Elizabethan pastiche of Lucan, perhaps the best in English.

APPENDIX C

The Player King before Shakespeare

THE scene in *3 Henry VI* in which York meets his death at the hands of Margaret and Clifford is one of the most violent in all Shakespeare's plays. But along with the savagery, elements of ritual and even of play are prominent in it. Margaret places a paper crown on York's head, and taunts him for aspiring to kingship: 'I prithee grieve to make me merry, York'. He is like an actor, whose mimic-grief is assumed for the pleasure of his audience. So for a few moments before his death, York indeed becomes king, but a king only in play whose crown is made of no solider substance than paper. Shakespeare's interest in the Player King has been much noticed in recent years, though the impression has sometimes been given that it was no more than a Shakespearian 'theme', original with him, rather than what it actually was, yet another item in his humanist heritage.

Shakespeare did not invent the Player King. This is another instance of Shakespeare developing—certainly in a highly original and subtle way—a topic made available for writers earlier in the century. I suggest that it may again have been Erasmus who acted as a mediator and that one of his *Adages*, brief though it is, played an important part in the transmission of this concept to Shakespeare. This is Adage LXXIX, 'Tragicus Rex' (*Opera*, Leyden, 1703–5, p. 574). The following is a translation:

> A ruler can be said to be a Tragedy King either if he behaves in a ludicrously affected and pretentious way or if he is king only in name, but in other respects is not worth very much. In the French proverb they call him a paper king—he has the title of king but no real power and wealth. Dionysius said that Pheraeus was a Tragedy King because ten months after ascending the throne he died. For in tragedies the king's power lasts only as long as the play is acted. When he steps out of his part, he who a few moments before had been Agamemnon, or even Jupiter, leaves for home no more than a shrunken little man hardly worth three coppers.

Erasmus's phrase 'Tragicus Rex' could by a very slight extension be translated as 'Player King', since he is concerned not so much with tragedies specifically as with any plays with kings in them. The 'Tragicus Rex' is merely a stage king, a king in show. As the King of France puts it in the epilogue to *All's Well that Ends Well*:

The King's a beggar, now the play is done.

Shakespeare's interest in the theme is one of many links between him and the early sixteenth-century humanists. Indeed no other dramatist took anything like the same interest in it. The idea of the actor who shares only his costumes and pomp with real kings occurs in a number of classical texts; it was a not uncommon Stoic trope. One of the most elaborate examples occurs in Lucian's dialogue *Necromantia*, which was translated into Latin by More and was therefore certainly known to Erasmus. Menippus is talking of the arbitrariness of Fortune's gifts, and develops a comparison between the world and the theatre: '. . . You know the kind of thing on the stage—tragic actors shifting as the play requires from Creon to Priam, from Priam to Agamemnon; the same man, very likely, whom you saw just now in all the majesty of Cecrops or Erechtheus, treads the boards next as a slave, because the author tells him to. The play over, each of them throws off his gold-spangled robe and his mask, descends from the buskin's height, and moves a mean ordinary creature . . .' (*Words of Lucian*, tr. H. W. and F. G. Fowler, Oxford, 1905, vol. 1, p. 164.) Quite apart from Lucian, Erasmus would also have remembered two examples from a favourite pagan moralist Seneca (whose works he had edited). These come in Letters 76 and 80, where the second is a livelier elaboration of the first:

Saepius hoc exemplo, mihi hic utendum est, nec enim ullo efficacius exprimitur, humanae uitae mimus, qui nobis partes, quas male agimus, adsignat: ille qui in scaena latus incedit et haec resupinus dicit:

> En impero Argis: regna mihi liquit Pelops,
> Qua ponto ab Helles atque ab Ionio mari
> Vrguetur Isthmus,

Seruus est, quinque modios accipit et quinque denarios.   (80. 7–8)

I must oftentimes make vse of this example, for by no other may this Mimick of mans life (which assigneth vs these parts which wee act very aukwardly) bee expressed. Hee that in the Scene staulketh proudly vp and downe, and looking vpward, vttereth these words:

> Behold I gouerne Greece, Pelops my sire
> He left me kingdomes, and the lands which lye
> From Hellespont vnto the Seas that tyre
> Th'Ionian shores—

Is but a Slaue, hee gaineth fiue bushels of Corne and fiue Pence.

(Thomas Lodge, *Seneca*, 1620, p. 332)

(Seneca's 'mimus'—Lodge's 'Mimick'—might be better translated as 'farce'.) This is probably behind Erasmus's adage, as is Letter 76: ' . . . after they have marched in their proud array and Buskins before the people, as soone as they depart from them they are disapparelled, and returne to their former estate' (Lodge, p. 319). Indeed some of Shakespeare's own theatrical metaphors probably also derive from Seneca's prose writings. Letter 80, for example, seems to have inspired not only Erasmus's adage but a few of the most famous lines in *Macbeth*:

> Life's but a walking shadow; a poor player,
> That struts and frets his hour upon the stage,
> And then is heard no more . . .

'Life's but a walking shadow' recalls Seneca's 'humanae uitae mimus'; 'a poor player' means 'a bad actor', an incompetent one (not, as editors usually say, 'an actor deserving of pity')—he acts 'very aukwardly', as Lodge puts it, translating Seneca's 'male agimus'. And like Seneca's posturing tragic actor in buskins, he 'struts and frets'. Elsewhere in the play, the image of Macbeth dressed in robes too big for him ('like a giant's robe / Upon a dwarfish thief') may also be traced back to Seneca's exemplum of the slave who plays a king.

Erasmus—and More—found theatrical imagery of this kind highly congenial, and they showed later writers how to use it in modern contexts. More uses theatrical metaphors at key points in both his *Utopia* and his *Richard III*. Even the association of kingship with dreams, which was noted in Shakespeare by Caroline Spurgeon, is matched in More. In a letter to Erasmus, More writes of having had a dream of being king: ' . . . but the rising Dawn has shattered my dream—poor me!—and shaken me off my throne and summons me back to the drudgery of the courts. But at least this thought gives me consolation: real kingdoms do not last much longer' (*St. Thomas More: Selected Letters*, ed. E. F. Rogers, Yale, 1967, p. 85). More's awakening anticipates Shakespeare's in Sonnet 87: 'In sleep a king, but waking no such matter.'

The most important play on an English historical subject before Shakespeare was Legge's *Richardus Tertius*; and it is interesting that the man who acted the title role—John Palmer—should have been associated, whether apocryphally or not, with the theme of the Tragedy King. According to Thomas Fuller, Palmer (Fellow of St John's, Cambridge, later Master of Magdalene and Dean of Peterborough) 'had his head so possest with a *Prince-like* humor that ever after *de did* what then he *acted*, in his *Prodigal Expenses*; so that (the *Cost* of a

Sovereign ill befitting the *Purse* of a *Subject*) he died *Poor* in *Prison*, notwithstanding his great *preferment*' (*Worthies*, 1662, p. 277). The confusion of roles, which is the essence of the matter, is clearly present here.

Erasmus's adage helped to focus the theme by giving it a name. Moreover the adage points in two directions, so suggesting different ways in which the theme could be explored. The first points to kings and the unrealities of their position, the second to actors and their momentary glory. Such a theme was capable of any number of permutations. It was open to Shakespeare to enlarge the perception that any king was a Player King, as More did before him '(real kingdoms do not last much longer') or to investigate further the ironies inherent in Erasmus's qualifying term *Tragicus*. So Shakespeare's Tragedy Kings may also be tragic kings. Richard II is both; so is Lear. Shakespeare's first Player King was the Duke of York who, as we have seen, was crowned with paper before being stabbed to death. His fate recalls the French proverb referred to by Erasmus. York too is a paper king, king for a minute—as, in a different way, is Hamlet, who also becomes king a few moments before he dies.

No one brought to the topic such powers of analysis as Shakespeare or such awareness of its ironical possibilities. But he never uses Erasmus's phrase in the text of his plays; the nearest he comes is Hamlet's 'He that plays the king . . .' (How common this English phrase was is not clear: the words 'hym that playeth the kyng' occur in the verse translation of Lucian's *Necromantia* published by John Rastell in the 1520s; for the whole passage see *The English Works of Sir Thomas More*, ed. W. E. Campbell and others, vol. I, pp. 208–9.) In the seventeenth century Marvell may be alluding to the Latin phrase in his lines on Charles I—

> That thence the *Royal Actor* born
> The *Tragick Scaffold* might adorn

—but it was another poet who actually used it in the title of a poem, and explored the topic in a way that might have pleased Erasmus. The poem is Herrick's 'Good Friday: *Rex Tragicus*, or Christ going to his Crosse' (*Noble Numbers*). It describes the Crucifixion entirely in terms of a tragic actor's performance on the stage:

> The *Crosse* shall be Thy *Stage*; and Thou shalt there
> The spacious field have for *Thy Theater*.
> Thou art that *Roscius*, and that markt-out man,
> That must this day act the Tragedian,
> To wonder and affrightment . . .

The poem is not remarkable except for its fundamental conceit; but it suggests the completion of a cycle. Shakespeare's first Player King, York on his molehill, was compared by Holinshed to Christ. Now, during the last years of the Renaissance theatre in England, Christ is himself compared to a Player King.

APPENDIX D

Shakespeare's Hubert

THE three most recent editors of *King John* have chosen to conflate the roles of the Citizen of Angiers and Hubert. E. A. J. Honigmann led the way with his New Arden edition (1954) and was followed by William H. Matchett in his Signet edition (1966) and by R. L. Smallwood in his New Penguin (1974). In his New Cambridge edition of 1936, J. Dover Wilson had favoured the conflation, but in his text did not break with tradition and so retained two distinct characters. It seems to me that the traditional position is right and that the conflation forms yet another obstacle to seeing the play as it really is.

The action of II. i takes place before the walls of Angiers. Both kings seek admission to the city and appeal in turn to the Citizens, or rather to the '*Citizen*' who, according to the Folio text, appears 'upon the walles'. This character has nine speeches in this scene, but in the Folio only the first four are prefixed 'Cit.'; the remaining five are given to 'Hubert' and 'Hub.' The nine speeches are clearly intended to be spoken by the same character, since this same 'Hubert' is more than once addressed as 'men of Angiers' and 'Citizens of Angiers'. The question is whether editors should call this character 'Citizen' or 'Hubert'. It seems clear to me that it is the 'Citizen' who speaks all these nine speeches and that as a character he is quite distinct from Hubert, who makes his first appearance in III. iii, where he is pointedly addressed by name several times (seven times in all in a passage of only fifty lines). The Citizen who speaks in II. i, is quite impersonally conceived; he speaks as a type, and after he has performed his part in this scene is forgotten. He does not (for example) appear in the following scene (III. i) in which Constance confronts King Philip with his broken oath. Hubert, on the other hand, enters the action exactly where he does in Holinshed: when John invites him to dispose of Arthur.

Hubert de Burgh was historically an important personage. He was the great justiciar not only of John but of John's successor Henry III. In the narratives of Foxe and Holinshed, which Shakespeare undoubtedly used, the name Hubert recurs. In his account of the early years of Henry III, Foxe says of Hubert that he was 'lord chief justice of England, who then, under the King, ruled most of the affairs of the realm' (ed. J. Pratt, vol. 2, p. 394). Later, Hubert was in grave trouble with the King, but Henry was unwilling to have him executed, saying

'That there was no such need to deal so straitly with him, who from the time of his youth first served mine uncle, King Richard, then my father, King John, in whose service (as I heard say) beyond the seas, he was driven to eat his horse; and who, in my time, hath stood so constantly in defence of the realm against foreign nations . . .' (p. 401.) When Hubert makes his first appearance in *King John*, Shakespeare makes certain that his audience identifies the new character by having John repeat his name: 'Come hither, Hubert. O my gentle Hubert, / We owe thee much!' (III. iii. 19–20.) And in his second scene, with Arthur (IV. i), Hubert's name is similarly repeated. Shakespeare's Hubert is in short a well-known historical figure, not a fictitious creation like the Bastard. The point must be stressed, since it has become the fashion to deny that the Hubert of *King John* is the historical Hubert de Burgh. Dover Wilson declares that there is no connection between them, and in this he has been followed by Honigmann, Matchett, and Smallwood.

Dover Wilson's argument rests in part on the humiliating treatment Hubert is subjected to by the English lords in IV. iii. Believing him to have murdered Arthur, Salisbury and Bigot call him a 'villain', Bigot making the difference in rank explicit: 'Out, dunghill! Dar'st thou brave a nobleman?' A reply to Dover Wilson on this point may be sought in another scene of *King John*. In III. i, Constance is told of the marriage treaty. Her informant is the Earl of Salisbury, who was historically a half-brother of the King. Constance is so outraged that she twice calls him 'fellow' (36, 62) and tells him that she cannot trust him: 'for thy word / Is but the vain breath of a common man' (7–8). Throughout the scene she addresses him with the contemptuous, or at least condescending, second person singular: 'thou', 'thou fellow'. Shakespeare's Salisbury obviously represents the Salisbury of history, and on that matter no inferences can be drawn from Constance's contemptuous treatment of him. Nor can any inferences be drawn to the effect that the Hubert of the play is not the Hubert of history.

Dover Wilson and his followers deny the historical basis of Hubert because they want to make him a Citizen of Angiers. Accordingly they invent for him a career in the play which will run parallel with the Bastard's. For W. H. Matchett, for example, Hubert moves from the cold neutrality of his first speeches at Angiers to his moment of crisis in the scene with Arthur when he is no longer in a position to evade moral commitment. Matchett's conflation of the Citizen and Hubert leads him to the following interpretation:

Hubert, the man who thought he could hold himself aloof from commitment, is caught between the claims of political allegiance and those of simple compassion. The warmth of John's fawning—'O my gentle Hubert, / We owe thee much!'—has a multiple motivation. John is not merely flattering

Hubert in order to bring him to murder Arthur, but indeed owes Hubert much, just as he says: he may owe him the very capture of Arthur, as the entry would seem to imply, and he presumably owes him Angiers, Hubert apparently having made his choice after France broke the league. John is promising a reward already due and hinting for just one further service.

(Signet edn., p. xxix)

This is a remarkable piece of misplaced ingenuity. There is no warrant for it in the text, and no audience would be prompted to understand the exchange in this way. For Shakespeare quite fails to make any link between the roles of the Citizen and Hubert, so that when watching the play we cannot do other than take them as being different men. The Citizen is never addressed as Hubert, but as 'men of Angiers', 'citizens of Angiers', etc. Hubert is never called anything but Hubert, and we are never told that he came from Angiers. Even if the same actors doubled the two parts (which has been a possible explanation for the problematical speech prefixes in II. i), the audience would still respond to them as two distinct roles. When Hubert appears, we are (as we have seen already) in no doubt of it: 'Come hither, Hubert', says the King: 'O my gentle Hubert', 'Good Hubert, Hubert, Hubert . . .' Consequently there is no justification whatever for Matchett's suggestion (following Dover Wilson) that Hubert 'apparently' handed over Angiers to John or that he 'may' have captured Arthur for him. Nor is there any basis for Honigmann's suggestion that Melun's reference to 'one Hubert' in his dying speech (v. iv. 40) can be explained by appealing to Hubert's past life: 'If Hubert was a leading citizen of Angiers . . . he might well be the friend of a French lord' (p. 136). Such novelistic conjectures can seem plausible only when we forget the realities of the theatrical experience. *King John* is entirely without the naturalistic continuity which such readings postulate.

That the two roles are distinct may be finally supported by the fact that the Bastard is essentially hostile to the Citizen of Angiers, who suggests the political marriage, and essentially friendly to Hubert, who is like himself a loyal servant of the King.

Index

Wilbur Sanders, The Dramatist and the
   Received Idea, Camb. 1962 ~ S & Marlowe

Bolgar (p. 14)